AMERICAN
RADICAL

AMERICAN RADICAL

INSIDE THE WORLD OF
AN UNDERCOVER MUSLIM FBI AGENT

TAMER ELNOURY

with Kevin Maurer

DUTTON

DUTTON

An imprint of Penguin Random House LLC
375 Hudson Street
New York, New York 10014

LIBRARY OF CONGRESS CATALOGING-IN-PUBLICATION DATA
Names: Elnoury, Tamer, author. | Maurer, Kevin, author.
Title: American radical : inside the world of an undercover muslim FBI agent / Tamer Elnoury with Kevin Maurer. Description: New York, New York : Dutton, an imprint of Penguin Random House, 2017.
Identifiers: LCCN 2017029950| ISBN 9781101986158 (hardcover) | ISBN 9781101986165 (epub)
Subjects: LCSH: Elnoury, Tamer. | United States. Federal Bureau of Investigation—Officials and employees—Biography. | United States. Federal Bureau of Investigation. | Terrorism—United States.
Classification: LCC HV7911.E42 A3 2017 | DDC 364.1/317092 [B] —dc23
LC record available at https://lccn.loc.gov/2017029950

Printed in the United States of America
1   3   5   7   9   10   8   6   4   2

Set in Adobe Garamond

CONTENTS

GLOSSARY OF ARABIC WORDS   xi

NOTE TO THE READER   xiii

CHAPTER 1. Super High   1

CHAPTER 2. I Am a Muslim   11

CHAPTER 3. No Fear   25

CHAPTER 4. Dirty Arabs Group   37

CHAPTER 5. Tamer Elnoury   47

CHAPTER 6. "Take His Temperature"   61

CHAPTER 7. The Bump   71

CHAPTER 8. Live Amongst Them to Defeat Them   81

CHAPTER 9. Uncle Ibrahim   93

CHAPTER 10. Gone Fishing   99

CHAPTER 11. Apartment 23   113

CHAPTER 12. The Road Trip   125

CHAPTER 13. The Imam Complex   137

CHAPTER 14. The Christian Burial Speech   153

CHAPTER 15. Best of the Mujahideen   163

CHAPTER 16. Pizza with Terrorists   171

CHAPTER 17. The Bridge   183

CHAPTER 18. Team Chiheb   199

CHAPTER 19. The Responsible One   207

CHAPTER 20. The Radicalizer   223

CHAPTER 21. Spitting in the Eyes of God   239

CHAPTER 22. Operation Happy New Year   253

CHAPTER 23. High Five   269

CHAPTER 24. The Sixth Pillar   279

CHAPTER 25. Eyes of Allah   291

CHAPTER 26. Stay True to Islam   301

CHAPTER 27. The End   315

CHAPTER 28. T-Bags   325

EPILOGUE: We're Everyone   341

ACKNOWLEDGMENTS   345

To my mother.
Everything I am and ever will be is because of you.
Rest in peace, Mom.

GLOSSARY OF ARABIC WORDS

Dunya: this world, Earth

habibi: brother, friend

halal: accepted and allowed in Islam; blessed

haram: forbidden in Islam; against the religion

insha'Allah: God willing

masha'Allah: an expression of appreciation, joy, or praise

mujahid (singular)/mujahideen (plural): one engaged in jihad

munafiq (singular)/munafiqeen (plural): an outward Muslim who is secretly unsympathetic and undermines the Islamic community

Muslim Ummah: the collective community of Muslims

NOTE TO THE READER

American Radical is the story of a group of extraordinary men and women whom I was lucky enough to work alongside for the past nine years and the human toll and sacrifice we make to do the job every day.

Only the first names of the actual agents are used. I do this to protect them from harm by enemies of the United States. I refer to publicly recognized senior agents and FBI management by their true names. I have taken great care to avoid going into specific detail about training, tactics, and procedures used by the FBI and law enforcement.

My intent in writing this book is to ensure that the content gives a clear and accurate account of the events and experiences in which I took part, but it is of paramount importance to me that I maintain the sanctity and secrecy of operational and security issues.

The majority of the material contained within this book was derived from reports and transcripts generated during the investigation. When no documents were available, scenes were reconstructed from my notes and memory. This book is my perception of what happened and when it happened. If there are inaccuracies in it, the responsibility is mine.

This book was reviewed and approved by the FBI, but it presents my views and does not represent the views of the FBI, the U.S. Department of Justice, or anyone else.

AMERICAN
RADICAL

CHAPTER 1

Super High

I was Rico Jordan before I was Tamer Elnoury. Hell, I was a lot of people before I ever got in front of a terrorist. I spent a lot of days looking and acting like a criminal. I had a knack for being able to relate to people. To pull them in and make them feel comfortable, even drug dealers.

I became Rico Jordan as soon as I tied my do-rag.

I stepped in front of the mirror and smoothed out my thick mustache and goatee that grew six or seven inches off my chin. Two hoop earrings went into my left ear. I tucked my baggy pants into my black Timberland boots and slid a pistol between my waistband and the small of my back.

It was close to 6:00 P.M. on September 10, 2001. I was working narcotics in New Jersey, so most of my days started when everyone else was headed home. For months, I'd been looking for the distributor of Super High, a potent batch of heroin coming out of New York. When Super High hit the streets, overdoses skyrocketed.

My target was Kit Kat's crew. She and her two sons ran a network of dealers working the towns and cities in central New Jersey. After months of buying from them, they agreed to let me meet their Super High source. The supplier's street name was Black. We'd heard of him, but we'd never gotten eyes on him. That was my job. Identify him and wait for the SWAT team to make the arrest.

Traffic was thick with the bridge-and-tunnel crowd coming home. Kit Kat's crew worked out of a row house at the end of an alley with lookouts positioned on the roof. I parked my green Mazda 626 behind the house after circling the block a few times. Most drug dealers will make a couple of passes to make sure the block isn't hot, and I needed to look the part. It also let me relay information back to the waiting SWAT team. While I drove, I narrated what I saw into a Nokia cell phone.

"Four guys at the front of the house," I said. "No one on the porch."

Billy, my sergeant, was on the other end of the line. He passed each mental picture back to the staging location, a makeshift command center. At the mouth of the alley, I saw the spotters on the roof watching me. With each step, everything slowed in my mind. I'd come a long way since my first drug buy three years ago.

My first buy was for "dip"—shards of crack cocaine chipped off a bigger rock. My hands were sweating as I approached the dealer. I pressed a twenty-dollar bill into his hand and waited for him to fish out a shard from a plastic bag. I was anxious. I couldn't catch my breath. My fingers tingled with adrenaline. I probably looked like a junkie. The dealer put the shard into my hand. I barely felt it as I ran back to the undercover car.

"How did it go?" Mike, my handler, said.

"Good, man," I said. "Look."

I held out my hand. The dip was just a smear. The rock melted in my sweaty hands.

"That's great," Mike said. "What was his name?"

"Who?" I said.

"The dealer," Mike said. "What was he wearing?"

I stared out the windshield trying to conjure an image.

"Was he black or white at least?"

I didn't know. I found out later the dealer had an enormous eagle tattoo on his neck. I was so full of nerves and fear I missed everything. It was embarrassing.

After that, I started to study. I found a junkie who taught me how to cook crack, cut heroin and cocaine. But the biggest lesson was the power of addiction. Just the thought of getting high aroused him. He carried a razor blade in his pocket. If he got arrested, he sliced up his leg through his pants and poured heroin into the wound. It was the only way to stave off withdrawal in jail. Rico Jordan was born out of those meetings. There was no respect in the drug world for a user. I had to be a dealer.

The key to a good cover story was keeping it close to your own experiences. I was a college graduate, so Rico Jordan had a few credits but no degree. He was a former business major—like me— who'd turned entrepreneur drug dealer. Rico Jordan was all business, which earned respect on the street and avoided the hassle of explaining why I wasn't using.

I'd been Rico Jordan for about a year and a half. People didn't know if I was Hispanic, light-skinned black, or Middle Eastern. All they knew was that I wasn't white. I didn't earn a second glance in the neighborhood.

A guy near the front of the alley—security—was sagging to the left as I approached. He likely had a gun on his right hip. He nodded to me as I passed. Kit Kat's crew knew me and I was ushered into the house.

"G-Money's in the kitchen," he said.

I'd been in the house before, so I knew the way. The house stunk like feet. Weed smoke hung in the air. The TV was on, but no one was watching it. About a half dozen men were too busy joking, talking, and smoking. No one acknowledged me as I walked into the dining room.

Two men—one of the guys was part of the crew—looked up. Money was being counted on the table. Glassine bags of heroin were piled in the middle. One of the guys had a bulge—likely a pistol—in his waistband. They kept talking.

I took a snapshot of each room. This wasn't about protecting the SWAT team any longer. This was self-preservation. If the deal went south, I knew my escape route and each room's biggest threats.

G-Money was leaning against the counter. I have no idea how he got the nickname. Probably because he thought it sounded cool. He was scrawny with short-cropped hair. I never saw him in anything but a FUBU shirt or a baggy sweatshirt and jeans.

Scumbag chic.

"Yo, what's good?" he said. "Where's your whip?"

I nodded toward the back of the house.

G-Money nodded.

"Black should be here any minute."

I looked around the kitchen. No one used it to make food. The counter was grimy and sticky. The sink stunk of stale beer.

"Good looking out putting him in front of me," I said.

"You're good people," G-Money said. "Don't forget me when you start moving up."

I laughed. He didn't have to worry about that.

"How much do you think he'll shave off?"

"If you buy twenty bricks, he'll knock it down," he said. "Just get to know him first."

Heroin is packaged into bags or decks, bundles, and bricks. In New Jersey, a brick of heroin is five bundles, or fifty bags. The street value of a bag of heroin is about ten dollars. I wanted a bulk discount.

I heard Black's Acura pull up outside the back door. I could see the car's rims and spinners from the window. He grabbed a black gym bag out of the back seat. G-Money greeted him with a handshake that turned into a hug.

Black was tall and thin with skin so dark it looked like it hurt. He had baggy black jeans that he had to constantly pull up over his ass. Black wore his tan Timberland boots untied. A comically large gold medallion hung around his neck. When he got to me, we shook hands.

"This is Black," G-Money said. "This is Rico, short for Tarico."

Black's face changed. His hands went to his sides as he eyeballed me, skeptical of what he'd just been told. The look startled me. Did he know me? Had he seen me somewhere? Had he made me as a cop? The mental pictures started flicking through my head. Threats. Escape routes. Seconds started to drag. Then he smiled.

"My name is Tariq," Black said.

"No shit," I said, my stress bleeding away.

Black chuckled.

G-Money had a big smile on his face. It was the best possible ice-breaker. Before we could get to business, Kit Kat staggered into the kitchen. She walked like a sailor on deck in a storm. She smiled at Black and then hugged me. I could feel her skeletal body against mine.

"Hi, baby," she said, kissing me on the cheek.

"What's good, Kit Kat?"

My luck was getting better and better. I could see Black check-ing us out as the matriarch of the family was hugging me. G-Money was making jokes about my name. Black was relaxing.

"Since we sort of share a name, you have to hook me up," I said.

"I got you," Black said. "I got you."

There were seventy-five cops staged around the house. Everyone was waiting for him to open the bag. This part always got my heart racing. He unzipped the bag and I looked at the bricks of heroin. A calm came over me. We had him.

"Let me grab a couple of bricks now," I said. "I'll get the rest later."

I had money to buy twenty bricks. Once we made the deal, his charge went from possession with intent to distribute to distribution in a school zone. An elementary school was only a block or two away.

"Yeah," Black said. "That works. Here, take these."

He stacked the bricks on the kitchen counter. My heart started to race again, because I knew when I gave the word, SWAT was going to hit the house.

"Want to give me your number?" I said. "I'll hit you up later for the rest."

Black was closing the bag.

"Absolutely," he said.

Every operation had a takedown word and a distress signal. The distress signal meant "Come and get me, I'm in trouble." The takedown word signaled "The deal is done. Take it down." This operation's takedown word was "soft pretzel."

"Man, you guys eat yet?" I said. "I missed lunch. All I had to eat today was a soft pretzel."

Black didn't answer. He just gave me his mobile number. I put it in my phone while Black and G-Money made small talk. Black started to pack up.

Hurry the fuck up, I thought.

Then I heard it.

"5-0! 5-0!"

The spotters saw SWAT coming. Everybody stopped. Fight or flight took hold. G-Money and one of the guys in the dining room bolted for the back door. Black froze. His eyes darted back and forth as his mind tried to figure out his next move.

I pressed my back against the refrigerator. My eyeballs went to Black's hands and waist. If he went for a gun, I was going to shoot him.

I heard the front door open with a crash.

"Police! Search warrant! Get down! Get the fuck down!"

Black's mind finally engaged. He grabbed the gym bag and went out the back door. SWAT officers with MP5 submachine guns met him on the steps. He came barreling back into the kitchen and tossed the bag as soon as he got inside. The heroin went everywhere.

Twelve seconds of yelling. Furniture breaking. Chaos. One of the guys in the dining room got slammed on the table, shattering it.

I knew Bobby, one of my closest friends, was coming for me. A few hours before the operation, I briefed the team dressed as Rico Jordan. That was common practice so that everyone knew what I was wearing. It was an officer safety thing.

"I'm going to put the cuffs on him this time," Bobby said during the briefing.

Bobby was Jewish. I am Muslim. I called him "Jew Boy." He called me "Camel Boy." The unit nicknamed our corner of the office the Gaza Strip. Political correctness had no place in our office. Every day was about the mission and the brotherhood in that order.

I could hear Bobby yelling at suspects to get down. His voice got louder and louder. Bobby hit the kitchen at a sprint. He was headed for me.

"Get down! Get down!"

I stepped to one side and bitch-slapped him. The crack of my hand hitting his face cut through the chaos. Everyone stopped for a second. I tried not to laugh just as hands grabbed me and slammed me to the ground.

"Get the fuck down, asshole."

I covered my head as Bobby and the guys flipped me on my face and cuffed my hands behind my back. You don't hit a cop without getting your ass beat, and I took a few slaps too. But it was worth it to see my handprint on Bobby's face a few hours later.

Bobby took me out to a waiting car. I could see the guys from the living room lined up along the wall. Everyone had their heads down. At the police station, Bobby took me in the back door. Billy, my sergeant, met me at processing. He dressed in old faded jeans and white Reebok sneakers. His disheveled brown hair needed a comb. When he was doing undercover drug work, we called him Charles Manson because of his long brown hair and thick beard.

"You all right? You good?"

I nodded. We spent about an hour going over the buy. It turned out to be a huge hit. We flipped some informants and found the source of Super High in Spanish Harlem. We also broke up Kit Kat's drug ring. After the briefing, Billy led me to a cell where they held the others.

"This fucking guy has a warrant," he said.

The fake warrant was from another town.

"I took care of that shit," I said, playing along.

"The fuck you did," Billy said. "It says it here. They want you."

A sheriff's deputy escorted me out of the cell. Right after we were out of sight, the cuffs were off.

"Just because I'm going home doesn't mean I won't get those overtime hours," I said.

Billy waved as he headed back into police headquarters.

"You'll get it. Get some rest," Billy said. "You've got that crack buy in the morning."

CHAPTER 2

I Am a Muslim

I was back on the street the next morning.

It was before 8:00 A.M. on September 11, 2001. The weather was perfect. Not hot, but not cool yet. The only hint of fall was football dominating the morning sports talk. Week one was over. My Bills dropped the season opener to the Saints, but it was week one. There was still hope.

I was tired as I drove my Mazda to the buy. Even though Billy cut me loose early, it still took me hours to come down. When I finally got to sleep, the alarm went off. I dragged myself to work, praying for a weekend.

It was only Tuesday.

I parked my car after doing a lap around the block. My spotter, James, was set up across the street as I approached the dealer. He was a young black guy. A low-level guy. He was just a cog in the machine. The start of a thread that hopefully led to his supplier.

The crack buy was routine. Money and drugs exchanged in one

fluid motion. The dealer was chatty. I wasn't interested in talking about the weather or if the Seattle Mariners, on their way to winning more than one hundred games, would challenge the Yankees when the playoffs started next month. But sports turned to current events before I walked away.

"Yo, did you hear some drunk guy just flew a Cessna into the World Trade Center?" he said.

"What?"

"Yeah. A plane hit one of the towers."

I didn't believe it. A drug dealer wasn't the most reliable source unless you were looking to score. I got back into my car and tossed the drugs onto the passenger seat. I tuned the radio to a news station. Initial reports had a Cessna striking the north tower at 8:46 A.M., a few minutes before I made the buy.

As I drove back to the office, details started to come in about the plane. It wasn't a Cessna. It was American Airlines Flight 11. The Boeing 767 aircraft had left Boston's Logan Airport headed for Los Angeles. I'd learn later that Mohammed Atta and four other hijackers took control and flew it into the North Tower of the World Trade Center. There were eleven crew members and seventy-six passengers on board.

I got back to the office just as United Airlines Flight 175, a Boeing 767 with a crew of nine and fifty-one passengers, hit the South Tower. I ran into the conference room. Guys from the unit were watching the news on a TV in the corner. A stunned silence hung over the room as the footage of the plane hitting the South Tower was replayed. The pit in my stomach grew each time I saw the plumes of smoke and fire shoot out of the towers.

———

American Airlines Flight 77, a Boeing 757 aircraft, with a crew of six and fifty-three passengers, crashed into the Pentagon thirty minutes later.

Oh God, please don't let this be a terrorist attack, I thought. That's how naive I was at the time, how naive many of us were.

My cell phone rang. It was my girlfriend. She was crying. Our mutual friend was trapped in the South Tower. He was a few floors above the damage and called his wife. She could hear the sirens in the background as he tried to reassure her.

"I love you," he told his wife. "I don't know what is happening. We're going to try and get out now. Don't worry about me. Take care of you."

That was the last time they talked. Everybody in the office was getting the same kinds of calls. The first reports about al Qaeda shook me out of my stupor. Images of Osama bin Laden in his military field jacket firing an AK-47 filled the TV screen. Then news broke that the hijackers were all Arab Muslims. All of a sudden my religion was front and center. The hijackers had killed thousands of innocents in the name of the most precious and private thing in my life. My gaze was fixed on the TV, but my mind was back in Egypt.

I was born in Alexandria. I arrived in New Jersey in 1977. My father was looking for a better life, so he packed up his wife and two kids and flew three thousand miles to a foreign country. Even at four years old, moving to the United States was a culture shock. My preschool teacher called home after the first week with a good report.

"He is doing well," she told my mother. "He is very talkative. He is a good little boy. But no one has any idea what he is saying."

My father was a medical engineer, but his first American jobs were modest. He pumped gas and worked in a chocolate factory and as a security guard on a department store's graveyard shift. My mother was a chemist. She worked side jobs before getting a job at a chemical company that made fabric dyes. She was lucky. It took my father six years to get a job designing orthopedic implants. His claim to fame was Bo Jackson's hip. Each passing year my family got wealthier. When my father bought a house with a pool in North Jersey, we knew we had settled into the American dream.

Being Muslim in America in the 1980s wasn't a big deal. We lived across the street from a church. A synagogue sat behind our house. I had sleepovers at my Jewish friends' houses. Most people thought I was Hispanic. But at home, my mother only spoke Arabic to me. She never wanted me to lose my culture or religion.

Islam was something I practiced privately. My mother made sure I studied the Quran and made Islam a daily part of my life. I still strive to say my prayers every day. Do I miss a day? Yes. Have I missed fasting during Ramadan? Sure. I'm no different from Catholics who go to church only on Christmas and Easter. That doesn't make me less religious. It just makes me a human who, at the end of the day, is a Muslim.

It was a trip to the mosque with my father that set me on my path. I was in college, struggling to get a degree in business. The prospect of being chained to a desk in a cubicle farm made my skin crawl. My favorite college class was an introduction to criminal justice. I knew it would be a hard sell to my parents. They'd accept lawyer, but not cop.

It was Friday and I was headed home for a visit. My father met me at the house and we went to the mosque together. As I prayed, I noticed a Turkish man in a Bureau of Alcohol, Tobacco, Firearms and Explosives (ATF) shirt nearby. I watched as he prayed with his gun strapped to his hip. I didn't know the man, nor did I talk to him afterward. But seeing him planted a seed. In his own way, he gave me permission to consider law enforcement.

The next semester, I switched my major to law and justice. It was a hybrid prelaw and criminal justice major. I told my parents I wanted to be a lawyer, but my sights were set on federal law enforcement. My grades went from solid Bs to straight As. Right before graduation, I broke the news to my parents that I wanted to be a cop. Not a street cop, but a federal agent. The FBI was recruiting me, but I didn't have a formal offer.

I papered the region's police departments with my resume. I was in the running for jobs in Maryland and with the Secret Service, but a New Jersey police department hired me. They promised me an investigative position and a spot on the fugitive task force. I couldn't say no. The day I graduated from the police academy, the FBI recruiter pulled me aside.

"Can I have a minute of your time?" he asked.

Agent Butler was a former SWAT Team member who was finishing up his career recruiting. I had met him during career day in college. Butler had checked in on me at the police academy, but this meeting was different.

"So, son, are you ready to join the FBI?"

"Let me ask you something," I said. "You and I have been talking for a couple of years now. You don't really know me. Why are you pushing the FBI so much on me?"

Butler smiled.

"I don't really know you," he said. "But you speak a language we need. You're in law enforcement, and before your face is known and before you forget about us, we'd love to have you start the process."

The Bureau was looking for Middle Easterners to help with terrorism investigations. It was the late 1990s, and terrorism was on their radar after the 1993 World Trade Center bombings. The FBI saw a gap in its ability to track and understand the Islamic terrorism threat.

"What are the chances of me ending up in a van in Detroit or in New York listening to a bunch of dirty Arabs?" I was trying to get a sense of how typecast I'd be.

Butler shrugged.

"Very astute," he said. "I'm not going to lie to you. A high likelihood. You're twenty-two years old. We don't hire twenty-two-year-olds to become agents unless they have one of a handful of things that we need. You speak Arabic. You're hired for that reason. They're not going to stick you in a bank robbery squad."

The FBI was one of my career goals, but more than anything I wanted to get my hands dirty.

"Okay," I said. "Can you give me some time to figure out what it means to be a cop? Get that out of my system, and maybe our paths will cross later?"

Butler shook my hand.

"I respect that," he said. "Good luck, son. Stay in touch."

I graduated from the police academy on a Friday in 1996. On Monday, I joined a fugitive task force in New Jersey. A couple of years later, I moved over to narcotics and guns. Back in the conference room on 9/11, I couldn't shake a feeling of guilt. Had I missed my calling? If I'd gone a different route, could I have prevented this? Should I have taken the FBI's offer?

"There's nothing we can do about this," one of my coworkers said. "I'm going back out on the street."

I couldn't move. At one point, a sandwich showed up for me. It sat untouched. People shuffled in and out of the room. But I stayed in my seat. An evidence bag of crack cocaine sat in front of me. All day I could feel the rage building in the conference room. There was a twinge of anger in Peter Jennings's tone as he read the updates. I understood it. But this wasn't Islam to me.

The sun had set when I felt a hand on my shoulder. It was Billy, my sergeant. He didn't put his hands on anyone unless they were getting arrested.

"We know that is not your religion," he said. "I hope they get those fucking animals. Go home. Get some sleep."

It was dark when I finally stood up. I'd been physically, mentally frozen all day. I locked up the office and walked to my car. I didn't turn on the radio. I just drove to my house in silence. I couldn't take any more talk about al Qaeda or the attack. I was angry, embarrassed, and hurt. Some asshole in a cave turned me and my family into the enemy. I hadn't felt this lost since my mother passed.

As I drove home, my mind drifted to 1997. It was July 4th weekend and I'd been a cop for a little more than a year. I was standing in my kitchen when my father called. I could tell something was wrong immediately. There was a hitch in his speech.

"Pop, what is going on? You're freaking me out."

He paused.

"I don't want to worry you, but your mom started dropping things in the kitchen," he said. "Being clumsy. She hit a shopping cart at the A&P parking lot. She clipped the mirror pulling out of the garage. I took her to the doctor. They found a brain tumor."

When my father said "brain tumor," I felt sick to my stomach. My legs felt weak and I sat down. My father sounded confident as he talked about how one of the best brain surgeons on the East Coast was going to treat her. I knew he was being positive for me and I took the lifeline. She was going to be fine, I told myself.

My mother was in and out of the hospital the next few weeks. The biopsy confirmed the tumor was malignant and aggressive. The treatment plan was to use chemotherapy to shrink it, and then the surgeon would go in and remove it. My father called me after one of her stays in the hospital. My mother wanted to have a party.

Our house had a cabana with a fireplace and furniture. I helped set it up for the party. Growing up, my friends spent from morning to when the streetlights went on swimming and hanging out at the cabana. My mother waited on us with drinks and snacks, but she was more than that to many of my friends. They spent hours talking to her. She knew more about their aspirations and problems than I did. I spoke to my mom every single day I was away at college. So did my roommates. They would run to answer my phone just to talk with her.

On the day of the party, guests arrived in small groups. There were lots of smiles. Some tears. Many laughs. I stayed busy helping with drinks and food. It was around dusk when my father asked me to help my mother to the pool deck. The guests were outside and my father wanted my mother to be in the mix. I trotted across the thick green grass of the backyard and in through the back door of the house.

"Dad wants you to come out," I told her.

She smiled and reached for my hand. She clung to me as we walked from the family room to the back door. Each step was a grind.

Left. Right. Left. Right.

I used to yell from the pool for more chips or soda. She had walked these few steps with ease and a smile. Now nothing flowed. Her joints were like hinges in need of oil. She was leaning on me so much that I practically carried her across the lawn.

I had leaned on her my whole life. Now she was leaning on me just to get across the yard. My mom wasn't getting better. She wanted this party to say her goodbyes.

My mother returned to the hospital less than a week later. I lived about an hour south, but I came up a couple of times a week to visit. One evening my father called me and asked if I could keep my mother company.

"I'm going to be late," he said. "I have a meeting in the office."

"No problem," I said.

"Just help her out with dinner," he said. "Sit with her until I get there."

I left work early the next day and headed to the hospital. Traffic was terrible and I arrived about ten or fifteen minutes late. She was alone in her room. Her dinner was on the tray across her bed. She had her knife and fork, but her brain wouldn't let them work together. The fork fell out of her hand. She held the plate with her elbow and tried to cut a piece of meat.

Tears rolled down my face. I froze at the door. I didn't want her to see me because I knew she'd console me. I wasn't there for me. I was there to help her. I wiped the tears from my cheeks and walked into the room. My smile hid the pain. I hugged and kissed her.

"I'm so sorry I'm late," I said.

I made no mention of the fork or knife. I just started cutting her meat and talking. I tried to keep a happy face, but my mother saw right through it. She knew I was hurting.

After her tray was cleared, I sat by her bed. I held her hand. I still wasn't ready to accept what was happening. But she was. She squeezed my hand and told me it was Allah's will.

"It is everything I ever taught you," she said. "You need to believe it in your heart."

She told me to take care of my father and sister.

"One day we will all be reunited," she said, the hint of a smile on her face. "Never spend a day being sad. Remember all the love and the memories we had. Wear them. Use them. Be the good man I know you will be. Help people. Do as much good in this world as you can. I will see you in heaven."

It was calming, yet devastating. Our bond was for eternity. I needed to hear it. But I still wasn't ready for the end.

My father called me the following week.

"You should come up," he said. "Your mother slipped into a coma."

I rocketed up the Garden State Parkway. It was just a setback. It happens. I kept repeating that to myself while I drove. When I got to the hospital, the nurses were standing around crying at their stations. In the short time my mom was there, she knew every nurse by name and everything about them. They adored her.

My father was in the doorway of her room. His arms were crossed.

He was crying. It was the first time I'd ever seen him shed a tear. I touched his shoulder and entered the room. In the corner was my sister in a ball. She was hugging her knees and sobbing.

The doctor was at the foot of my mother's bed looking at her chart. I was struck by how thick it was. He flipped page by page like he was looking for a cure. His eyes never left the chart. I ran to my mother's side. She was wearing her favorite purple robe. She had a breathing tube in her mouth. Her head was leaning toward me. I grabbed her hand and touched her head. My mouth was dry. My head was throbbing. I wasn't sure what to do. There was only silence and the hum of her respirator.

Why weren't we game-planning? Why wasn't this like a war room? I didn't want peaceful. I craved action. A plan. Anything but surrender. I stared at the doctor. He kept his gaze on the charts.

"The tumor clearly didn't reduce in size," I said, struggling to engage him. "It's obviously getting bigger. What if we go in and we just try to take it out? You said it would be like arthroscopic surgery. We can just reduce it, right?"

I wanted him to order the nurses to prep my mother for surgery. I wanted him to tell me he was going to save her. The doctor put down the chart and looked at me.

"Look, kid, it's over," he said. "Say your goodbyes."

"You motherfucker," I said.

Then I dove across my mother's legs and reached for his shirt. My pistol—slid into the waistband of my pants—was visible. The doctor recoiled and stayed just out of my grasp.

Then I felt someone grab me. It was my father. He was in shock. He went from watching his wife die to stopping his son from hurting the doctor. I was screaming and yelling as the doctor ran for the door.

"Call the police," the doctor told a nurse as he left.

Jasmine, one of my mother's nurses, took me to a neighboring room. She was a Middle Eastern woman in her late forties. Not much younger than my mother.

"I was with your mother before she slipped into the coma," she said. "Your mother kept looking at something in the room."

The story calmed me for some reason.

"What was she looking at?" I said.

"She saw light," Jasmine said. "She told me everything was going to be fine. She said, 'I know it is going to be fine. I am so relieved. Tell my family it is all going to be okay.'"

I didn't know what to say.

"It's going to be fine," Jasmine said.

A police officer arrived a few minutes later. He was wearing sergeant stripes and a stern look. Jasmine met him at the door. She said a couple of words to him just out of earshot before he walked over to me.

"Son, are you on the job?" he said.

"Yes, sir," I said.

"Can I see your ID?"

I showed him my badge. He looked at it and put his arm on my shoulder.

"I'm sorry for your loss, son."

My mother died later that day. I didn't sleep for weeks. I paced. I stared out the window. When I got home on September 11, 2001, I felt the same profound sense of loss. But unlike with my mother, there was something I could do to help. The next day, I met Billy in his office.

"They're going to need help," I said.

Billy was confused. "Who is going to need help?"

"The FBI," I said. "I speak Arabic. I know the religion. I know the culture."

I needed Billy's permission to talk with the FBI. Billy signed off immediately. The next day Jim, the FBI resident agent, met me.

"We're a little slammed," he said.

It was three days after the attack. The Bureau was running down every lead they had on the hijackers. There were reports of meetings in a northern Virginia mosque, of trips to flight schools in Florida, and of post office boxes and checks cashed in Virginia Beach. Every FBI agent seemed to be working the case.

"What can I do for you?" Jim said.

He looked haggard. His suit jacket was absent. His shirt was wrinkled and he moved with a nervous energy. He hadn't slept for days and likely wouldn't for the next few at least.

"I speak Arabic," I told him. "I'm Sunni Muslim. If there is anything I can do, let me know. I cleared it through my chain of command. I want to help."

"We really appreciate it," Jim said. "We'll definitely be reaching out to you if we need you."

I got the message. Don't call us. We'll call you. The meeting had lasted less than thirty minutes. I followed up with Jim for weeks after the attacks, but he was always too busy to talk. The FBI was waking up to a new war. They could no longer just be cops. They had to adapt to meet a new enemy.

When I arrived in America, Islam just *was*. Now it was the only thing that mattered.

CHAPTER 3

No Fear

The first rule of undercover work is: The day you're not scared anymore is the day you have to get out.

It was the summer of 2008 and I'd been working drugs for ten years. Rico Jordan's cover story led me from the fringe into the heart of the drug scene in New Jersey. I'd picked up some informants who knew I was a cop. One of my best was Jose, a fat Hispanic guy from the neighborhood. His information got more drugs off the street than most detectives. He also elevated Rico Jordan's profile. In the drug world, you're only as good as who you know. Jose was connected to all the players, so by extension, so was Rico Jordan.

My new target was a Dominican crew led by two guys named Manuel and King, who used their limousine service to bring drugs down from Spanish Harlem. Billy only agreed to take on the case after the DEA asked us for help. They wanted Manuel's crew, but they didn't have an undercover who could do it. My source, Jose, already had an in, so the DEA agreed to front the cash.

We met at the office before the first buy. I sat around the table with Billy; Mike, the case agent who would run our side of the investigation; Steve, who used to work with us before transferring to the DEA; and two other DEA supervisors.

"These guys are pretty badass," one of the DEA supervisors told us.

I was bored from the jump. I knew how to handle myself. I lived it every day. I didn't need a bunch of DEA guys in suits who hadn't made a drug buy in decades—if ever—telling me anything. I zoned out for most of the meeting. Then one of the DEA agents mentioned something about Bangkok.

"Sorry?" I said. "What did you say?"

"We've gotten information about a large shipment of heroin coming in from Bangkok," one of the DEA supervisors said.

I smiled like a junior high school kid. I caught Mike's eye. He and I had worked together for years. He was a big Italian guy with piercing blue eyes. I was his undercover. We had made a lot of great cases together. We also had the same sense of humor.

Mike giggled.

I snorted, trying to hold in a laugh, and covered my mouth with my hand. The DEA supervisor giving the briefing hesitated for a second. I could feel Billy's eyes on me. I glanced up. He had the look of an embarrassed parent.

"What the fuck is going on?" he said.

"Sorry, boss," I said. "He said Bangkok."

Billy and the DEA agents just stared at me and Mike. Steve knew us too well and laughed.

"Excuse me," I said.

I stepped out of the room. Looking back, I'm embarrassed. The DEA was about to trust me with tens of thousands of dollars and I'm laughing at "Bangkok." I was too cavalier going into the operation.

Living up to his reputation, Jose set up an introductory meeting with Manuel at a downtown row house in New Jersey. They were sniffing me out. If this meeting went well, I'd meet the supplier.

The humidity hit me the second I climbed out of my car, but everything else seemed right. My spotters were in place. Jose was waiting in front of the house. He was holding a can of Coke. I never saw him without a can, and never the diet stuff.

Jose knocked and a tall Dominican opened the door. He had a scraggly beard and was wearing a tank top with a pile of chest hair climbing out the front.

"Your boy is downstairs," he said.

We followed him through the house to the basement door. I cased the place as we walked. There were toys on the floor and the table was clogged with mail. The row house looked lived in and not by a bunch of gangsters. A family lived here.

Jose went down the wooden stairs first. I followed. The Dominican bolted the door. Manuel was standing in the middle of the room with another bodyguard. He had a massive gut. It stuck out like a pregnant woman's stomach. A skinny beard framed his face. He was still dressed from his shift driving one of the limos; his dress shirt was unbuttoned at the neck and his black slacks were wrinkled.

The basement was unfinished. Everything had a musty smell, but it was cooler than being on the street. A small table sat in the middle of the room. Chairs were arranged around it. I spotted some trash bags in one corner. The only way in or out was through the bolted door at the top of the stairs, but I wasn't worried. I wasn't going to die in this basement. Something about doing a drug deal with a guy in business casual set my mind at ease.

We gathered around the table. Manuel and Jose made the introductions. I wanted to buy a few ounces of cocaine to start. My goal was to make Manuel believe this was an ongoing thing. Five kilos a month forever and ever, amen.

"Give me the right price," I said. "I don't want it to go up."

Manuel wanted five thousand a month on top of the price for the cocaine.

"Fuck you, I ain't paying that shit," I said.

I was flippant. Dismissive. Cocky. It didn't matter that I was in a basement with only one way out.

Manuel insisted. The extra money was for delivery. He was offering to bring five kilos of coke to my door once a month.

"You're out of your fucking mind," I said. "Why am I going to pay so much? I can drive up to New York myself and buy it anywhere in Spanish Harlem."

The second rule in undercover work is to always deescalate. Don't take control of the situation like a cop. You don't control the room. But I wasn't following the rules. A smirk creased my lips as Manuel explained the economics of drug dealing.

"I get what a delivery charge is," I said, leaning back in my chair. "But you're fucking bending me over."

Jose was looking at me. His eyes asked what I was doing and his face said stop.

"Come on, Rico," he said when I ignored him. "Let's just get a taste to start and work out the price next time."

He calmed everything down with one sentence. Manuel looked at him and then at me.

"Let's get the taste and then we'll see what's what," I said. "We can finalize the price when I meet your guy."

I made the first buy without incident. Now we were in business. Manuel agreed to deliver one kilogram of cocaine and a thousand pills of Ecstasy. He also agreed to bring the supplier.

Billy was pissed when he heard we met in a basement.

"We're not meeting there again," he told me during the debrief. "Find a new place."

We set the next buy in a row house we could control. It was wired with video cameras and microphones. Billy staged the arrest team around the corner. Jose and I waited for Manuel and his boss, King, to show up. They were driving down from New York. We had them under surveillance the whole ride.

Mike picked them up when they got near the house. He was driving a gold Ford Taurus and drove right up behind the limousine as soon as they got close.

"Got 'em," he said over the radio.

Mike was notorious for bumper-locking suspects. Instead of shadowing them on parallel streets, he jumped into their backseat and hounded them like a guy late for a meeting. I warned him about it before the buy, but he ignored me. Mike followed Manuel for a few blocks and then peeled off just before they arrived.

Jose and I saw the limousine pull up. It sat idling for a few minutes. No one moved. I could hear Manuel put the car in gear. He eased it off the curb and drove off.

"Where is he going?"

Jose just shrugged.

"We've been burned," I said. "Fucking Mike."

I lit a cigarette just as Manuel rolled to a stop at the curb again. He walked to the trunk and took out a gym bag. King climbed out of the back and joined Manuel in front of the house.

King was about forty years old with a lean build, short cropped black hair, dark brown eyes, and a scar on his forehead. He was dressed like a drug dealer trying to look like a businessman. Nice pants, but baggy. A designer button-down dress shirt with rolled-up sleeves and opened in front so you could see his Guinea tee and gold chains. He wore a gold pinky ring. His pinky had a very long fingernail—a coke nail—used to scoop and sniff cocaine.

Manuel and King were speaking in rapid-fire Spanish as they walked up to the house. It took Jose a second to figure out what was being said.

"There was a white guy in a gold car," Manuel said to me in English. "He was following us."

"You're talking about crazy Eric," I said, waving my hand like I was shooing him away. "That fucking guy follows people around all the time out here."

To this day, I still have no idea how I pulled that out of my ass. Even now, guys in the department still talk about Crazy Eric. Manuel wasn't sure if I was kidding or not. But it wasn't what I was saying. It was how I said it. I was calm and they believed I was taking the same risk as they were.

"He's a crazy white guy that follows everybody," I said, shrugging and turning to enter the house. "Don't worry about him. He's a nobody."

Jose laughed.

Manuel relaxed.

Ice broken.

We settled into the living room. King's English wasn't very good, so Manuel translated. King took out a kilo of cocaine and started to unwrap the tape. Then the foil. Then the plastic. At one point, Jose handed King a butcher knife to cut through the wrapping. I shot him a glance. Nice job giving the drug dealer a weapon. King got through the tape and plastic, but he couldn't get through the foil. I was losing my patience.

"Who the fuck wrapped this?" I said.

King stopped and looked at me.

"I did," King said.

"Yeah, that's right," I said, nodding like I approved. "You've got to keep that shit tight."

My frustration changed to a compliment in a breath.

King finally got it open enough for me to dip a finger into the powder. Cops can't take drugs. Well, they can in extraordinary situations, but it becomes a lot of paperwork. But I had this trick. I dipped my middle finger into the cocaine and moved my hand up to my mouth to taste it. I turned my head just a bit so King couldn't see my hand and I swapped my middle finger for my pointer finger. The movement sent a subliminal message to King that I tasted it. But I really put my clean pointer finger into my mouth.

"Yeah, that's good," I said. "Jose, why don't you go and get the cash."

We didn't want Jose in the house when the raid happened. Plus, a good drug dealer would never have the money and drugs at the same location, so it didn't seem out of place for Jose to leave.

Jose knew to leave the front door unlocked for the arrest team.

He had a cold Coke in his hand and left the can on a table by the door. I stubbed out my cigarette. I knew once Jose left it was only a matter of time before we got hit. I tried to chat with Manuel and King, but it was hard. I just wanted to get arrested so I could finish up my paperwork and go home. I had plans that night.

The front door opened with a bang. We all froze. I knew they were coming, and it still scared the hell out of me. There's nothing like staring down the barrel of a dozen Glocks and machine guns.

The DEA agents crashed into the table, spilling the soda all over the linoleum floor. Manuel bolted for the front door and ran head-long into Steve. They scuffled for a second and then Steve slipped on the spilled soda. They both tumbled to the floor.

"That is a classified DEA technique," Steve told me later as we watched the video of the takedown back at the office. "I can't tell you any more about it."

Since everything was going to be on video, Billy had reminded us to be professional just before we started the operation. He didn't want his men to look stupid in court.

"Let's put everybody in custody," he said. "Once the house is secure, shut that shit off."

I went right down. No slapping. No fighting. I didn't talk shit. The agents arrested Manuel and King. Both men were on the couch and I was facedown on the floor. Billy was the last one inside. He saw the drugs on the table. A smile spread across his lips.

"Po-lice, muthafuckers," he said, like a true professional.

A few weeks later, I had to listen to all of the recordings. We were preparing the file for court. I sat for hours at my desk listening to myself talk with Manuel. That was when it hit me. I didn't give a fuck. I wasn't scared anymore. Contrast that with my first buy. That was fear. I was so scared I missed an eagle neck tattoo. Somewhere in between, I found the happy middle. Just the right amount of fear to keep me focused and safe. But after ten years on the street, I had traded my fear for arrogance. I refused to acknowledge it because I was the unit's eyes and ears. But I knew it in my heart. I was burned out.

Billy came by my desk the night before we started a new investigation.

"Hey," he said. "You need to go down to the state police office tomorrow at ten and get a new license. It's all set up. They're waiting for you."

The New Jersey State Police had a special office for undercovers. I arrived wearing my scumbag clothes. I skipped the lobby and snuck into the office from a side door. I didn't want to sign in or be seen. The office wasn't far from where I made my buys.

"Hey, Sarge, I'm here for my ten A.M.," I said to the state trooper in the waiting room.

The state trooper waved me toward a line of chairs along the wall.

"Have a seat," he said. "I'll be right with you."

I found a chair near the end and stretched out my legs. Even in our special DMV we still had to wait. A few minutes later, a man stomped into the room in black jeans and motorcycle boots. He looked like the love child of a mobster and a biker. He was Joe Pesci short, with a slicked-back salt-and-pepper ponytail and a huge cross tattoo on his right forearm. He took a seat nearby.

Who the fuck was this guy? Why was he back here with me?

I could feel my blood pressure building. I couldn't believe they let a shithead in here with me. I looked over at the state trooper. He was shuffling papers and didn't notice the guy.

The biker fished a silver BlackBerry out of his jacket and powered it up. He held it at arm's length, like it might bite him. The font on the screen was huge. I could see the screen from where I was sitting. The first e-mail header was from the Department of Justice. I relaxed.

"Yo, my man," I said. "Who you with?"

He took off his tiny round John Lennon sunglasses and looked me up and down.

"Who you wit?"

He sounded like an extra from *Goodfellas*.

"How are you doing?" I said, breaking the ice. "I work undercover narcotics."

"I'm Vinnie," he said. "I'm the assistant undercover coordinator for the FBI's Newark division. Great to meet you. What are you doing here? Is it for a case?"

I shook my head.

"Nah, it's not for a case," I said. "It's all I do."

Vinnie cocked his head. He wasn't tracking. Most local departments didn't run long-term undercovers.

"What do you mean?" he said.

I just do undercover drug work, I told him.

"Really," Vinnie said. "What nationality are you?"

"I'm Egyptian."

He turned his whole body to face me. Ten minutes later he knew I was born in the Middle East. He knew I spoke Arabic and I had ten years of undercover experience.

"When we're done here, can I buy you a cup of coffee?"

"Sure," I said.

I found out later the FBI was having trouble getting Arabic speakers through the undercover program. Vinnie was of the mindset that it was great if you could speak a language, but the undercover skill set was even harder to find.

We found a coffee shop a couple of blocks from the office and took a table near the back. At a glance, we looked like two scumbags enjoying coffee. *The Wire* meets *The Sopranos*.

"It's funny, I reached out to the Bureau right after nine-eleven," I said. "I went in there to offer my services."

"Listen, after nine-eleven, it was a cluster fuck," Vinnie said. "We've come a long way since then."

We talked for a little while longer. He was interviewing me. Finally, he gave me his number.

"We'd love for you to come and help us out with a case," he said.

Back at headquarters, I went into Billy's office and shut the door.

"I met this guy," I said. "He is with the FBI. They want me to help them with a case."

Billy folded his hands. The urgency of the attacks on September 11 had worn off. It was 2008. He wasn't keen on losing his only undercover. But he also knew this was something I wanted to do. It was something I needed to do.

"Have him reach out to me," Billy said.

A few days later, Vinnie called Billy. Vinnie's team was investigating a gang of Turks bringing in Middle Eastern illegals from Mexico. The FBI feared the human traffickers were also bringing in terrorists. None of Vinnie's men could get close to the ringleaders. They needed a Middle Easterner.

Billy knew once I was exposed to the Bureau there was no way I was coming back to drug work. But he couldn't say no to the FBI's request. He knew what it meant to me. So when Vinnie called, Billy had only one request.

"Look out for my boy."

CHAPTER 4

Dirty Arabs Group

I met Vinnie at the FBI office in Newark a few weeks later.

"Kid, you need a legend," Vinnie said.

"What's that?"

"Come up with a name," Vinnie said. "And then leave the rest to us. We'll make you real."

It was pretty much what I did with Rico Jordan, but I didn't know the terminology. I picked an old family name and cooked up a story about a property manager who didn't want to bother with the visa process because getting people in from the Middle East was a pain. I was looking for a way around immigration laws. Vinnie loved it.

The next week I pulled into an abandoned strip mall in southern Jersey, just across the Delaware River from Philadelphia. It was a crisp day in early fall of 2008 and I was going to meet Ali—the gang's leader.

The strip mall was deserted. I pulled around the back. A fleet of government sedans with blacked-out windows and antennas sticking out like porcupine quills was parked behind the empty stores. Everything screamed feds.

I knocked on the back door and an agent showed me to a makeshift command center. Computers and recording equipment were set up on plastic folding tables. All the FBI agents were in 5.11 Tactical pants and blue polo shirts.

I sat down on a folding chair and started to put on my wire. The case agent, Victor, began to go through the operation. I was headed to a hookah bar owned by Ali. He usually arrived in the early evening for dinner. My job was to meet him and start building rapport.

"These guys are your backup," the agent said, nodding toward four guys in polos. "Where do you want us to set up? There is a parking lot in front of the place."

It was culture shock. I was used to my guys. My spotters could blend into the neighborhood. They looked the part and knew the streets. These guys looked like lawyers or accountants with guns.

"No," I said. "How about you guys stay here. If you want to drive up and down the highway, be my guest. Don't pull into the parking lot. Hell, don't get those vehicles near that parking lot. I'm a new face. If they put together a new face with your cars, this case is over before it starts."

The FBI guys looked around. I could tell they thought I was a diva. I was. But I was also the guy going into the bar.

"We'll do it your way," Victor said with a shrug.

The hookah bar was tucked into a modest shopping center with a grocery store, a sandwich shop, and a pharmacy. The place was packed. I checked my watch. It was barely five o'clock.

———

Don't these people work?

The cacophony of backgammon and card games and the low roar of men arguing sports and politics over thick Turkish coffee hit me when I stepped inside. The clank of spoons hitting cups of the thick brew mixed with the smell of coffee and roast meat attacked my senses. Waitresses moved around the room delivering plates of food and drinks from the bar.

Ali was supposed to arrive in a half hour. I wanted my face seen first. At the bar, I ordered a plate of kofta, a grilled dish of minced meat made from a mix of lamb and beef and served with tzatziki, or yogurt sauce. I met a Turk who ran a construction crew. He was sipping a cup of coffee. I introduced myself. He asked me what I did, and all of a sudden my legend kicked in.

A waitress brought over my food, and I turned and surveyed the room. The only open table was in the back. I walked over and put my plate down. I got looks from everyone in the room.

Who are you?

I sat down with my back to the front door and started to eat. I wanted to look like a guy enjoying a meal, not a cop. As I dipped into my kofta, I felt someone standing behind me. I cut another bite and then looked over my shoulder. Ali had a grin on his face. *Do you have any idea how badly you messed up?* it said.

Ali was in his late forties. His dress shirt was unbuttoned one or two buttons too far. A shock of gray hair peeked out of the fold of his shirt. His more-salt-than-pepper hair was slicked back and his cheeks had a calculated level of scruff—more groomed than missing a razor. Fit and lean, Ali could handle himself.

I heard Rico Jordan in my head. *"What the fuck are you looking at?"*

My new legend said the opposite.

"I'm so sorry," I said. "Is this your table?"

"It is," Ali said. "But you're already eating."

"No," I said. "I'll stand by the bar. I'm sorry."

I started to gather my plate and utensils.

"No," Ali said. "Finish your dinner."

My Middle Eastern manners kicked in.

"Sit with me," I said. "Please. I didn't mean to take your table and interrupt your dinner."

Ali moved to one of the open seats. He signaled the bar with a wave and sat down. A waitress came out a minute later with a plate of mixed kabobs with rice and a plate piled high with fresh vegetables. That spoke volumes and he knew it. Between bites, I told him how I was in town looking at some properties. A friend told me about the restaurant. I decided to stop for a bite on the way home.

"I didn't realize how crowded it was," I said. "I didn't mean to step on your toes by sitting here."

Ali just shook his head.

"Absolutely not," he said. "You didn't step on my toes. How is your food?"

"Spectacular," I said.

And it was. It was the only thing I wasn't lying about. Over tea, I started to dump more of my legend.

"I'm having trouble finding workers," I said. "Good Muslim brothers."

"That is a problem," he said.

Ali told me he owned two restaurants as well as a cell phone shop nearby. We talked about the area and business opportunities. He liked being seen as a player with his hand in as much of the action as possible. So I did what I do. I made him like me. I made him laugh. I made him feel happy to be around me. I made him feel good about himself without kissing his ass. At the end of the meal, he gave me his contact information. Cell phone. E-mail.

"Next time you call me," he told me, handing me a card with a couple of numbers written on the back, "I'll take you to a better spot for dinner. I'm a part owner there too."

"I'll call you when I know I'm coming back," I said, shaking his hand.

An hour later, after making sure I wasn't followed, I sat down at the abandoned strip mall. The 5.11 pants were huddled around me as I debriefed. I walked them through the room, giving them details about the patrons and Ali.

"Should we record this?" one of the agents asked.

"No," I said. "We recorded the meet. I'll write a detailed report of the other stuff."

I saw a couple of agents exchange glances when I got to the part about Ali's table.

"You sat down at his table?"

"There was nowhere else to sit," I said. "What do you want me to do? I went there to eat. I couldn't stand at the bar. That would be weird."

I handed the agents Ali's card.

"Holy shit, he gave you his personal cell?" an agent said. "We didn't have that number."

Victor high-fived a fellow agent. It was so dorky it made my teeth itch.

"Hey," I said. "Let's not start sucking each other's dicks just yet. I just got a phone number."

The air went right out of the room. They didn't get the reference. *Pulp Fiction.* The Wolf.

Two of the agents looked horrified. One guy put his hands in his pockets and looked down at his boots. Victor, who was trying to be cool, looked away. I didn't know what to do. Explaining the joke felt weirder.

"I'm out of here," I said, patting Victor on the back. "I'll get you that report."

I got in my car and drove off. I could only imagine what they told Vinnie. During the investigation, Victor kept him in the loop. He called me a few days after I met Ali with some pointers. He told me if I did well, there was a good chance I could do some work on the dark side of the house.

"The dark side?" I said.

"The FBI is split into two," Vinnie said. "We have a CT [counterterrorism] side of the house and we have a criminal side of the house. Right now, you're helping the criminal side. Do a good job on this case and you'll get a chance at the CT side."

I was used to doing drug operations. In the drug world, it was hurry up and make the buys because funding and manpower were always at a premium. The FBI's mind-set was slower. Undercover work was an art form. I had months to ingratiate myself. Become friends. Be there for them. Then take them down. My legend had to be fully rounded. It couldn't be like Rico Jordan—an attitude with a name. It had to be a real person. A guy Ali liked.

After several more meetings at the hookah bar, we met at his

Turkish restaurant. It wasn't far from the hookah bar but didn't cater to an almost all Middle Eastern clientele. Ali again had the best table in the place, toward the back and away from the noise of other diners.

Dinner was a whole fried fish. It sat in the middle of the table. We picked at it with our hands. Plates of fresh vegetables and bread crowded around the fish platter. As we ate, I had to make up stories about a fake wife and a fake uncle who owned the properties. Some of the stories were taken from my own life with the details switched. At the end of dinner, Ali took out a bottle of raki, or Turkish moonshine. He poured a few glasses, for me and some of his associates. When he added a little water to it, it turned milky.

"Şerefe!" he said.

Cheers, or literally, to honor, in Turkish.

We all drank. It tasted like water with a kick. After a couple of glasses, Ali started to talk about his time in prison. He had been convicted of passport fraud. An informant—a rat—dimed him out.

"Fucking rats," I said. "I hate them."

Ali stopped talking and looked at me. I had yelled it so loud I'd startled him. Hell, I startled myself. A silence fell over the table. I took another bite of fish.

What the fuck was that? I thought.

"Excuse me," I said.

I was drunk. It felt like someone tipped the room on its side. I practically dove into the bathroom. Gripping the sink with one hand, I splashed water on my face.

I hate rats? What is wrong with you? Why is your face so red?

The agents listening to the wire told me later they couldn't stop laughing. When I got back to the table, Ali eyeballed me for a second. When it was clear I wasn't wasted, he was ready to do some business. He explained how the immigrants fly into South American countries with no visa requirements. He gets them to Mexico and trucks them into Texas, where he gets them fake identities. That was enough to lock him up. We had everything on tape.

After Ali was arrested, Vinnie called me with an offer. The New Jersey State Police had asked the FBI to do a weeklong undercover school. The Bureau agreed, as long as I could take one slot. As a student. At first I balked. I had ten years of experience. What was I going to learn in a school?

"Yeah, I know," Vinnie said, anticipating the pushback. "But there are some FBI-type scenarios I'd love to run you through. I want my guys from Headquarters to take a look at you in action."

They wanted to see if I could come close to passing the FBI Undercover School. The weeklong course at the New Jersey State Police Academy was intense. We did classroom work and role-playing. The scenarios ranged from drug buys—which were second nature—to murder for hire. I impressed the powers that be and got a formal offer from the FBI. They wanted me to join the Bureau's Joint Terrorism Task Force, a local, state, and federal law enforcement partnership spearheading the fight against terrorism. I had to go through all of the background investigations and polygraph tests before I received my security clearance.

The final hurdle was the FBI Undercover School. It didn't matter that I passed the state version. To work as an undercover in the FBI, you have to be certified. The school has a 50 percent graduation rate. It's a small and elite fraternity.

The location of the FBI Undercover School alternates among

major American cities. It's two weeks of the most intense training I've ever received. Every minute was planned. If we weren't in a classroom learning about techniques, we were practicing them in role-playing scenarios. Sometimes it was a fake bar meeting. Sometimes a meeting in a hotel room. Since the techniques are being used every day to keep America safe, I won't get into too much detail. By the end of the two weeks, I was exhausted both mentally and physically. But I also felt more confident in my abilities. One of the proudest moments in my career was getting pinned.

I returned to the Newark office after training. The FBI is a collection of kingdoms. Each special agent in charge runs his region. Everyone is territorial, and Vinnie kept me on a tight leash. He had one of the few Arabic-speaking Muslim undercovers and wasn't keen on letting me out of his sight.

But Headquarters had other plans. They were putting together a counterterrorism undercover unit. I nicknamed it the "Dirty Arabs Group." It was designed to eliminate the red tape and bureaucracy of getting an undercover in front of a potential terrorist on U.S. soil.

I met the team in Los Angeles. We were headed to the Howard Fine Acting Studio and then to our first briefings. Our acting coach, Howard, had trained some of the biggest names in Hollywood. He shut down his school for the week to work with us.

Howard taught us how to tap into emotions that we already had and use them to be believable. He helped us focus on character so our legends came to life with real emotion. I have no doubt his training saved my life as much as any training I got from the FBI.

Before we left Los Angeles, our supervisor held a final meeting. We gathered around a conference room table as he read down the caseload.

"I need someone in Chicago," he said. "And we need a couple of you guys in Jacksonville. A DirecTV installer saw a map of a military base along with 'religious paraphernalia' in an apartment."

I knew right then I was going to want every case. That this was where I belonged.

CHAPTER 5

Tamer Elnoury

The beach house overlooked Monterey Bay.

Every morning, I took my cup of coffee outside after prayers. I walked down to the sand and stood watching the waves. A pregnant sea lion I named Whiskers lived nearby and usually sunned herself on the beach near the house. The sound of the surf and the sea air soothed me. I could feel the stress drain out of me. It was my few minutes of peace before I rejoined the terrorist living in my guest room.

After working a few low-level cases, I got my first big one. The FBI had a source with connections to al Qaeda's leadership. The group was looking for a financier, and the FBI was happy to provide them with one. The objective was to sell my legend to an Afghan emissary to get face-to-face with his boss. From there, we could follow the chain from boss to boss, eventually getting to al Qaeda's leaders.

Chris, a former marine turned FBI agent, had the case in the San Francisco office. I flew out there a few days before the Afghan arrived. I already had worked up my legend—Tamer Elnoury—a wealthy Egyptian-American real estate developer whose views had become more radical in recent years.

Tamer's story started with his uncle in the 1980s. Tamer's uncle bought two row houses for twenty thousand dollars in New Jersey. He went down to city hall and convinced them his investment would expand the tax base. That investment turned into one hundred and fifty thousand in less than two years. Tamer's uncle sold the pair of row homes and bought more. In five years, he owned more than twenty houses in New Jersey and had created the Elnoury real estate empire. Eventually, Tamer's uncle needed help and he asked Tamer to come on as a property manager after Tamer's mother died.

But I had to change my mind-set. It wasn't enough to be a criminal. I needed an ideology. A reason why my legend wanted to commit terrorist acts.

During our acting training, Howard had urged us to come up with a backstory. We took that idea and created our "point of radicalization." For Tamer, it was his mother's death. I used my own mother as the basis, but twisted up the facts. After her death, Tamer was ready to leave the country, but his uncle convinced him to stay. Run the business and send the profits to al Qaeda in the Arabian Peninsula.

In my legend, Tamer took the business to the next level. Elnoury Investments bought beach houses and commercial property and the profits flowed overseas. Tamer grew the business from slumlords in New Jersey to commercial developers in New York.

Real estate was tricky because so many people know it or think they do. I was on the fence about using it at first. But then I remembered that James, one of my spotters when I worked drugs, was a slumlord. He got into buying homes and flipping them. It was his side business. I stole the idea for Tamer's background.

The FBI unit that backstops our legends brought Tamer to life. They created Tamer's company's website, Facebook page, and financial accounts. All the things that mean you're alive in the modern world. The FBI made sure someone answered the phone at Tamer's office. All e-mails and correspondence had a company logo and letterhead. When the FBI was done, Tamer was a real guy, ready to meet al Qaeda.

The Afghan arrived from the Middle East in the fall of 2011. He was coming to vet me before I met al Qaeda's leadership. We planned to spend about a month together.

The Afghan was tall with a little potbelly. His beard was thick and his eyes were hooded under thick eyebrows, which made him look drowsy.

I took him back to the beach house, which was wired with cameras and microphones in every room. FBI agents monitored the cameras twenty-four hours a day. The first night, I asked the team to disconnect the one in my room. I couldn't sleep knowing someone was watching me. They refused. It was for my security. I hated living in a fishbowl.

The first few days were slow. The Afghan slept off his jet lag and we got to know each other. His Arabic was learned and hard to understand sometimes, but we managed. After three days of being cooped up with him, I took him and the FBI source, who introduced us, to dinner at a nearby seafood restaurant. There were no halal places nearby, so seafood was the easiest choice. The Afghan was dressed in a galabia, the long white Arab robe. Everyone else was in business casual. We stood out.

The waiter came over and I started to order for the table.

"None of us eat pork here," I said. "So if anything has pork in it, will you do us a favor and just let us know? We're going to have water. I'd like to have an iced tea. With extra lime on the side and no lemon."

I stopped and looked at the Afghan.

"Do you want something else instead of water?" I asked in Arabic.

He couldn't muster a word. I was spooked.

"That's it for now," I said to the waiter.

I turned back to the Afghan.

"What's wrong, brother?" I said.

He just shook his head.

"*Masha'Allah,*" he said. "You sound just like they do."

It was the first time he'd heard me speak English. That was the minute I got him. I was what they were looking for—a jihadi, but I talked, dressed, and acted like an American in public.

I spent two more weeks with the Afghan as his people in South Africa, Southeast Asia, and the Middle East vetted me. The FBI was working overtime as they pinged my businesses, checked my records, and made sure Tamer was who he said he was. The vetting allowed us to map their network. After the vetting, the Afghan told me his boss wanted to meet me and Yasser, another undercover posing as a bomb maker. Yasser arrived a couple of weeks into the operation. I wanted the Afghan to know I could recruit.

After a stop in Germany to meet the overseas team, we flew into a country on the Arabian Peninsula. We looked like the odd couple as we walked toward immigration. Yasser was tall—six foot two— with a thick, unruly beard. He was dressed in dress slacks and a button-down shirt. I was the opposite: shorter, groomed, and dressed in a nice suit. As we walked from immigration into the main terminal, I spotted four police officers corralling us.

"Stop talking to me," I said to Yasser.

I thought they were going to grab him. He looked down and I started to move away from him.

"Mr. Elnoury, right this way, sir," one of the officers said.

They were very polite. But they formed a wall blocking me from exiting the terminal.

Keep walking. Keep walking, I thought, as I watched Yasser from the corner of my eye. He walked right past. The police ushered me to a side room. I was met by a supervisor with wavy black hair and piercing eyes that never left my face.

"What brings you here?" the supervisor said, as the other four officers started opening my luggage.

I told him business and pleasure. I was looking for investment properties and on a short vacation. The officer nodded. After he asked me the same question a couple more times in different ways, I realized he was fishing.

"Why did you stop me?" I said after a few minutes.

"You're well dressed," the supervisor said. "You come from America. But you were born in Egypt. You know how Egyptians can get a little crazy sometimes."

He figured I was an Egyptian radical with a U.S. passport, and he was right about Tamer. He knew within the first two minutes not only that I was Egyptian, but from which city and neighborhood based on my accent. He was a brilliant young guy and very good at his job. As we talked, another officer was checking my passport against a database. That was the first real test for my legend and the FBI's backstopping.

The supervisor nodded at my bags.

"Do you mind?"

I smiled.

"No, go ahead."

Three officers started to go through my toiletry bags. The supervisor noticed I had two.

"One man, two toiletry bags?" he said.

"I can't look this good on my own," I said, giving him a smirk.

He laughed. After that, we just made small talk while the officers finished searching my bags. They let me go an hour later and I made it to the hotel, which overlooked the Persian Gulf, around three in the morning. I called Yasser.

"You in your room?"

"Yeah," he said. "You made it? What happened?"

"Come to my room."

"You're all the way on the other side."

"You need to come to my room right now," I said. "You've got to see this place."

My suite made the nicest apartments in New York look like a slum. Each room had a balcony that overlooked the water. Four full bathrooms. The furniture was ornate, decorated with gold accents, and straddled the line between nice and gaudy. The whole country did.

Yasser was floored when he walked into the suite.

"What the hell?" he said, poking his head into the empty rooms. "I thought my room was nice. Do you know you have a bathroom over here?"

"There's a bathroom there too?" I said.

Yasser just shook his head.

"Hey, man, you wanted to be the bomb maker," I said. "I'm the money."

The next morning, the Afghan took us around the city. We saw the malls and the iconic buildings. My eyes darted among the authentic Gulf architecture that seemed to spring up between the glass and steel. Cranes dotted the horizon as newer and taller buildings climbed skyward. Everything was clean and new, like the city had grown out of the desert sand.

We had dinner in a working-class part of town. This was where the guest workers—Bangladeshis, Pakistanis, Indonesians—lived. The Afghan took us to a buffet restaurant with huge silver domes filled with lamb, rice with raisins, and grilled kabobs. Sliced fruit and vegetables took up one whole table. As we dug into our first plate, the call to prayer echoed across the city.

Waiters put cloches over our plates to keep the food warm. People left their bags as we walked across the street to the mosque. For a second I lost myself in prayer. I forgot I was there to meet with a terrorist until we returned to dinner.

"The Sheikh wants to meet you," the Afghan said. "I will pick you up tomorrow afternoon."

The Sheikh was the Afghan's boss, but he answered to the people we wanted: al Qaeda's planners and leaders. We were slowly climbing up the chain.

The Afghan stressed to us this was only an introduction when he met us at the hotel the next day. We picked up the Sheikh around the corner. He was dressed in a suit. Older than the Afghan, he was in his sixties, with a neatly trimmed white beard and deep black eyes.

He climbed into the front seat of the Afghan's SUV and we drove around the city talking about current events, the war in Afghanistan. It was all very vanilla, but I knew the drill. He was checking me out.

"I want to hear your English," he said after almost an hour.

I said a few words to him. He looked at the Afghan and smiled. The Afghan must have told him I spoke perfect English with an American accent. I could tell he was impressed. The Afghan pulled to the curb.

"Let's meet tomorrow in private," the Sheikh said. "We will pick you up at the hotel in the morning."

Every time I left the hotel, the country's security services or al Qaeda tossed my room. They were subtle. Nothing was out of place. But they always missed a piece of tape across the door or something I balanced on the drawer that fell when it opened. I was on everyone's radar, which I took as a compliment. I was doing something right.

But it was also a reminder that, unlike in my drug days, backup wasn't a few minutes away. I was on my own. My only link back home was two proof-of-life calls. Twice a day at a certain time, either Yasser or I had to call our handlers in Europe. This was our signal that we were safe. Code words were in place to relay whatever message we needed to at the time. Missing a proof-of-life would set off alarms. Our handlers would send help, regardless of whether it blew our cover.

After our first meeting with the Sheikh, I didn't sleep. My mind kept running through all the scenarios. I rose at dawn, prayed for the courage to do my job, and dressed for the meeting. The Afghan was out front and we all climbed into his SUV. He drove us in circles for the next hour. Finally, he pulled into a parking lot across the street from a beautiful mosque right on the water and shut off the engine.

"Come on, I want to show you this mosque," the Afghan said.

I shot Yasser a look. Bullshit. The parking lot had only one way in or out. It was easy to see if we were followed. We walked over to the mosque but only visited for a minute before the Afghan ushered us back into the car.

He drove the SUV across the street to a tall apartment building. The biscuit-colored building wasn't shoddy, but it lacked curb appeal. A middle-class workingman's building. The lobby was dark and dusty. The elevator took a minute to arrive. The Afghan hit the button for the twenty-seventh floor and the elevator clattered up the shaft. The door opened into a pitch-black hallway. As soon as the Afghan stepped off the elevator, the lights popped on. Motion sensors.

We followed the Afghan down the hall. He stopped about halfway and opened a door into an apartment. No furniture. Every room was empty. The blinds were open, and we could see the deep blue of the Persian Gulf and the mosque across the street.

The Afghan opened one more door. The Sheikh was sitting on a sectional couch. He stood up when we walked inside. We all greeted one another while the Afghan got a tray with tea and dates. The Sheikh never touched his tea or the dates. I wondered if we were getting poisoned. But to not drink the tea would have been an insult. When the Afghan finally took a sip, I relaxed.

"It would be great if you could support the hospitals and schools in Afghanistan," the Sheikh said.

His cover was the head of a charity, but it was clear before I came that I wanted to support the fight. I was here to help kill Americans. I let him do his pitch. When the Sheikh paused, I cut in.

"Let me ask you something," I said. "You know where I am coming from. You've already checked me out."

The Sheikh nodded.

"We're sitting here and you're telling me about building schools and hospitals," I said. "Let me put it to you this way: You're telling me that one of our brothers has cancer. And you're asking me to buy him a suit. To dress him up. Why don't you ask me to help remove that cancer? We'll worry about what he looks like after."

The Sheikh gave the Afghan a nod. He stood up and left the room. Another door opened and closed. I heard voices in the hall. Yasser shifted in his seat. No one said anything.

The Afghan came back with a twelve-year-old boy in a white robe and kufi—the white skullcap—carrying a laptop. The boy didn't look at anyone. He just sat down next to the Sheikh and put the computer on the table. The Sheikh gave instructions in Dari and the screen soon filled with charts and spreadsheets.

"These are the areas I was describing," the Sheikh said. "But clearly you can be an asset to the brothers in other areas, such as military aid. But these are sensitive areas."

The Sheikh never touched the computer as the boy scrolled through the information.

"We'll have to shield your assets," the Sheikh said.

"Of course," I said. "You have my e-mail. Send me the proposal. If you have a way to receive the money, I'm all ears."

"*Masha'Allah*," the Sheikh said. "We will contact you."

I was ready to talk specifics, but the Sheikh put his hand on the boy's back, who closed the computer and left. We had an understanding but nothing more. The Afghan stood up and we followed him out.

We were leaving the next night. Our flight departed near midnight, so Yasser and I lounged by the pool the rest of the morning. Just before lunch, I got a call from the Afghan.

"The Sheikh wants to meet," he said. "I'm coming to the hotel."

We met the Afghan in the lobby. There was a seriousness to his movements. This was important and had to be done before we left. The Afghan turned to leave and we followed. He stopped after a few steps.

"I'm going to get the car," he said. "The Sheikh just wants to meet with Tamer. Finish up their discussion from yesterday."

The Afghan walked out, leaving us.

"No fucking way," Yasser said once he was out of earshot.

"Listen, he bought what we were selling," I said. "Let's see what he has to say."

I checked my watch. It was just after 1:00 P.M. and our last proof-of-life call was scheduled for 2:00 P.M.

"I'm not going to make the call," I said. "Make the call for us. Trust me. I'll be fine. We've got to make this happen."

Yasser didn't like it, but he didn't stop me. I jumped into the car and the Afghan drove around the corner to a coffee shop. The Sheikh was waiting there. He climbed into the front seat and we drove a few minutes to an underground garage. The Afghan found a spot in the lowest level. It was dark and quiet.

"Take the battery out of your phone," the Sheikh said as he turned to face me.

I showed him the battery. He smiled.

"Thank you for coming," he said. "You're going to be the reason we win this war."

The Sheikh laid out the plan. They needed money for weapons.

My point of contact was the Afghan. The Sheikh wanted me to wire him money that I raised through my business. I had an envelope with a few thousand dollars in it and handed it over as a goodwill gesture.

"It is very important to me that this money go directly to our leaders," I said to the Sheikh. "Can you assure me of that?"

I also had a message for al Qaeda's leaders.

"I can help brothers come to America," I said.

Our business was done. I checked my watch. It was close to time for the proof-of-life call, but the Sheikh kept talking. We were friends now. The Sheikh asked me to fly to his home in South Africa in a few months. Not for business, but because he wanted to host me at his home. We also talked about setting up bank accounts so I could send them money.

I watched the hands of my watch blow past 2:00 P.M.

A half hour.

One hour.

Finally, the Sheikh thanked me for the money and agreed to pass along my offer to get American visas for like-minded brothers.

By the time I finally got back to the hotel, I was three hours late. The Afghan dropped me off and I walked into the lobby. Yasser was in the same spot as when I'd left. He was a mess. He had tried to call me, but of course my phone didn't work.

"I don't know whether to punch you in your fucking face or kiss your lips," Yasser said.

He hugged me.

"Let's go to the room," I said.

In the suite, I told Yasser that the Sheikh confirmed everything. Tamer was now going to provide money to al Qaeda, and the Sheikh agreed to deliver my visa offer.

For the next few months, I kept in touch with the Afghan and the Sheikh. No money was exchanged, but we were both working toward it. We'd set the trap with the visa offer; now we just had to wait for the Afghan to deliver it. I was working with Chris to set up another trip overseas to visit the Sheikh when he called me.

"Our boy is on his way to Kabul," Chris said. "Looks like they took the bait."

"That's awesome," I said. "We have coverage?"

"Yeah," he said. "I'll let you know."

The very next day I got another call from Chris. The Afghan had been picked up.

"They took him into custody for special conversations," Chris said.

"What does that mean?" I said.

"Don't know," Chris said. "I'll let you know when I do."

Then, in late spring, I noticed a breaking news scroll flash across the TV screen. A drone attack in Pakistan. The target was one of the al Qaeda planners on our list.

My phone buzzed. It was a text message from Chris.

"It's over. I'll call you later."

A few hours later, Chris called. After he was brought in, the Afghan had held out for two weeks before he gave up his mission and Tamer. His confession had led to the drone strike. Because of it, one of al Qaeda's chief planners was dead. The operation was a success.

"What about Tamer?" I said.

"You're good," he said. "The military folks scrubbed everything. Tamer's clean. Your legend is still intact."

CHAPTER 6

"Take His Temperature"

My cell phone rang as I lounged in my undercover apartment in St. Louis.

I recognized the number. It was FBI Headquarters in Washington. Suhel, my supervisor, was on the line. I could tell he needed a favor as soon as I answered.

"Hey, we've got a case out of New York," Suhel said. "It's a Canadian guy in Montreal. We need you to take his temperature."

Shit. I rubbed my temple and took a deep breath. I hated to say no, but I was jammed. I didn't have a moment to spare. Since returning from the Middle East, I'd jumped back into my caseload.

"I'd love to help, but I'm in St. Louis today," I said. "I've got to be in Jacksonville at the end of the week and I've got a case in Tennessee. I've got to be in L.A. for two weeks at the end of the month."

Suhel was prepared for my answer. He must have studied the large board that took up one wall of the unit's Washington office. Each undercover agent had his own row with color-coded magnets for each case he or she was working. The colors—red, yellow, green—signified where each case stood. Next to my designation were two rows. I had six cases across the country in addition to the overseas mission.

"We know," Suhel said. "But we think this is a very bad guy and we need a Muslim and Arabic speaker. He is flying to California for a conference in a month or so. Just take his temperature. It's a three- or four-day babysitting assignment."

"Fine," I said. "I'll drive up to New York and meet with the case agents when I get back from Florida."

I had no choice. I wouldn't be able to live with myself if this guy killed people and I hadn't intervened. This is what I signed up to do.

A week later, I fought the Holland Tunnel traffic and arrived at the Joint Terrorism Task Force offices on the west side of Manhattan. I badged my way in and was ushered into a conference room. I shook hands with the two case agents, who had come straight from central casting: drab suits, conservative haircuts, no regional accent. They introduced themselves and I started the meeting by telling them all about myself, the different legends I had, and my level of experience.

"We think we can get you in front of him," the male agent said, looking at the case file. "Which legend do you want to use?"

I had several. But I needed more information before I could figure out which one would work.

"Do you have any idea when he'll be flying?"

The agents looked at each other.

"No."

That was weird. Headquarters said he was going to California in a few weeks.

"He speaks Arabic, right?"

More confusion.

"We don't know if he speaks Arabic," the female agent said.

"I'm sorry," I said. "I thought he was Tunisian."

"No, he is Bangladeshi," the male agent said.

Now everyone was confused.

"Are you looking for CT-1?" the female agent said.

"Yeah."

"This is CT-4."

I was in the wrong room. I gathered up my notebook and stood up to leave.

"Sorry," I said. "Can you point me in the right direction?"

The male agent shut the door.

"Now you can't leave," he said with a smile. "You're ours now."

I laughed. We talked for a few more minutes about the case. They were investigating Quazi Mohammad Rezwanul Ahsan Nafis, a native of Bangladesh who had links to al Qaeda. I knew the undercover officer they were going to use.

"Listen, the guy you're getting is a great guy," I said. "But I'll make myself available if you need me."

A couple of months later, after meeting with another FBI undercover agent, Nafis was arrested for plotting to remotely detonate a bomb in front of the Federal Reserve Bank of New York in lower Manhattan. He pled guilty in February 2013 and was sentenced to thirty years in prison.

The male agent walked me over to CT-1. Nelly—a short Colombian with coffee-colored skin—greeted me at the door.

"I almost got sucked into that," I said, looking back as the agent from CT-4 walked away.

"Fuck those guys," Nelly said. "You're with us."

CT-1 was the task force's international, extraterritorial squad, known historically as the al Qaeda squad. It worked the 1993 World Trade Center bombing, the 2000 USS *Cole* attack in Yemen, and arrested and thwarted the 2007 plot to blow up jet fuel supply tanks and pipelines at JFK Airport. The squad was known across the FBI as the premiere counterterror unit in the country.

Nelly ushered me into their conference room. A New York City detective assigned to the Joint Terrorism Task Force, Nelly joined CT-1 in 2005 after working in a citywide anti-gun unit. Besides working terrorism cases in the United States, he assisted with cases worldwide, including going overseas after a suicide bombing attempt in Stockholm, Sweden, in 2010.

We were joined by Johnny, another NYPD detective on the task force, who worked homicides and robbery before joining CT-1. His nickname was "mini-Hulk" because he looked like a giant muscle with his short and stout build. His New York accent was so thick, it sounded fake.

Kenny—a barrel-chested Italian from Boston—was one of the primary case agents on the JFK bombing case. He came off as more of a cop than an FBI agent. Most of the other agents were lawyers with guns. A navy veteran, he also maintained all the surveillance equipment. Without him, we couldn't gather the records needed for a conviction.

The supervisor of CT-1 came and popped his head in to say hello just before we started. He reminded me of Karl Childers—Billy Bob Thornton's character in *Sling Blade*. As he talked, all I could hear in my head was *"I like them French fried potaters."*

When he left, I looked at Nelly.

"What's up with *Sling Blade*?"

Nelly's face lit up and he tried to stifle a laugh.

"That's my boss."

We both started laughing. I know in the first five minutes if I like someone. I loved Nelly. He reminded me of Billy, my old boss when I worked drugs. They were both street cops. I found out later Nelly had also worked drugs in the Bronx before he came to the task force.

Johnny led the meeting. He handled all the intelligence on the case. Our target was Chiheb Esseghaier, a Tunisian citizen living in Montreal. Chiheb had popped up on the FBI's radar after he made contact with some al Qaeda operatives online.

"Over the last two years, the target traveled to Iran twice," Johnny said. "We're not sure why he went to Iran, but we think he went there to train."

While Johnny talked, I flipped through a bunch of top secret folders. I stopped on a flowchart showing the guys Chiheb was talking with and how they were connected to al Qaeda's leadership.

"He may be in the pre-operational phase," Johnny said. "The Canadians have seen an escalation of his countermeasures and recruitment."

Basically, once he was on our radar, we had notified Canadian intelligence. They opened up their own investigation and believed he was acting suspiciously.

"What's he doing in Canada?" I said.

"He's going to school," Johnny said. "He's getting his doctorate."

Chiheb was a doctoral student at Institut National de la Recherche Scientifique, Canada's top research university. He was world-renowned for his work in biological nanotechnology. His research was part of a project developing optical and electrochemical biosensors. But his trips to Iran were a red flag, because as part of his research he had access to infectious diseases.

I looked at the pictures of Chiheb. Thick beard. Shaggy, curly hair. He wore glasses that softened up his jihadi look. He looked more scientist than killer. I compared the current pictures with ones shot soon after he arrived in Canada. He didn't have a beard and looked like an innocent kid.

"The Canadians tried to bump him in Cancún, Mexico, during a conference in 2011," Johnny said. "They weren't able to get close to him."

A bump is a casual meeting. It seemed random and was used to meet a target. The Canadians didn't have a Muslim, so they used a Peruvian Christian. Chiheb's English wasn't that good. The hope was a native Arabic speaker would have a better chance.

"What is his family like?" I said.

Johnny flipped through some pages in the file. Three brothers. Mother and father both alive. The family was mainstream.

"What flipped him from 'As salamu alaikum' to 'I'm going to kill your ass'?" I said. "Something happened."

No one could tell me. Johnny had all the facts, but not his pattern of life.

"What does he do on Saturday night? Where does he eat? What does he do after the mosque on Friday? Is he an early riser?"

Everyone looked at one another like I had two heads. Why did I want to know all that?

"You're asking me to get in front of this guy and develop a relationship with him," I said. "We've swung and missed in the past. I need to know how I'm going to craft my legend to make sure he chooses me. I want him to go to bed at night thinking about me. I want him asking himself what he can do for me. How can he make me his friend?"

The lightbulb went on. Nelly and Johnny both nodded in agreement.

"We're on it," Nelly said. "We'll get you a better pattern of life."

The meeting ended with Nelly taking down my list of questions. As he walked me out, he promised to get on the phone with his counterpart in Canada. We agreed to meet a week later to review the findings and work on my legend.

On my ride home, I went over the facts of the case. A lot of these bumps get blown out of proportion. Most times it is just some asshole talking shit. All bark. But something wasn't right with Chiheb. His trip to Iran was troubling. He met with and talked online with bad guys.

But first, I had to learn more about him. Did he like to smoke hookah? Was he like the September 11 hijackers and have a thing for strippers? I needed a thread to pull. A week later, I was back in New York in the same conference room with Nelly, Kenny, and Johnny.

"The guy is all about Islam," Johnny said.

"What do you mean?" I said.

"All he does is talk about religion," Johnny said. "But he stopped going to the mosque."

As soon as Johnny said that, my heart sank. It was said in passing, and Johnny was already on to his next point when I stopped him.

"Johnny, did you say he stopped going to the mosque?"

Johnny flipped back through his notes.

"Yeah," he said. "He used to go to a mosque around the corner from his place in Montreal. Every Friday. He stopped going shortly after he got back."

"From overseas?" I said.

"Yeah. Why? What's wrong?"

"Was it a radical mosque?" I asked. "The one in Montreal."

"It's a legit stand-up mosque," Johnny said.

"What about the Imam?"

"Nope. Nothing on him."

"Did he go to another mosque?"

"Nope," Johnny said. "He stays home on Fridays. If he's not at work, he's at home."

Mainstream Muslims go to the mosque. If you're radicalized, Muslims in the mosque who aren't as "dedicated to the cause" are going to drive you nuts. They are an affront to Islam, more so than nonbelievers, because radicals feel they should know better.

"I need you to ask what his dialogue was like in Cancún," I said. "Did he say anything about women on the beach?"

"Women?" Johnny said.

"What was his reaction to women in bathing suits?" I said. "Was he angry? Disgusted?"

I saw Nelly and Kenny exchange a puzzled glance.

"In the eyes of the mujahideen, the women on the beach are the types you grab off the streets," I said. "You cut their throats or stone them for not covering themselves. They're whores."

"We'll call the Canadians tomorrow and hit you back," Johnny said.

But he didn't wait until tomorrow. On my way home, my cell phone rang. It was Johnny.

"I don't know how you figured this one out, but he was spewing all kinds of shit in Mexico when he saw the women in bathing suits," Johnny said. "He said those women are going to rot in hellfire. He went out of his way to talk about it."

These were all signs that he was already gone, and the only thread I had to get close to him was Islam. Chiheb didn't have any bad habits. My only way in was to be a recruitable asset. I'd have to be a Muslim, but I'd be hiding my supposed jihadi beliefs. I had to convince him he needed me.

A week before the bump, I was back in New York with Nelly. The plan was to intercept Chiheb on his flight to California. Kenny was working with headquarters to set everything up while Nelly and I worked out my legend.

With little lead time, we decided to use Tamer Elnoury. You're not supposed to use the same legend for multiple cases, but this was just a bump. Plus, Tamer was fully backstopped after his trip to the Middle East. Al Qaeda had already vetted him and he had some attractive qualities. He was born overseas but living in the West. Chiheb could relate. Tamer also had money.

"I have to be wealthy," I said.

"Why?" Nelly said.

"For two reasons. One, I'm going to be traveling a lot. I need a reason to go anywhere and be anywhere. Two, I don't know what his intentions are. Does he want to bring people in? Does he want to just recruit? Whatever his reasons are, you're better off having money."

Nelly got it immediately. Money was the world's best superpower.

"I'm down with that," he said. "Tamer Elnoury is the most interesting man in the world."

"Stay thirsty, my friend," I said.

We were ready. Now all we needed to do was get on the plane.

CHAPTER 7

The Bump

Nelly returned from the hotel's breakfast buffet with bacon piled high on his plate.

I was sitting across from him. Unlike during my drug days, my hair was thicker and my beard was untrimmed like the Prophet's. Most days I could pass as Hispanic or light-skinned black, depending on my haircut, but not now. I was an Arab and there was no mistaking how I felt about pork.

Nelly took a bite of bacon and looked at me. The realization hit him as fast as the salty flavor.

"Shit," he said with a sheepish grin. "I forgot I'm eating breakfast with a Muslim."

I laughed. I didn't know him well yet, but I already felt like I was back with my old narcotics unit. I loved that he was already breaking my balls.

"Bro, we're good as long as you're not stuffing it down my throat."

We were in Houston. It was June 2012 and we had a few hours before Chiheb's bump. For the past several weeks, Nelly and Kenny had worked to set everything up. First it was to be in Chicago. Then Minneapolis. Houston was a last-minute change.

We arrived the night before, and Nelly went over to the FBI office to coordinate everything. I stayed at the hotel alone. I was already Tamer. I'd been in legend since I left home. In my pocket was Tamer's driver's license. His credit cards. His business cards. His phone was in my jacket pocket. My FBI work phone was packed away.

My transformation started before I left my house. Like a batter getting ready to hit, I had a routine that always ended with me sitting on the beach watching the waves. It started with a shower. I washed my true identity away and got dressed in Tamer's clothes. I put on his watch, slid his wallet into my pocket, and charged up his phone. From my house, I drove out to the Jersey Shore. There was something about being near the sea. The natural rhythms of the waves helped me focus. I watched set after set of waves crash against the sand, each one clearing my head so I could fill it with Tamer.

"Hello, my name is Tamer Elnoury," I said out loud as I stared into the surf. "Nice to meet you."

I recited his mother's maiden name, his social security number, and his address over and over until it sounded natural. Passersby figured I was nuts. But it was the only way I knew how to get ready. A half hour later, I put the car in gear as Tamer.

At the airport, I stopped at a restaurant in the terminal to get a bite to eat. At the bar, I introduced myself as Tamer. I even handed out business cards and offered some real estate advice.

Usually I traveled alone, but Nelly forced me to straddle both worlds. As we ate breakfast, he started to fill me in on Chiheb's movements from his apartment in Montreal to the airport.

"He boarded his flight early this morning," Nelly said. "He's headed for Orlando now. From there he will make a stop in Houston before going on to California. We're going to get on his connecting flight from Houston to San Jose."

"Okay," I said. "What are you looking for in this bump?"

I needed to know Nelly's goals. It helped me to know what buttons to push once I was in front of Chiheb. For some reason, it always came out in baseball terms.

"What's a base hit?" I said. "Do you want to just figure out if he is jihadi? Are you looking to develop a relationship with him? Uncover a plot? What is a grand slam in your eyes? What would be the greatest thing I could do to make your case go forward?"

Nelly finished a strip of bacon as he thought about it.

"I want to know if this guy is who we think he is," Nelly said. "And if he is, I want you to get close to him. If you do, I want you to find out everything there is to know about his intentions."

Nelly was treating this as more than just a bump to take his temperature.

"Thanks," I said. "That's what I needed."

I pushed my food around my plate for a few more minutes and then excused myself. I wasn't hungry and I needed to reset. I wanted to get fully into Tamer's legend. Back at my hotel room, I showered again and got dressed. Tamer had money, so I wore a tailored shirt, expensive slacks, and Italian shoes. Except for the untrimmed beard, I looked put-together.

I took a taxi to George Bush Intercontinental Airport and went straight to the gate. I was early, so I took a seat in the corner and fished out my BlackBerry Torch. At a glance, I was checking my e-mail. But my attention was on the waiting area. I'd only seen a picture of Chiheb once. I didn't want to see another picture of him, because I wanted it to seem natural when I saw him at the gate.

When my group was called to board, I saw him. He was wearing a button-down shirt and jeans rolled up so his pant legs never touched the dirty ground. He had an overstuffed laptop bag over his shoulder. He was fidgeting with his ticket. There was a nervous energy. He rocked his weight from foot to foot, trying to burn it off.

I relaxed when I saw him. I was no longer dealing with the unknown. He was right in front of me. I could see him. I could almost touch him. He was two people ahead of me as we boarded. I kept looking down at my phone when he looked back in my direction. I wanted to be surprised when we ended up sitting next to each other. Our seats were in the second row just past first class. But when I got into the cabin, a family was sitting in our row. The man was on the end, with his wife seated in the middle next to their young daughter by the window.

Chiheb was staring at them. He checked his ticket and then looked back at the full row. He waved his hand at a male flight attendant helping passengers with overhead baggage. The flight attendant didn't notice him. I turned my back to Chiheb and flagged down the female flight attendant in the first class section.

"Excuse me," I said. "I believe my seat is messed up."

The female flight attendant looked at me and smiled.

"Sir, I'll be right with you," she said.

She had to wait for the line of passengers to clear.

I kept my eyes on my boarding pass. I could feel Chiheb behind me. Suddenly, he stuck his head around my shoulder.

"Do you speak Arabic?" he asked in Arabic.

"Of course," I said.

"*As salamu alaikum,*" Chiheb said.

"*Wa alaikum al salam wa rahmat'Allah wa barakatu,*" I said, the extended Arabic greeting.

It sent a message about who I was and my religious beliefs.

"I knew it," he said. "I could tell you were a brother."

By now we'd moved to the front of the plane so the other passengers could board. I was doing my best to stay out of the way as passengers brushed by us.

"Where are you from, brother?" I said.

"Tunisia," Chiheb said. "Where are you from?"

"Egypt."

"By the grace of God, what are the chances?" Chiheb said, visibly relieved to have someone to talk with in his native language.

"Sorry, dear brother," I said. "They messed up my seat."

"Me too," he said. "Hold on."

"Sir, we need to sit together," Chiheb told the male flight attendant in heavily accented English. "You have to put us together."

He chose me.

The flight attendant found two open seats next to a European guy in the exit row. I took the middle seat. Chiheb grabbed the aisle. The row was right in front of the female flight attendant's jump seat.

As I sat down, I spotted Nelly and Kenny. Two air marshals were also taking the flight. The flight attendant knew four armed federal agents were on board, but not why. She had no idea who I was. When the flight attendant took her seat, I noticed she kept looking toward Nelly and the other agents.

You're here for them, right? her eyes said. *Please tell me you're here for them.*

It was a three-and-a-half-hour flight to San Jose. After takeoff, Chiheb and I picked up our conversation in Arabic. We covered family, my work, his work, and our hometowns. I mentioned that my uncle still lived in Egypt. Before the drink cart got to us, Chiheb flipped to politics. Islamic politics.

"This *Dunya* doesn't matter," he said.

In his mind, everything a Muslim did in this world, or *Dunya*, was a test. He was earning his place in paradise.

Chiheb started to rail against the munafiqeen, Muslims who are secretly unsympathetic and sought to undermine the Muslim community. The Quran calls them the most dangerous enemies of Islam.

"They are worse than the infidels," Chiheb said. "They have been shown the way and have elected not to choose it. As opposed to the infidels who never had the opportunity."

This was classic fundamentalist talk. It didn't mean he was a terrorist. It just meant he took his religion very seriously. It was a flag, but not necessarily a red one. Not yet.

So far, I was able to balance the conversation. It's a very fine line between agreeing and kissing ass. I wanted to push his buttons. Put him in a position to be the Imam and educate me. Show me what it means to be a real Muslim.

Chiheb's demeanor changed when he talked about the drone strikes in Afghanistan and Pakistan. The Imam was gone. There was anger in his voice.

"The West is killing our women and children," he said. "They are raping our women."

I agreed, citing a passage from the Quran.

"'A life for a life, and an eye for an eye, and a nose for a nose, and an ear for an ear, and a tooth for a tooth, and for all wounds, like for like.'"

Something similar appears in the Bible and the Torah. But I left off the last part:

But whosoever forgoes it by way of charity, it will be for him an expiation. Those who do not judge by what Allah has revealed are indeed the wrongdoers.

The Quran makes it clear human beings are not supposed to be judge and executioner. That is God's job. Humans forgive and forget.

But I knew Chiheb rejected any notion of forgiveness. That is what the jihadis do. Edit out the parts of Islam that get in the way. Leaving it out was a signal. In skipping the last lines, I was like him.

As the flight went by, his body language changed. I could feel his passion and excitement building. He knew I was a like-minded brother. He was leaning so far forward he was practically in my lap.

"What started out as a disastrous trip turned out to be a fateful trip," Chiheb told me just before landing.

Chiheb had no idea when he left his apartment in Montreal that morning that he would fly all over the United States. His itinerary was supposed to have been a more direct route. At each stop he got searched.

"What do you mean, brother?"

"I almost didn't come," he said. "I was so fed up. I kept asking Allah why am I going on this trip if you keep putting roadblocks in front of me? And here we are, dear brother. I was meant to meet you. Allah put us together, Tamer. This is Allah's will."

I believed him. Allah put me in his path to take his temperature. The pilot came over the intercom. We were on final approach.

"Where are you staying?" I asked.

He told me his hotel was a long way from the airport. He planned to take a taxi, but I shook my head no.

"Absolutely not," I said. "I've got nothing until late tomorrow. I want to make sure you're okay. I'm going to drive you myself. My job is to protect you and make sure you're safe. If my brother is visiting me in this country, I am going to make sure my brother is okay."

"May Allah reward you for your blessings and your kindness," Chiheb said.

It was close to midnight when we landed. The airport was deserted except for the cleaning crews. Chiheb followed me to the rental car area after we retrieved our bags. We bypassed the desks and went to the VIP area. Nelly had arranged a luxury rental car. Chiheb followed me as I was greeted by a clerk. The car was running next to the curb.

"Hello, Mr. Elnoury," the clerk said. "Your car is ready."

No signatures. No paperwork. He just took our bags and put them in the trunk. I climbed into the driver's seat of the Mercedes sedan and punched in the address of Chiheb's hotel. It was 1:00 A.M. by the time we arrived. I helped him get settled in his room. It was a modest room with two double beds. Chiheb put his suitcase on one bed.

"Look, I have two beds here," Chiheb said. "I insist you stay with me."

He was trying to return my hospitality. I thanked him but declined.

"I've got meetings tomorrow," I said. "I'm going to go to my hotel and check in and get settled."

"Can we have dinner tomorrow?" he asked.

"I'd love to," I said. "I should be done by dinner. Give me a call."

Chiheb walked me to the door of his room.

"Brother, do you need anything else?"

Chiheb shook his head no.

"I'm eating," he said. "I'm sleeping. I'm praying. I have all that I need, dear brother."

CHAPTER 8

Live Amongst Them
to Defeat Them

The streets were deserted when I left Chiheb's hotel.

Before I could go to bed, I had a meeting with Nelly and Kenny. Nelly met me at the door of his room at the Residence Inn Suites in San Jose. I took a seat on the couch. Nelly and Kenny sat in chairs in front of me. We went through the bump and the ride to the hotel.

"What is he doing tomorrow?" Nelly asked.

"The conference," I said. "I'm going to dinner with him afterward. I need a good halal restaurant in the area."

"I'll check in with one of the San Jose guys," Nelly said. "We'll get you a place."

The rest of the meeting we talked about the flight and laughed about the seat mix-up. I left the suite just before dawn and went to my hotel. That morning, I waited to hear from Chiheb. He e-mailed me in the late afternoon. Chiheb's phone didn't work. I fired back a response.

No problem, brother. Let's communicate via e-mail. See you at
6 p.m. for dinner. I'll pick you up at the hotel.

I called Nelly after Chiheb confirmed dinner. He had a restaurant for me.

"Menara Moroccan Restaurant," Nelly said. "It's on East Gish Road. Four stars. High-end."

"It's halal, right?" I asked.

"Definitely," Nelly assured me.

"Perfect," I said. "I got an e-mail from Chiheb. His phone doesn't work here."

Nelly chuckled. I knew what he was thinking right away.

"I'll run it by the team," Nelly said. "See you at the safe house to wire up."

I got to Chiheb's hotel at 6:00 P.M. He was waiting for me in the lobby. When he saw the car pull up, Chiheb got into the passenger side. After saying hello, I handed him a smartphone. Nelly and the team had gotten the phone for me.

"Here, take this," I said. "So you can reach me, brother."

Chiheb wouldn't touch it.

"Absolutely not," he said. "You can't do this. What did it cost?"

I refused to tell him. He reached into his pocket and took out his wallet.

"Let me pay for it," he said.

I refused to take his money.

"While you are in my country, it is my honor to give you what you need," I said. "You need a phone, brother. Nothing else. Just call me this week. It can dial international. Feel free to talk to anyone you want."

Chiheb finally slid the phone in his pocket. He took it because it would have been rude not to, an insult to my hospitality. Plus, he felt like I was being a good brother. But now we had coverage on his calls and e-mails.

"Thank you, brother," he said.

I put the car in gear and eased into traffic. The restaurant was in North San Jose, near the airport.

"Where are we going to eat, brother?" Chiheb said.

"I called a buddy in New York," I said. "I told him, 'Do me a favor, you've been to San Jose. Can you tell me a halal restaurant for a couple of good Muslim brothers?' He gave me this place. I've never been there. I don't know anything about it. But he said it's delicious."

Another rule in undercover work was never pretend to know something or someplace, because it will always bite you in the ass.

I could tell he was uncomfortable with the restaurant. He'd rather eat at a fast-food place and save the money. A true mujahideen wouldn't waste anything. Everything Chiheb did was for Allah. It was a sin to waste money on frivolous things.

I had to justify my choice.

"We kind of have to spend money because my company makes so much money a year," I said. "We have to spend a good amount to have a business write-off. This whole trip. My flight. The car. My meals. Your phone. Everything is being billed to the company. At the end of the year, say we make a million dollars. In order for us to pocket the profits, we have to show expenses. If we don't spend it on ourselves, the government gets it in taxes."

Better to spend it than let the American government use it on guns and missiles to kill the brothers overseas. Chiheb listened carefully. His scientific mind started processing my logic.

"That makes sense," he said, content that he understood it. "So basically, if we don't spend it here, the haram government is going to get it."

"Exactly," I said.

He smiled.

"Bon appétit."

Menara looked small from the outside. But once inside, it opened up into a large, low-lit room with a fountain at the center. I got three steps into the restaurant when I noticed the bar. It was massive, with top-shelf liquor on the shelves. The place was supposed to be halal, which means blessed by an Imam. Chiheb noticed the bar too. My heart sank when I saw his face turn.

"May Allah forgive me," he said quietly in Arabic.

The hostess met us at the podium. She gathered up two menus.

"Can I get a table in the back corner," I said. "We want to be away from the bar area."

She led us through the dining room, which was decorated with a Middle Eastern aesthetic. The tables were low, with pillows or low benches for seats. I took off my shoes and sat on a pillow. Chiheb sat opposite me. He was angry.

"How can a Muslim owner possibly have liquor in this establishment? I don't understand it."

I was trying to calm him down when our waiter showed up with glasses of water. He was an Asian kid. Mid-twenties. Scruffy goatee.

"Can I get you anything to drink?"

Chiheb folded his hands on the table. His inner Imam was fighting to get out.

"No," he said.

Chiheb was angry.

"How can you call this place halal?" he said. "No Imam should bless a place that serves alcohol."

He went on and on.

"Look, man, I just work here."

I cut Chiheb off.

"Yeah, okay," I said. "We'll figure out who the owner is and we can talk with him later."

Chiheb agreed.

I ordered some fruit juices and appetizers. Hummus. Grape leaves. Olives. A feast. When the waiter left, we started talking. He wanted to know about my uncle in Egypt. The one who started the Elnoury Investment Group. We were headed toward my "point of radicalization," the incident that led me to embrace radical Islam, when the lights in the restaurant dimmed. I noticed two disco balls come down from the ceiling. I turned toward the front of the room. Two guys dressed like extras in *Aladdin* were banging on drums.

Are you fucking kidding me? I thought.

I glanced at Chiheb. His mouth was open in stunned silence as a gorgeous Arab woman started belly dancing. She moved around the room shaking and gyrating. Chiheb covered his eyes.

"Stay right here, brother," I said.

I stood up and walked toward the bar. Our waiter was coming with a tray of drinks. I flagged him down.

"Do me a favor, ask her not to go anywhere near our table," I said, pressing a twenty-dollar bill into his free hand. "As you already know, I have a very religious man with me."

"Absolutely, I understand," he said.

He started to walk away.

"Hey, when is she dancing again?"

The waiter started laughing.

"Six o'clock Thursday," he said.

"Thanks," I said, and headed back to Chiheb.

"What did he say?" Chiheb said as I sat down.

"Clearly this owner is munafiqeen," I said. "I berated him. I told him do not let that woman anywhere near our table."

"Good for you," Chiheb said.

The dancer stayed away and the first plates arrived.

"Let's just finish our meal," I said.

I sampled all the dishes. After about a half hour, I stopped eating. I was full. There was plenty left and Chiheb kept eating. For pleasure at first. Then to finish each dish. One of the hadiths tells Muslims not to waste food, water, anything. I watched Chiheb hold the plate at an angle with his left hand as he scooped the hummus into his mouth with his right hand. It was clear he was full. But he couldn't waste a drop. When he was done, the plate was spotless. He did it with every plate. He knew the waiter was going to throw it out, and that is haram. Waste not, want not to the one-hundred-thousandth degree.

While he ate, I talked about my mother. I told him how much she meant to me and how I felt when I got to the hospital on her last day. Chiheb sat quietly as I described the room and my mother in her bed. The doctor was there with some nurses. We were the only Muslims. I ran to my mother's side. I grabbed her hand and touched her head. Everyone was silent. They just stood by and watched my mother die, I told him. I looked at the nurses. They were joking. Laughing. They didn't care about my mother because she was Muslim. I told Chiheb how I could feel my rage building. I wanted to smash the doctor's face against the wall. I wanted to beat the nurses for not helping. For hating my mother and my family for being Muslim. Even telling the fictionalized version of my mother's death was hard. Tears welled up in my eyes. I took a moment and sipped my water.

"I tried to fit in so much," I said. "I lost my religion. I looked like them. Dressed like them. Talked like them. But when my mother needed them the most, they weren't there for her."

Chiheb held my gaze. There was a hint of empathy. He believed me.

"My father died four months to the day after my mother," I said. "I was ready to go back to Egypt. I was done with this country. I was done with everything it stood for. I was disgusted with myself. I wanted to go back to Egypt and dedicate myself to Islam. Then my uncle Ibrahim, God bless him, he put his arm around my shoulder after my father's funeral."

Chiheb leaned in as I explained how Uncle Ibrahim left me the business and went back to Egypt to help the brothers in the Sinai Peninsula. Ibrahim was one of the group's financiers. There was a good bet Chiheb was going to check my story, so making Ibrahim a financier was safe. Al Qaeda's revenue streams were kept secret even from the group's leaders. No one was going to talk about who was funding whom, so it would be impossible to debunk.

"My uncle told me to live amongst them, as them, to defeat them," I said. "I've been helping my uncle with the profits from my company."

Chiheb had a knowing look on his face, like he had found what he was looking for in me. It's a look that I don't normally see so early on in a bump, but it was there. I was hesitant to give him so much so soon, but I felt like I only had a few days.

"Your uncle is a brilliant man," Chiheb said. "He is exactly right."

"I don't know if you know of the true brothers in Sinai," I said. Chiheb nodded. He knew the brothers.

"I don't know why I'm telling you this much already," I said. "I just met you. But I can see Islam is in your heart. I am confiding in you. I beg you to never tell people."

"Of course not," he said. "You have my full trust and confidence."

Chiheb was especially taken with my uncle's strategy to live among the West to defeat it.

"I will tell you hypocrisy is haram in Islam, but it's not during times of war or necessity," he said.

He explained how Muslims can break rules in order to survive— eat pork if it is the only food—and pretend to be American in order to blend in during times of war. Chiheb forgave me for straying from the path of Allah and pretending to be American when I desperately wanted to be like them.

"My God, my brother, how many years younger you are than me and look how well-read you are," I said. "Look how smart you are with your job. Look how educated you are in our religion. God bless you, brother, and may Allah keep you for all the Muslims, because we need you. We need your brain."

I found out later that his al Qaeda recruiter told him the same thing. Al Qaeda needed his brain. As we waited for the check, Chiheb leaned in closer. Now Chiheb felt the need to reciprocate.

"With you in America and me in Canada, we can do great things together, my brother," he said.

Off the cuff, it was an innocuous comment. But it was clear to both me and Chiheb what he meant. He just confirmed what we knew. That was as close as I needed to get.

"Chiheb, I will do anything for you," I said. "You and I think alike. You and I are the same. We have the same thought process. Thank God, it is nice to know that I have a Muslim brother like you, but I don't know you like that brother."

My job was done. We had confirmation that he was a legitimate threat.

At the hotel, Chiheb seemed reluctant to get out of the car.

"We need to spend every night together," Chiheb said. "There are a couple of Muslim brothers in this conference; maybe we can go to dinner, all of us?"

I was due in St. Louis at the end of the week. There was no way I was going to stick around, since he'd already given me what I wanted to know. I had other cases, but it was easier to tell him yes.

"You know, brother, I would love that," I said. "But be careful what you tell them."

"Oh no, I'm not telling them anything about you," he said.

"Get some rest," I said. "Call me tomorrow on your new phone and we can go to dinner."

At the Residence Inn suite, I settled into a couch across from Nelly and Kenny.

"Who suggested Menara?" I said.

"One of the San Jose guys," Nelly said. "Why?"

"There was a full bar when we walked in," I said.

Nelly was stunned. "Shut the fuck up."

I took a sip of my water.

"Yeah," I said. "But wait, it gets better."

I then told them about the belly dancer. Nelly looked at Kenny.

"Holy shit, that didn't happen," Kenny said.

I just sat back and smiled.

"Was she hot?" Nelly said.

"Oh, yeah," I said. "Smoking hot. That was my first question: When is she dancing again?"

"When?" Nelly asked.

"Thursday night at six."

"Nice," he said.

But the joking was over after that.

"So, what is this guy's deal?" Kenny said.

"Better tell the Canadians they have a shit storm on their hands," I said.

"Really," Nelly said. "You're sure?"

"Yeah," I said. "I've been in front of posers. I've been in front of the real deal. This guy is the real deal. He is up to something. He was recruiting me tonight."

I went over the dinner.

"He went that far with you already?" Nelly said.

Both Kenny and Nelly were suspicious. A seasoned sleeper wouldn't reveal himself so easily. I could tell they thought this guy was an amateur. But I saw something different.

"I think this guy is a very suave recruiter," I said. "He asked all the right questions on the plane. All through dinner. I jumped through all of his hoops before he opened up to me. When I gave him my POR [point of radicalization], I think I tipped the scales. They need a full detail on him. I don't know what he is up to or where he is going. I believe he is looking to go operational."

"And then he recruited you," Kenny said, checking his notes.

"Yeah. That's why I pushed him away."

"Why did you push him away?" Nelly said.

"Because he isn't our fucking problem," I said. "He's Canada's problem."

Nelly laughed. "You're fucking right he is."

"I also pushed him away because I'm part of six other cases right now and I was hoping tomorrow night I could leave."

"No fucking way, you're staying the whole week," Nelly said.

Nelly knew what we had. A clean bump on a potential al Qaeda sleeper. I was going to dinner.

"He is going to ask some Muslim brothers from the conference to dinner tomorrow. A Paki guy from London and an Iraqi dude from Germany."

"Great, a dinner party," Nelly said.

"Let's see how he deals with others," Kenny said.

The next night, I picked up Chiheb and his friends and drove them to San Francisco. We had dinner at McCormick & Schmick's near Fisherman's Wharf. Chiheb made small talk. They talked about the conference. Politics and religion. But it was all surface talk. The jihadi Chiheb never came out.

After dinner, I picked up the tab and we walked to the car. I was in front with Chiheb. The Paki and the Iraqi were several steps behind us. A plane bound for San Francisco Airport thundered overhead. Chiheb looked into the sky and at the buildings nearby. He pointed to one.

"Look at that building right here," he said. "Perfect rooftop. With all these planes coming, get a surface-to-air missile and take them all down. You could probably take down three or four before they knew where you were."

He said it nonchalantly. Like pointing out a nice sunset. No matter what he'd said and done at dinner, he was still focused on his purpose. The look in his eye was pure evil as he watched the plane fly overhead. His purpose from Allah was to kill the infidels. Before I could dig further, the Iraqi interrupted us. I walked back to the car in silence.

When I dropped off everyone at the hotel, I knew one thing: Chiheb loved Tamer. In Chiheb's eyes, Allah had given him what he needed. A wealthy American jihadist with money to fund his operations. I promised to keep in touch but knew I wouldn't.

But it was clear Chiheb was a threat.

CHAPTER 9

Uncle Ibrahim

For my part, I was ready to forget Chiheb. I had to—it was Thursday and I was due in St. Louis on another case. My mind was already transitioning to my new legend when I sat down for my final debrief with Nelly and Kenny.

"I would love to tell you he was all talk," I told Nelly and Kenny. "But I have no doubt this guy is a true mujahideen. You need to tell Canada that this fucker is for real and they can't take their eyes off of him."

"Are you sure?" Kenny said.

In all the years I've been doing this, no one has made the hair on my neck stand up like Chiheb Esseghaier. I had an opportunity to be out in public with him. To be on an airplane with him. To see how he interacted with the public. Interacted with other Muslims. But the look in Chiheb's eyes when he talked about killing infidels was something I'd never seen before in my life. It was a look of hatred and death. It turned my stomach.

The debrief took a couple of hours. Most of it was settling up receipts for the hotels, dinners, and rental car. Death by paperwork. When we were done, I grabbed my backpack and suitcase and headed for the door. I had a plane to catch in San Francisco.

"If you ever need a dirty Arab, call me direct," I told Nelly.

"You good? Need a ride to the airport?" he asked.

"No," I said. "I'll take a cab."

"We'll take you. When is your flight?"

"You sure?"

"Yeah," Nelly said. "We're meeting the San Jose guys in San Francisco for drinks after we get Chiheb on his flight. His flight doesn't leave until tonight. We've got time."

Nelly and Kenny dropped me off in front of the terminal an hour later. I was happy to be done with Chiheb, but I'd miss working with Nelly and Kenny. They were good dudes.

"Tell those assholes thanks for the restaurant suggestion," I said as I got out of the car.

After I landed, the St. Louis case agent picked me up from the airport and took me to my cover apartment. It was a spectacular loft with views of the Gateway Arch. Of all my cover apartments, this one is still one of my favorites.

I had a meeting with the target scheduled for the next morning, so I stayed in and watched the Cardinals game. I was about to switch off Tamer's phone when it started to ring. A second later, my FBI phone started to ring. I checked the caller ID. Only Chiheb had Tamer's number. Nelly was on my FBI line.

I answered Chiheb's call first. I heard the sound of a metal detector beeping and the noise of the airport security gate in the background. Chiheb's voice was breathless. Frazzled. He spoke in Arabic. It came out in short bursts.

"Peace be upon you, my brother," he said, still trying to be polite. A brief pause.

"They are trying to touch me on my private areas. You know it's haram. I don't care if it is a man. He can't touch me there. He has no reason. They are not touching anyone else."

I closed my eyes and let out a long exhale.

"Slow down," I said. "What's going on?"

"I'm at airport security and they won't let me on the plane unless they search me," he said. "There are police officers around me. They are threatening to arrest me."

"Chiheb, do me a favor," I said. "Take a deep breath. Calm down."

I knew what was going on, but I had to get through to Chiheb without alerting him that he was under investigation.

"Let me call my lawyers in New York and see if there is a way around this," I said. "I'll call you right back. Don't let go of your phone."

I heard him let out a sigh of relief.

"May Allah reward you for your troubles," he said, and hung up.

I called Nelly. No greeting. He was agitated like Chiheb.

"What the fuck, bro?" Nelly said.

"What's going on?" I said.

I could hear the same background noise on Nelly's phone. He had to be less than thirty feet from Chiheb.

"They are going to lock him up," Nelly said. "It's going to be over unless you get him on this plane."

"What are you talking about?"

"It's protocol," Nelly said. "TSA will not let him on the plane without a physical search. He is wigging the fuck out. As soon as they try to move him out of line, he flails his arms. He is causing a scene. I tried to tin the supervisor, but he isn't getting it."

Nelly had showed the TSA agent his badge, or tin, and asked them to let Chiheb pass. But they refused. Chiheb wasn't getting on the plane until TSA searched him.

"I really didn't want to go down this road with him," I said.

"I know," Nelly said. "I hear you. But we have no other choice. He has to get on that plane or this is over."

"All right. I'll call you back."

I tossed my FBI phone onto the table. If Chiheb got arrested or detained, he'd know he was under surveillance. He'd go underground. His sleeper cell, if he was part of one, would disappear. I took a deep breath. I had to tell him something to get him on that plane. I dialed his number, hoping something would pop into my head.

"Hello, brother," I said. "I just hung up with my attorney in New York. He said it is their right in this country to search anybody whenever they want. You know it's because you have a beard and you're a Muslim. This shit happens to me every time, brother. But you need to take a deep breath. It's okay."

"It's haram," Chiheb said, his voice rising an octave.

I was going to lose him. I knew what I needed to say, but I didn't want to say it. I couldn't push the words out of my mouth. My fist was clenched. My jaw hurt from grinding my teeth.

"Chiheb," I said. "Chiheb! Listen to me. Are you listening?"

"Yes," he said.

"Do you remember what Uncle Ibrahim said to me when I

was ready to leave this country? You're in the same place now. You're leaving this country but you plan on coming back, don't you?"

Chiheb's voice was even again. He understood what I was saying to him.

"Yes," he said.

"He told me to live amongst them, as them, to defeat them. And you told me hypocrisy is not haram in a time of war."

There was a pause. At this point I was pacing. I pressed the phone closer to my ear. I could hear the low murmur of people talking. The beep of the metal detector. TSA officers telling passengers to remove their shoes.

Chiheb was silent. Did he hear me? Was I getting through?

"Are you there?"

"Yes," he said.

"If you draw attention to yourself today by getting arrested, you draw attention to me," I said. "We just spent a week together. You draw attention to us. And then they know who we are."

We were now a team. Two mujahideen. Two brothers doing their part in the war. But no undercover moves this fast. It went against everything I was trained to do. But it had to be done.

"May Allah reward you," he said. "Thank you, my dear brother, for everything. I'll call you when I'm in Montreal."

The line went dead. I relaxed. Chiheb told me later that my speech set a flashbulb off in his head. It wasn't worth fighting now. Better to wait for the greater good. I didn't know it at the time, but his al Qaeda trainers told him the same thing in Iran.

A few minutes later, Nelly was on the line.

"What happened?" I asked.

"He hung up with you and tossed the phone on the x-ray belt," Nelly said. "Then he put his arms out and TSA searched him."

"Okay," I said. "So we're good."

"Yeah," Nelly said. "He just got through security. What the fuck did you say to him?"

"I gave him my uncle Ibrahim's 'live amongst them, as them, to defeat them' speech."

I could feel Nelly's smile through the phone.

"Great work," he said. "I'll call you later."

I hung up the phone and mixed a drink. I wasn't looking forward to Chiheb's next call. After my speech, I knew it was coming.

CHAPTER 10

Gone Fishing

It was just before Labor Day weekend in 2012 and I was headed to the Caribbean.

I had promised some very dear friends a year earlier that I would be around for their destination wedding. It was a swanky affair with rooms at the Ritz-Carlton and a big reception on the beach. My friends knew my job kept me on the road, so they gave me plenty of lead time. I had jealously guarded that weekend.

I needed a break. After St. Louis, I'd worked cases in Tennessee, California, Washington, D.C., and Florida. I'd also taught terrorism indicators to local law enforcement, counterterrorism techniques at the FBI undercover school, and the "mujahideen mind-set" at the FBI profiler's school. The Bureau was getting their money's worth out of me, and I'd loved every second of it. But I was burned out and needed a few cocktails on the beach to recharge.

It was Wednesday and I was off the rest of the week. I planned to bum around the house before I went to the airport. I had just finished packing when my phone rang. It was John, the special agent in charge in New York.

"Hey, boss, what's up?"

"Listen, Nelly tells me you're getting ready to ship out on vacation tomorrow," he said. "What time is your flight?"

I checked my flight confirmation.

"I'm taking a late flight out of New York."

"Any way possible you can run by the office tomorrow?" John said. "We have the assistant director of CSIS flying in. He has a bunch of questions about your new best friend."

CSIS was the Canadian Security Intelligence Service, and my new best friend was Chiheb. Chiheb and I had talked almost every day since San Jose. I'd gotten him out of the country safely—or he thought I did—and it turned out to be the catalyst for our relationship. But the conversations were about keeping up appearances. For the most part, I had punted the case to Nelly and the Canadians.

"Sure thing," I said. "No problem. I can come up."

I was headed to New York anyway, so what was a few hours earlier? I could hang around the city and catch up with Nelly and the guys before my flight.

"Thanks," John said, the relief evident in his voice. "I really appreciate it."

"Formal attire?"

I eyed my suits hanging in the closet.

"Come as you are," John said. "You're on vacation."

The next day, I pulled on some shorts and flip-flops, tossed my bags in the car, and shot up to New York. I hit midtown just before noon and parked at the office.

We were meeting in the special agent in charge's conference room. It overlooked the Hudson River. Artifacts from Ground Zero hung on the wall as a constant reminder of why we did the job. A flat-screen took up the wall on one end. Over the TV were clocks with the local time in different time zones. It was the "Hollywood" conference room, meant to impress visitors.

The CSIS officials were sitting with their backs to the Hudson. Big visitor badges with "Escort Required" printed in huge red letters on the front hung off their suit jackets. They couldn't go to the restroom alone. Nelly and his team were sitting on the opposite side of the table. John was standing at the head of the table when I walked into the room. Everyone was in suits. Nelly smiled.

"He said casual, not beach wear," Nelly said.

I just shrugged and smiled at him. Nelly pulled an empty chair out for me. I dropped my backpack next to it.

"Give me one second," I said. "I've got to use the men's room."

I ran to the bathroom and hustled back to the conference room. On my way back, I clipped my ID badge on and turned it backward so my true name was facing my body.

John waited for me to sit down.

"Are you ready now?"

"Yeah, boss," I said.

We went around the table introducing ourselves. I studied the CSIS assistant director. I didn't catch his full name. He looked like Danny DeVito. His suit was two sizes too small.

"They've got some questions for you," John said after the introductions were finished.

The Canadian looked at me.

"What can you tell us about Chiheb?"

It seemed like a pretty broad question to ask this far into the investigation. I looked at Nelly and then John. Both nodded for me to give them my take.

I turned to face the Canadian.

"He is the real deal," I said, folding my hands on the table in front of me. "He is not a poser or a pretender. I wholeheartedly believe he is here to commit a terrorist attack. I don't know where. And I don't know when. But I do believe he is here to hurt us."

It was clear to me that Chiheb followed the "path of Allah." There was no way for a believer to remain a believer without trying to live a life of total obedience to Allah. This was the path that every Muslim tried to walk every day, but Chiheb twisted it and made it extreme. He brushed his teeth to keep them healthy so he didn't have to waste time going to a dentist to fix them. He ate not because he was hungry; he needed food to continue on the path of Allah. He slept to regenerate his body to do Allah's work. Even his conversations were focused on staying on the path.

Chiheb never mentioned any terrorist attacks on the phone. But he did probe my legend. During one of our conversations, he asked me about the deal I was working on when we met in San Jose.

"I bought both buildings, brother," I told him. "Then I flipped one of them and made more than a million dollars. My uncle was happy. I was able to get most of that to him. My uncle said the brothers are praying for me. I said they should pray for you too. Your face was good on me."

I explained to the Canadians that we were speaking in Arabic and the saying "your face was good on me" was like saying Chiheb brought me good luck. And now he felt like he had a hand in getting the brothers a million dollars.

The FBI told me people connected to Chiheb overseas researched my business, my financial holdings, and my background. They made sure the building deals I mentioned happened. Each verification made Tamer more valuable. He was already vetted by al Qaeda operatives, so to Chiheb's handlers, Tamer was clean. And his wealth gave Chiheb's plans—which he hadn't revealed to me—some serious muscle. I was the jihadi bank. I was the fuel for his jihad engine.

Our conversations fell into a familiar pattern. Greetings followed by talk about family and work. We seemed to always talk about the brothers overseas. I always asked him if he needed anything at the end of the call. His response, like the first night I met him, was the same.

"I'm eating. I'm sleeping. I'm praying. I have all that I need, dear brother."

It was his reminder that he was still and would always be on the path of Allah.

"Thank you very much," the Canadian said after I was done.

But that's not what he was really saying. His tone was off. He was being polite, but his body language rubbed me the wrong way. I felt like we had shared a lot of information and insight, and now I wanted him to help connect some of the dots. What was Chiheb planning? What had they learned about him that we didn't know? I still wasn't clear why they had called me in for this meeting.

But the Canadian was keeping his cards close. It was his nature as an intelligence officer not to share. I was used to working with cops. At the end of the day, all cops are sheepdogs. We want to protect people, and for the most part, we share information in order to do it. But these were intelligence officers. Information is currency to them. Being in the know is more important than anything else.

"We know he is going fishing this weekend," the Canadian said. "We just wanted to get some insight because we don't know the people he is going to meet yet."

I leaned over to Nelly.

"There is no way Chiheb is going fishing."

"No way," he said.

Fishing didn't make any sense. But I did know the guy he was going to meet.

"You're talking about the Palestinian guy, right?"

The Canadian looked at me and then at John.

"Yes," the Canadian said.

"He just told me on the phone last week that he was going to visit a Palestinian brother in the Toronto area."

The Canadian perked up when I said Toronto. He hadn't mentioned it yet.

"How far is it between Montreal and Toronto?" I asked.

Six hours, one of the CSIS staffers said. I started to do the jihadi math. There was no way Chiheb was going to spend twelve hours in a car to go fishing for a day. That would mean being thirty-six to forty-eight hours outside of the path of Allah. He couldn't stand being off the path for ten minutes.

"Sir," I said. "Based on everything I just told you, it really doesn't make sense that Chiheb is going to go fishing."

There was an awkward silence. Both sides of the table looked at me.

"Let me put it to you this way," I said. "If I asked anybody in this room if you had plans this weekend, even if you didn't have anything firm, you'd have something in the back of your mind. Some of you might be going away on vacation. I'm going to the

Caribbean. We all have plans. This is how normal people live their lives. We take breaks. We travel for pleasure. Chiheb does not take a vacation. Every action he takes is to support jihad. There is no way he is going to cast a line and sit and have a conversation with an old Muslim buddy."

Silence. The Canadian was looking at me. He raised his hand, signaling me to stop talking. He turned to face John.

"We know for a fact he is going fishing," the Canadian said. "He rented a boat and we know the area he is going to is a popular fishing location."

Just as he finished his sentence, I stood up.

"I gotta roll," I said to Nelly.

"I don't blame you," Nelly said.

I looked at John.

"Hey, boss, I've got a flight to catch. Are we good here?"

John nodded.

"Thank you so much for coming up."

Everyone stood up. I gave Nelly a hug and shook hands with the rest of the team. I was being an undercover diva. CSIS made it clear they just wanted my insight and that was it. It was a Canadian problem. I had done my job. I hoped to God they got to this guy in time.

"Take care, guys," I said. "Have a good weekend. Enjoy your holiday. Good luck with that fishing trip."

At the airport, I shut down my FBI phone and didn't plan to be sober the rest of the weekend. Two days later, I got a call from Nelly on my private phone.

"Hey, remember when you said it probably wasn't a fishing trip?" Nelly said, trying not to disclose classified information over an open line.

"Yeah," I said.

"You were right," Nelly said.

"What was it?"

"Can you get to Bu space?"

A Bu, or Bureau, space is a secure location. I was standing on a beach with a drink in my hand.

"No."

"We'll fill you in later, but let's just say it is very nefarious."

Nefarious could mean anything. Was he recruiting? Did his Palestinian friend want to head overseas to fight? I wasn't sure what Nelly was getting at, but I did know something was up. There was tension in his voice. A sense of urgency. Whatever Chiheb was up to, he had our attention.

CSIS quickly realized Chiheb wasn't fishing. He was on a recon mission for an attack. The target was a train bridge. That weekend, CSIS dropped the case in the lap of the Royal Canadian Mounted Police, or RCMP. Since Chiheb was now talking about committing a crime on Canadian soil, CSIS was no longer involved. This was a law enforcement matter. In Canada, CSIS and the RCMP operated much like the FBI and CIA pre–September 11. There was an immovable wall between the agencies that existed to protect intelligence agents and techniques from the court system. But after September 11, the wall came down in the United States. Terrorism straddled both sides. The FBI had to learn intelligence, and the CIA had to get comfortable sharing information that could lead to arrests. I was the change personified. When I went overseas, I was a spy. When I worked in the United States, I was a cop. Everyone in the Bureau working counterterrorism undercover operations became this hybrid agent.

CSIS told the RCMP a terrorist was planning an attack and his best friend was an undercover FBI agent in New York. The RCMP called the FBI, and eventually I got the call from Nelly. I spent most of the weekend on the phone. I couldn't even give one weekend to my friends.

My flight landed Monday afternoon and Vinnie, my boss in Newark, met me at my house and drove me to the FBI office. FBI executive management wanted to discuss the case.

"Do I have time to change?"

"No," Vinnie said. "The boss is waiting for us."

I was wearing board shorts and flip-flops. Vinnie shrugged.

"It doesn't matter," he said. "It's Labor Day."

I grabbed my credentials and stuck my gun in my waistband.

"I'm really sorry you had to work through the one weekend you wanted to yourself," Vinnie said.

"It is what it is," I said. "Is the threat real?"

"Very real," Vinnie said. "I listened to everything and it's as real as it gets. They want to blow up a train from New York to Toronto."

I shook my head.

"I'm going to give you some kudos," Vinnie said. "You nailed it. You knew this guy. You put it out there to everyone and no one listened to you. Shame on them. Good for you."

That felt good. But I didn't want to be right. I think deep down I had wanted him to go fishing.

"We've got to figure out how we're going to get you in front of him now," Vinnie said.

"When do I leave?"

I was ready to get on a plane the next morning. But Vinnie warned me there were still some details to be worked out.

"We've got protections in place for you," he said. "The Canadians don't. There are a ton of questions we need answered. The problem is, this attack is a week away."

"How do we know that?"

"Because they called it an anniversary attack," Vinnie said.

September 11 was eight days away. Al Qaeda isn't known for anniversary attacks. It didn't add up. But if they were getting ready to attack, the chatter made sense. The recon made sense.

"Shit," I said. "We don't have a lot of time."

Mike, the FBI special agent in charge for Newark, met us in the conference room. We were all dressed for a cookout, but Mike looked like he had just stepped out of a DeLorean in 1984. He was wearing a pair of corduroy OP shorts. I couldn't take my eyes off his pasty white legs as we shook hands. Bill, the assistant special agent in charge, shook my hand next. He was one of the first bosses I met in the FBI. A cop's cop. He was in charge of the counterterrorism side of the house for Newark.

I took a seat next to Vinnie. Mike wanted to talk before we turned on the videoconference with Headquarters in Washington, D.C., the legal attaché in Ottawa, and Nelly and the team in New York.

"You comfortable with this?" Mike said. "We don't know if the Canadians are going to honor your protections."

Basically, my true name was protected, even in court documents, in the United States. It was unclear if the Canadians would grant me the same protections. If they didn't, there was a good chance my true name would come out if there was a trial. I didn't care. All I thought was—*the clock is ticking*. We had eight days to stop an attack.

"I'm sure," I said.

Bill started the videoconference. Nelly summarized the case for everyone. The fishing trip turned out to be a recon of a bridge used by Canada's VIA rail line. The train line went from New York City to Toronto. CSIS watched Chiheb and his Palestinian friend rent a boat and row it underneath the bridge. They didn't carry fishing poles.

Chiheb talked about the very shallow water underneath the bridge in a recording of their conversation. He didn't want the water to put out the flames as the train derailed and ran off the bridge. His goal was to kill every passenger on the train.

Nelly said the operation came from al Qaeda leaders overseas. Chiheb was getting direction from the highest levels, according to intercepted communications. His contacts were all on the FBI's Most Wanted list. Everyone agreed Chiheb gave us a chance to generate intelligence on al Qaeda operations.

Nobody was denying the evidence. Everyone knew it was real. The question was whether it was worth risking my identity in the process. But that was never a question for me. I knew I was doing it. I just needed to wrap my head around the fact that this could be my last mission.

"I'll clear my schedule," I said when they asked if I was ready. "As soon as you give me the green light, I'll be on a plane to Montreal."

But Bill wasn't ready for the green light.

"Time the fuck out," he said. "No one is taking my guy anywhere until we meet with their brass and they match our protections."

I looked down the table at Bill. What was he doing? I didn't care about protections. The clock was ticking and I had a relationship with a terrorist planning an attack in a few days. There was no time for posturing and politics. People's lives were in danger.

"Well, Bill, I've got to tell you, I doubt they will play ball," said one of the suits from Headquarters.

Bill shrugged.

"If they don't, they're going to have to figure out how to stop these guys on their own, because they're not going to get my guy up there."

The videoconference ended at an impasse. Headquarters promised to work on getting my protections. Bill agreed to have me ready. The screen had barely faded to black when I confronted Bill.

"I have to do this," I told Bill.

I didn't understand what Bill was doing.

"I know you do," Bill said. "And you will do it. But you're going to do it on our terms. They need you more than we need them. Go home and get some rest. You're going to have a fuck of a week coming up."

Bill called Headquarters' bluff. The FBI was under pressure to produce an undercover who could help Canada, one of the United States' closest allies. They also had the juice to make sure I was protected. They just needed the right motivation. Bill's refusal to send me was that motivation.

After the videoconference, Heidi, a lawyer in the FBI's National Security Law Branch, wrote a thirty-three-page affidavit asking the Canadian courts to grant me the same protections I had in the United States.

While she worked, we planned. Since it was Nelly's and Kenny's case, they were headed to Montreal with me. The plan was to get on the ground in Montreal, figure out the conspiracy, and then arrest Chiheb. It was a weeklong operation.

Every major FBI undercover operation has a contact agent who makes sure the undercover has everything they need to be successful. The contact agent is never someone with a stake in the case. His only agenda is the undercover's well-being.

The undercover picks the contact agent. I picked Joey after Vinnie suggested him. We had gone to undercover school together. He was the Italian mob version of me. What made him so talented was his ability to read people. It didn't matter if you were a foreigner or a crack dealer, Joey could figure out your motivation. It was uncanny. I was excited when Vinnie told me he was available.

"That's my family," I said. "Is he okay with it?"

"He can't wait to get started," Vinnie said.

It was almost Tuesday when Vinnie finally drove me back to my house. Neither one of us talked on the way home. My mind was working through all the scenarios. Only one scared me: What if the Canadians didn't give me the protections? The FBI went to extreme lengths to protect my identity. I never had to testify in open court and my true name would never be revealed. I could do my job over and over again without ever having to worry about being compromised. I knew I had to go, but then my true name could be revealed, putting my father and sister in harm's way. I'd signed up for the job. They hadn't.

"What would you do?" I asked as Vinnie pulled into the driveway.

Vinnie put the truck in park and rested his head against the seat. He let the question sit out there for a minute. I could tell he was mulling it over. He was like me. An undercover who had been in the same room as killers. He loved the work as much as I did, but he also understood the cost. This wasn't going to be a simple or quick case. We had an al Qaeda sleeper in our sights. He was a direct link to the organization. A link that could lead us deeper into the network. I was convinced the risk was worth taking. I just wanted to hear him say it.

A wry smile creased Vinnie's lips.

"You're fucked, buddy," Vinnie said. "You're damned if you do, damned if you don't. But this is why you joined the FBI. This is why we recruited you. This case is going to change your life."

Over the next week, the team went to Toronto to work out the details with the RCMP. Three days later, I got word to get packed. The RCMP agreed to protect my identity after Heidi argued that revealing my true name would cause severe damage to the United States' national security efforts.

As she put it, I was a non-fungible asset.

Yeah, I had to look it up too.

CHAPTER 11

Apartment 23

I took a deep breath as the plane made its final approach into Montréal–Pierre Elliott Trudeau International Airport.

It was September 2012 and the air was crisp. I retrieved my bags from the carousel and took a cab to the hotel. I was alone and traveling under Tamer's identity, just in case Chiheb had someone waiting for me at the airport. I had told him I was coming in a day later so I could meet with my team. Nelly, Kenny, and Joey were already set up at the Marriott Château Champlain, a luxury hotel in the heart of downtown Montreal.

"Get checked in and then give me a call," Joey said when I called him from the car.

The hotel was a time warp back to the 1950s. The lobby was all gold and marble. The echo of footsteps bounced off the walls. The bellman took me to Tamer's suite. I called Joey after he left.

"We're in the penthouse," he said.

Joey gave me the room number and the code for the elevator, which took me to the top of the hotel. The hallway was deserted. I knocked on the double doors and a woman opened one.

"Do I have the right room?" I asked.

"Are you Tamer?" she said in a slight French accent.

"I am."

"Come on in," she said, kissing me on both cheeks and giving me a hug. "You're here to save our country. Thank you."

"Man, did I make the right call coming up here," I said, laughing.

The team was sitting in the living room. Benny, the RCMP undercover boss, stood up and shook my hand. He was a handsome guy who looked like he read a lot of fashion magazines. He was wearing a corduroy sport coat and a puffy white shirt. A scarf tied the whole outfit together. My mind went to the *Seinfeld* pirate shirt episode. I stifled a smile and reminded myself to mention the shirt to Nelly.

We nicknamed Benny "the party planner" because he took the team to the best bars and restaurants when we weren't working. Always without me, of course, because I couldn't be seen with them in public. And I made sure to remind him of that on a regular basis.

"We'll get you anything you need while you're here," he said.

Frank was next. He was the RCMP Toronto liaison, a former undercover. Frank's long ponytail from his biker days was now gray. He introduced me to Doug, my RCMP handler. He was lean with a receding hairline that he wore as a buzz cut. Like Frank, he was a former undercover.

"You're doing God's work," Doug said, giving me a firm handshake.

Doug motioned me to a seat near Kenny, Nelly, and Joey, who smiled. Joey shot me a knowing glance as I sat down. He had already figured out the room. Joey looked like George Clooney in both appearance and spirit. He made life look easy, but the façade hid one of the Bureau's best minds. He was a grinder who didn't miss a detail.

The meeting started like all the others. The Canadians wanted all the same information that CSIS did in the New York meeting.

The next evening, I waited until my "flight" landed, then I walked down to the lobby to call Chiheb. When I'd told him I was headed to Montreal, he had made it clear never to call his cell phone because my mobile phone account was tied to my name. It seemed he wanted to protect me. So perhaps it wasn't a surprise that the phone rang and rang. It was after 7:00 P.M. and people walked in and out of the lobby on their way to and from dinner. A generic message finally answered my call. His voice mail wasn't set up. I tried two more times and then sent him an e-mail asking if he wanted to meet up. Chiheb picked up when I called just before nine o'clock. His phone was out of minutes, he told me.

"I was hoping it was you," Chiheb said. "I've been waiting for you, brother."

"I just got in," I said. "Give me half an hour and I'll shoot over."

He wanted to give me directions, but I told him that wasn't necessary.

"I have a GPS in the car," I said. "I have your address from our e-mails."

"That's great," he said. "I'll be waiting for you."

I arrived at his apartment on Rosemont Boulevard at 9:34 P.M. Chiheb lived in a three-story brick building. I circled the block, a habit from my drug days. My GPS told me to make a U-turn. I ignored it and made a left. I went a few blocks and then pulled over.

I watched the cars pass for a few minutes. I studied faces. Did I see the same faces? Who was trying not to look at me? I returned to his building twenty minutes later, confident no one was following me.

I rang his apartment number. Chiheb came over the intercom and buzzed me up. His apartment was on the second floor. Chiheb, wearing jeans rolled up at the cuffs and a light blue button-down shirt, was waiting for me on the landing.

"Peace be upon you," I said in Arabic.

We almost always spoke in Arabic together. By now he'd mastered my Egyptian dialect. To the untrained ear, it sounded like we were speaking the same language. But to a native speaker, it was like hearing English spoken by a New Yorker and by a southern gentleman from Charleston. Same language. Drastically different sound. It amazed me that Chiheb could tailor his accent so that I could better understand him. I could hear my childhood in Alexandria coming from the mouth of a Tunisian.

"Peace be upon you," Chiheb said.

"*Habibi, habibi,*" I said, calling him a friend.

"How are you?" Chiheb said. He was excited to see me. "I really missed you, I swear."

"May Allah keep you," I said.

The apartment building was home to students and low-income workers. I could hear the other tenants watching TV or talking inside their apartments as we walked down the corridor. He stopped at the first door on the left. Apartment 23.

"Why didn't you have me pick you up at the airport?" Chiheb asked.

"I didn't want to disturb you, *habibi,* because I knew they would be giving me a car," I said. "They had a car waiting for me when I arrived, so there was no reason to put you out."

"No, that is not a problem, that is not a problem at all," he said. "Please come in, brother, please come in."

His apartment was small. The front door led into the kitchen. An old mattress was on the floor in the living room. His clothes, a laptop computer, and some random belongings sat in the corner. A sliding glass door led to a balcony. His roommate, a taxi driver from Algeria, lived in the only bedroom. His roommate was in Algeria, so we were alone.

Chiheb motioned for me to sit on the mattress. I hesitated. It was streaked with dirt. A massive brown stain covered more than three quarters of it. I found out later he took it from a dumpster. Why spend money on a mattress? His comfort was second to Allah's will.

"What's all this? I told you when we spoke not to prepare anything."

Chiheb smiled. Next to the mattress was a plate with oranges, plums, strawberries, and dates. He poured me a large glass of milk. He was excited to play the host because now I was in his country.

"No, no, no, it isn't much," he said. "Just cold milk, so it can help you sleep tonight."

Anything given to a guest, especially a drink, is personal in my culture. There was no getting out of drinking it. Thank God it wasn't spoiled and it was cold.

"How was your trip? Was it a long trip?"

I took a sip of the milk and put it on the stool next to the mattress.

"It was a long trip, the flight was a bit delayed," I said. "For about half an hour or so."

Chiheb nodded along. His eyes never left me.

"I really miss you, brother," he said.

"I miss you too," I said, looking around his apartment. "May Allah keep you safe. This apartment is nice."

"Yeah, what do you think?"

"Praise Allah," I said. "Everything you need."

"Tell me, how have you spent the time since Santa Clara?" Chiheb asked.

"Thankfully, things are good in terms of the building; we rented it out already," I said. "It's making money. And as for work in general, it's still very busy, but busy is good. But truthfully, Chiheb, after I met you, I see everything differently now."

Chiheb's weakness was his fatalism.

"May Allah bless you," Chiheb said.

He was staring at me intently.

"You understand," I said. "You understand what I mean?"

"Yes. Thank Allah."

"I know my Arabic isn't perfect, but bear with me for a bit so I can explain this to you," I said. "Right before I met you, I said to myself . . ."

I let the sentence trail off. I paused. I looked away as I pretended to search for the right words.

"I pray every day, and every time I pray, I ask Allah . . ."

Chiheb was getting swept into the moment.

"Tell me what I can do," I said. "I look at all the problems that are taking place in this world and the Muslims being oppressed by the infidels we are living next to and I just wish, O Lord, give me the strength and the courage, give me something more that I can do to help. You understand?"

"Praise Allah," Chiheb said.

"I asked Allah to show me how to help the Muslim Ummah. Give me any sign. Then I went to the airport. So, I got to Houston and then I met you," I said.

"Do you really want to help the Muslims?" Chiheb asked. "I mean, do you wish to help the Muslims?"

"Exactly. I wish to."

I wanted to talk about the plot. We only had a few days before September 11, but I wanted him to lead the conversation.

Chiheb's demeanor changed. His smile was gone. One second he was playing host. Pouring a glass of milk. Trying to coax me into eating some fruit. The next second his eyes got dark. He was still, but intense. He looked right through me and it gave me a chill.

"Is your cell phone on?"

One of two things was going to happen when he asked me to turn off my phone. One, he was going to rip my shirt open and look for a wire, or two, he was going to open up about the attack.

"Let's get the devil out of the room," Chiheb said.

I took my phone out of my jacket.

"Do you want me to shut it off?"

"Yes," Chiheb said, staring at the phone like it was a bomb.

I started to tap out a text message to Joey, claiming to be in touch with an employee.

"I have to let him know that I arrived; let me do it before I turn it off."

"Shutting the phone down," I wrote. "All is good."

I sent the text and deleted it before Chiheb could see. Joey knew the drill. He would never send me anything overt on my undercover phone.

Chiheb got up from his pillow and sat next to me. His chin was almost on my right shoulder as he watched me shut down my phone.

"That's it," I said, letting him see the screen.

"Is it off?" he said.

I put the phone back in my jacket. I had another phone. I pulled it out and shut it down as well. Chiheb smiled.

"It's not that we're afraid of them, but it's a precaution," he said.

"Talk to me, brother."

"I have brothers who I visited who are mujahideen for the sake of Allah."

"Praise Allah," I said.

"Yes, may Allah keep them," Chiheb said. "I visited them at the border."

"What does that mean?"

"The border. The border between Iran and Afghanistan."

"What do you mean?" I said. "They live here or there?"

"They live near the border between Iran and Afghanistan," Chiheb said. "They are in contact with our brothers in Afghanistan who are carrying out jihad for the sake of Allah."

"May Allah be with them," I said.

"The brothers told me, go back to Canada and stay there and, of course, we'll keep in touch, God willing. So I am in contact with them."

He studied me as he spoke. He seemed nervous, like he needed validation. I nodded with each sentence. I leaned in, held his gaze, and offered a slight smile at the end. I acted impressed.

Chiheb took out his passport and flipped a few pages.

"I mean, this is the visa," he said, showing me the page in his passport. "The Islamic Republic of Iran."

I studied the page.

"I went to Iran," Chiheb said.

"Who is that?" I said while I stared at his passport. "Is this one of the brothers?"

"No, that's me."

"That's you?"

I acted surprised, but I wanted him on tape talking about his trip to Iran.

"Yes, that's me," Chiheb said. "I went to Iran in April 2011."

"Praise Allah, you were in Iran?"

"Yes," he said. "Then I went again in February 2012."

"So it was this past February?" I said.

My mind started to put the pieces together. I reached for my passport and handed it to him.

"Hang on a second," I said. "So in February you were in Iran. And myself, let me see, in February . . ."

I let the sentence trail off. I had more evidence that Allah put us on the path together.

"Where were you?" Chiheb asked as he turned the pages of my passport to match the dates.

"I was near there," I said. "I went to see my brothers."

Chiheb was floored. He saw my stamps from February 2012, when I was in the Middle East.

"I mean, there was only a sea between us," he said.

"We were there together," I said.

I couldn't help but think that if he only knew why I was really over there, he would cut my throat right there on his shitty mattress.

"Do you know which city in Iran I was in in February?"

"Tell me," I said.

"In a city in the south of Iran."

"So that means it's not that far," I said. "You were in Iran. And I was meeting with the brothers."

"You?" Chiheb asked.

He was astonished. But I needed him to know I could do more for the brothers. For him.

"When I met with them, they told me that I was an asset to them in America. I know they're right, and I get it. But they also knew that I wanted to do more than just send money. But I'm still waiting. I haven't heard from them. But anyway, look at the path that you and I are on. We were overseas at the same time looking for the same thing. And look at how Allah put us together in Houston.

"Brother, let's keep the devil out of the room," I said. "I know Allah had a plan for us. But I've only met a couple of other good brothers like you."

I rattled off some names—aliases of my fellow Dirty Arabs Group members. I wanted to know if Chiheb had any brothers in Canada. I wanted to know more about the Palestinian he went on the recon with a few days ago. Chiheb had mentioned him in August, but I didn't have any firm details.

"You told me before, there are Muslims you want me to meet," I said. "I told you they have to be like us."

Chiheb nodded. He said we should meet Raed Jaser, the Palestinian brother in Toronto.

"If you want, we can visit him," Chiheb said.

"Of course," I said.

We agreed to drive to Toronto to visit Jaser the next day.

"If you finish at three o'clock, we can go straight to him," Chiheb said.

"Does he know that we are coming?"

"I told him, I said, there is a possibility that a brother from America is coming to pay us a visit," Chiheb said.

"He is like us, correct?"

"Yeah, he is truly into jihad," Chiheb said, smiling. "Don't worry about him."

"Okay, good," I said.

"Actually, him and I, we have projects together."

"You have what?" I asked.

"We have a project together," Chiheb said.

There was no mistaking what he was talking about.

"You mean plans?" I asked.

"Plans. We have plans."

That is all he would tell me in Apartment 23. But we both knew what "plans" meant. We were now brothers against all infidels, with a mission to kill.

CHAPTER 12

The Road Trip

Joey put his arm over my shoulder and guided me into the other room of the suite.

We talked about the road trip to Toronto for hours after I got back to the hotel. Nelly and Doug had a map spread out on the table and were going over the route for the six-hour drive. I made it clear I was not spending much time in a car with Chiheb.

"No way," I told Joey. "It's a forty-five-minute flight. Why would Tamer drive if he could fly?"

When I made the plan the night before, I forgot Toronto was that far away. My Canadian geography sucked. Now I was in a full-on diva shit fit. We already had Chiheb. He'd admitted to planning the attack the night before. There was no reason to spend the time driving.

"Let's just fly," I said. "I can get the Palestinian to admit his role and deliver the case to the Canadians with a bow."

But Joey had other ideas.

"Listen, I hear you," Joey said as we left the room. "I'm with you. I wouldn't want to spend any more time with him than I had to, but think of the evidentiary value of that six-hour conversation. Just the two of you. Phones shut off. Think of what he wants to tell you. Look how quickly you brought him around."

He was right, even if I didn't want to admit it. But I wasn't thinking about the case. I was thinking about me. Spending time with Chiheb required me to put my arm around him. To call him *habibi*. Tell him he was my brother. Plus, I hated who Tamer was. I created him to be recruitable. But a little part of me died every time I had to denounce my country or pervert my religion.

"Think outside yourself," he said, really driving home the point. "It's not a car ride, it's an interrogation. Do your thing. There is nobody that we would want more in that car to save these lives than you."

Joey, ever the smooth one, was basically telling me to shut my mouth and do my job. But doing it by tickling my ego. A little sugar to help the medicine go down.

"You're right," I said.

Just after 4:00 P.M. the next day, I picked up Chiheb in my Chrysler 300. It had a V8 hemi engine. Leather seats. GPS. It was flashy and expensive. It screamed Tamer. All Chiheb knew was that I "rented" it on business travel. But of course it was also wired up so everything we said was in surround sound. I jumped on the highway heading west. The road—immaculately paved—skirted Lake Ontario. There was little traffic and I pushed the gas pedal to the floor.

There were multiple surveillance teams on the road ahead of us and behind us. A plane circled overhead. My phone buzzed. It was Joey asking me to slow down. I was pushing it. I didn't want to prolong the trip. Once we got outside of Montreal, I poured on the speed. The second text was more urgent. What were they going to do, pull me over?

My phone buzzed a third time.

"SLOW THE FUCK DOWN."

I looked at the speedometer. We were going well over one hundred miles per hour. Surveillance vehicles couldn't keep up without giving themselves away. I let the speedometer fall to about seventy-five miles per hour.

About an hour outside of town, Chiheb flipped the switch. I handed him my phone and he shut it off. It was time to get serious.

"The project regarding the train," Chiheb said. "You are included in what we are planning. Do you understand?"

I said I did.

"You are included because we need you."

He told me the brothers in Iran—al Qaeda planners—ordered him to cut a hole in the train tracks and derail a train heading to Toronto from New York. He and his Palestinian friend were going to use jackhammers to cut out the track on a bridge near Toronto. When the train derailed, it would smash through the barriers on the side of the bridge and plunge the passengers into the shallow water below.

"The thing is that it needs two people, you know, the hole," Chiheb said. "When it's dug, there has to be one person on one side and one on the other side."

"Right," I said.

"They start together at the same time and when it starts breaking up, it's all going to fall. Do you understand?"

"Of course," I said. "Definitely."

"So, I mean we need only two people to do the work, but we
need a third person as an external partner to watch our back. Do
you understand? You are the external partner."

As he talked, I concentrated on my smile. I touched my heart. I
wanted him to know I embraced his beautiful plan and that I felt
like I was part of something real. It was firing him up that I wasn't
appalled. By being quiet yet reassuring, it made for better recordings. The jury didn't need to hear my voice.

"How do you know it's not going to be considered an accident?"
I asked.

Chiheb and Jaser planned to shoot a video taking credit and
warning the United States and Canada that the attacks would
continue until all foreign troops were removed from the Middle
East. I asked if they had a target. Chiheb smiled.

"I talked with the brother from Palestine about the operation,"
Chiheb said. "I asked him, 'Are you going fishing? Did you go fishing? When are we going fishing?' Understand?"

"Ahh," I said.

"He understands me when I say it," Chiheb said. "Like, there
isn't fishing."

"No, that's easy," I said, thinking back to the Canadians in New
York before Labor Day.

Trust me, we know it's a fishing trip.

Yeah, right.

Chiheb said he was instructed to cut a five-meter hole in the tracks. The hole would be big enough to derail the train, but Chiheb thought it would be almost undetectable to the engineer.

"You are in construction," Chiheb said. "What do you think?"

"Five meters is about fifteen feet," I said. "That makes perfect sense; if you're traveling at what, eighty kilometers, a hundred kilometers, you've got five meters, right, which is a good amount; it's going to drop at some point and it's gonna derail it, just like you said."

With the rail plot on tape, I switched gears.

"What other good ideas do we have to work on, Allah willing?" I asked.

Chiheb said his other plan was to hire a cook and send him to work on a military base in the United States. Once there, he would poison the soldiers' food. He wanted me to help find a cook.

"When you look for the cook you have to be careful," Chiheb said. "When you talk to a person you need to have a reason why you are searching. For example, 'I have some plans for buying a restaurant,' for example."

Chiheb asked me if I understood.

"My business is my cover," I said, which is probably the only truthful statement I made during the six-hour car ride.

Before I got in the car, Doug had asked me to confirm the timeline. We assumed the attack was set for September 11. He wanted to be sure.

"God willing, it'll be in December, when five o'clock at night is dark," Chiheb said after I asked when he planned to attack. "So the train would have no opportunity, no chance to escape, because the vision is poor. Do you understand?"

"Of course," I said.

"Because at night there is no traffic," Chiheb said. "So the train's speed becomes faster."

"It's brilliant," I said, relieved.

When CSIS picked up Chiheb and Jaser talking about an anniversary, they meant Christmas. The anniversary of Jesus Christ's birthday.

We were barely halfway to Toronto, and I had enough evidence on tape to charge Chiheb. With four more hours to kill, we started to talk about his training in Iran. An al Qaeda planner—El Massoul—trained Chiheb in Iran. One of my tasks was to figure out who El Massoul was, since we only had his nom de guerre.

"The brother, the one who is in charge, El Massoul, the Responsible One, that I met in Iran. He told me he has a soldier in the U.S.A. He's just sleeping, you know?"

"Yes," I said.

"Do you know the sleeping cell?" Chiheb asked. "One sleeping cell."

My heart started to race. Did Chiheb just tell me there was an American sleeper? I focused on the road as I regained my composure, because I had to work overtime not to show him I was losing my shit.

"Is he alone?" I asked.

Our Canadian problem had just turned into an American problem.

"I mean, he didn't tell me," Chiheb said.

"Better this way," I said.

"But El Massoul told me 'I will call you and I will make the soldier call you. Either the soldier comes to Canada or you go to him in the U.S.A.' I am asking myself, this soldier, is it you?"

Then it dawned on me why he'd brought it up. He thought I was the American sleeper.

"Praise Allah, may Allah keep you, oh God, God willing, I am a soldier of Allah," I said.

But I told him I wasn't the sleeper. Still, the fact that there might be an American version of Chiheb? That scared the shit out of me.

"Tell me about your time in Iran, *habibi*," I said. "Did you enjoy it there?"

I wanted him to talk about his training in hopes he'd give me something on the American sleeper.

"They had me memorize the symbols, the language. Memorize some of the projects, the plans. They taught me the symbolic language."

"Yes, the codes," I said.

"They taught me the project of the cook. I got the message from our Sheikh, you know him?"

"Our Sheikh?" I asked, hoping he'd say his name.

I wanted it all on tape.

"The Sheikh, the one who succeeded Sheikh Osama, without saying his name."

"Oh, you don't want to say his name?"

"Do you know Sheikh Osama?"

He was talking about Osama bin Laden.

"Of course."

"The one who succeeded him," Chiheb said. "He's from Egypt."

"The Egyptian."

He was talking about Ayman al-Zawahiri, the Egyptian-born doctor and a former deputy to Osama bin Laden. He took over after bin Laden was killed in Pakistan.

"I got a message from him personally," Chiheb said.

"Unbelievable," I said.

"Praise be to Allah," Chiheb said.

"Praise Allah, *habibi*," I said, trying to sound as impressed as possible.

"I got a message from him through the Responsible One," Chiheb said.

He was bragging. But I wanted to talk about the American sleeper.

"Do you know who this guy is?" I asked.

"No, I never met him," Chiheb said. "But I know he was there, because El Massoul talked about him a lot. When I'd do something good he said I reminded him of Al-Amriki [the American]."

"Wow, are you ever going to cross paths?"

"One day, we'll meet when the time is right," Chiheb said.

"Maybe one day I will meet him," I said. "I'd love a chance to meet a good dear brother like you."

We needed to rethink the case. Chiheb was our only link to the American sleeper. There was no way we could arrest him before we identified the other sleeper. About halfway to Toronto, Chiheb got quiet.

"Maybe you can advise me," Chiheb said. "So in the last period, my boss brought in one PhD student from Jordan."

"Okay," I said, not tracking where the conversation was going.

"She is a girl," he said.

It was clear he was uncomfortable. He was back to being the awkward Chiheb. The scientist with no social skills.

"A woman," I said.

"But it's a girl—she's not married," he said.

The Jordanian woman had the office next to Chiheb's. She was Palestinian but grew up in Jordan after her family fled Israel.

"The distance between her office and my office is just seven centimeters," he said. "Can you imagine?"

I tried to act surprised. But I still wasn't sure where Chiheb was headed.

"Almighty God, this is His wisdom. So, why this girl, she didn't come when I was not thinking about all of this stuff? But what makes things more serious, it's a test, Allah makes this girl love me."

"You're kidding," I said, more to myself than to him.

Chiheb needed dating advice. He was attracted to her, but was nervous that his feelings would take his focus off his projects.

"Yes, she tries to always show me that she loves me," he said. "I am very disappointed about this subject. Could you give me some advice about this issue, because I see her every day?"

"Are you sure she loves you?" I asked.

Knowing Chiheb as I did, it seemed strange that a woman would be into him. She hadn't been over to his apartment. I shuddered just thinking about that mattress.

"I am sure. When I talk with another girl, she became very mad."

He told me a story about a female colleague joking with him after he spilled something on the floor of his office. The Jordanian woman saw them laughing and shooed the other woman away and started to clean up.

"Can you imagine?" Chiheb said, smiling at the memory. "Just for the sake to stop the joke. So give me advice please."

It was obvious the Jordanian woman was important to him. Important enough to demand his attention and force him to think about something besides the path of Allah.

"Do you love her?"

"Sometimes I feel that I love her. When she disobeys Allah, I feel that I hate her."

This crush concerned me. I didn't want him talking to her about the plot.

"You can't talk to anyone about the project, because now it's not just you," I said. "It's you, it's me. The Palestinian brother. I know she's not your wife but if she's going to be your wife, think about it—does she have to know?"

"That she married a mujahid?" Chiheb said. "She didn't marry a regular person. She should know that she is married to a mujahid."

I nodded.

"That's true."

"But the issue is not me. I don't want my heart to become deviated."

Chiheb was always on the lookout for obstacles on the path of Allah. He feared the Jordanian was one.

"It's kind of a war inside myself," he said.

"If she loves you the way you're telling me, she knows that you are a mujahid and that's not the problem," I said. "The problem is you're telling me you believe you have a mission, but you're afraid that if you end up falling in love or getting married it will deviate you from the mission."

"Either I cut any kind of relation with her and I leave her forever or I marry her forever. One of the two."

"And if you marry her forever are you going to walk away from being a mujahid?"

"No. And if she pushes me to do this, I will divorce her immediately. So what is your advice?"

"Okay, before I give you my advice I have one very important question that you have to make clear for me," I said. "If you walk away from her and you cut ties or if you go the other way and you marry her, either way, you are still staying focused to go straight ahead with the missions and stay mujahid?"

"Yes," Chiheb said.

"No matter what?"

"No matter what."

"So there is no issue," I said. "Follow your heart."

"You don't think that what is in my heart is just simple desire?"

"You're thinking it's the devil in the path of Allah?"

"Do you not think that what I have for that girl is just simple desire?" Chiheb said. "Because of Satan?"

"That's a possibility, I'll give you that, but let me ask you something. With love comes desire. Marriage isn't haram and it isn't always Satan. If you love someone, you desire them."

"Yes."

"That's not haram and that's not Satan," I said.

Chiheb seemed grateful.

"You are not only professional advisor but you are also personal advisor," he said. "Another advice?"

Chiheb looked out the window. He hesitated before he spoke again.

"She's trying to show to me that she doesn't love me."

I smiled. "They call it in English 'she's playing hard to get.'"

But I wasn't convinced she was even interested. My hope was to force the issue. Get her to reject him and end any chance that he'd tell her about the plot and derail the case.

"When you return to work, ask her, Could we talk? Talk to her. The best route is honesty. Be straightforward with her, tell her, Look, instead of playing any games, you know me, let's be straight. What's your feeling? Where are we going?"

Chiheb seemed discouraged.

"She won't say. She hides her feelings."

"You tell her and then she'll tell you, that's it. No more of this talk, that's it, no more games. You go in straightforward now. You're a man of business, go in straight and tell her, Look, I swear by Allah this is the story and I'll say it to you straight, do you want me or not?"

I laughed. This was kind of fun.

"It's my business mind, okay?" I said. "No games, no more playing games, get to the point. Give me the bottom line."

As we got close to Toronto, Chiheb asked me not to mention the plot to the Palestinian brother.

"No, no, I would never say anything until you tell me we could talk," I said.

Chiheb relaxed.

"Yeah, like, I have to prepare him psychologically. You let me talk to him."

Chiheb tried to call the Palestinian, but his phone didn't work. I handed him my phone.

"Tell him this is the brother's cell phone," I said.

After a few tries, Chiheb finally reached him. It was around eleven o'clock and we wanted to make sure it was still okay for us to visit.

"Of course," the Palestinian said. "I'm waiting up for you."

CHAPTER 13

The Imam Complex

Raed Jaser, the Palestinian, lived in a quiet suburban neighborhood in northern Toronto. His house was a mother-daughter home converted into apartments. Jaser lived in the apartment around the back of the main house.

We arrived a little after 11:00 P.M. and followed the path to his front door. Chiheb was in the lead. I started shooting mental pictures of everything. I memorized the license plate numbers in the driveway and made mental notes of the layout, because at some point the SWAT team would want to know.

Jaser's entry was a sliding glass patio door. Chiheb knocked. A few seconds later, Jaser came to the door. He was wearing a long white robe, a red-and-white checkered scarf on his shoulders, and slippers. He was heavily bearded, with a pronounced nose and dark eyes. He wore a kufi on his head. His face lit up when he saw Chiheb. They embraced and exchanged kisses.

"This is my dear brother from America," Chiheb said, turning to me. "He's Egyptian."

"Welcome, brother," Jaser said, looking me up and down before hugging me.

Jaser's apartment was quaint. There was one bedroom and a bathroom. With men in the house, Jaser's wife hid in the bedroom. Fruit and snacks were spread out on the table.

"Brother, can we use your restroom to make *wudu*?" I asked. "We'd love to pray Isha. Do you want to pray Isha together?"

The Isha prayer is the fifth and final prayer of the day. But before we could pray, we had to clean ourselves, or make *wudu*. Jaser showed us the bathroom, but shook his head no when I asked if he wanted to pray.

"I already prayed," he said. "You guys go ahead."

Chiheb excused himself and used the bathroom. I thought it was strange Jaser hadn't waited to pray with us. He knew we were coming, and you get extra credit from God when you pray in a group.

When I got out of the bathroom, I joined Chiheb. Jaser sat on the couch nearby. Isha requires four *rakk'ah*—the movements and words of the prayer. The first two *rakk'ah* are prayed aloud. I could feel Jaser's eyes on me as we recited the Quran during prayer. He watched my every move. He wanted to hear my Quranic voice. He listened to the way I said each word in the prayer.

This was a test.

Mainstream Muslims pray a certain way. But the mujahideen have little idiosyncrasies, tells that signal to others they are "more religious," like not crossing your legs or spreading your fingers when you kneel and bow. There are certain ways to enunciate the words.

It was hard to pray for real with Jaser watching. It annoyed me that I couldn't concentrate and instead had to focus on making sure I passed the test. Saying my prayers was never an act, even when I was Tamer. But I trusted that Allah understood what I was doing.

When we were done, Jaser relaxed. He poured us each a cup of tea. It was clear he and Chiheb were friends. They jumped into talk of religion and how the brothers overseas were being oppressed by the Jews and America. Jaser started quoting from *Milestones,* written by Egyptian Islamist Sayyid Qutb. He was one of Osama bin Laden's idols.

Qutb called for Muslims to re-create the world based on the Quran. He argued Muslims lived in a "state of ignorance of the guidance from God" because they didn't follow Sharia, or traditional Islamic law. He considered Sharia no different from the "laws of nature," like gravity. Anyone living under any law other than the law of Allah was a *kaffir,* or nonbeliever. He called for the rejection of secular leaders and "the rubbish heap of the West" and wanted to form a "vanguard" that resembled Mohammed's first followers. The vanguard would cut itself off from Western thinking and any non-Muslims. They would inspire people to become "true" Muslims and throw off the shackles of secular leaders and systems.

Sharia Law has become code for oppression in the United States, but for me it was just the rules a Muslim must follow to be religious. It has nothing to do with violence or extremism. Books like *Milestones* created confusion and omitted the parts of Islam that didn't support radical Islam. The Quran specifically states that Muslims must abide by the country's laws in which they reside. That is the word of God, not some Egyptian scholar's interpretation.

I knew Jaser was quoting Qutb even though he never said the

name. With each quote and idea, I responded enthusiastically. When Jaser's testing me was over, we agreed to meet the next day for prayers at a mosque on Victoria Park Avenue.

Back at the hotel, I waited in my room for an hour—to make sure Chiheb was asleep in his room—and then texted Joey.

"You good?" he asked.

"Yeah, but I need to meet."

"Do you want to do it tonight? Is it too risky?"

The plan was to complete the trip and then meet, but I had to dump the audio and make sure they picked up Chiheb talking about the American sleeper.

"We have to meet tonight."

"Stand by for a location."

A half hour later, I grabbed the recorders and drove over to a nearby parking lot. Nelly, Joey, and Doug were waiting in a black SUV.

I jumped in the back.

"Did you hear?"

Nelly nodded.

"Yeah, most of it," he said. "But it was muffled a lot of the ride."

The cell coverage was spotty between Montreal and Toronto, and the audio must have cut out. They had no idea about the American sleeper.

"There is an American sleeper."

Nelly and Joey looked at each other.

"What?" Nelly said. "Are you fucking kidding me?"

"That's why I wanted to meet."

"Does he know who it is?" Nelly said. "Has he met him?"

I shook my head no.

"The American sleeper trained in Iran before Chiheb," I said.

As I rehashed the conversation, I could tell by Joey's face that everything had changed. This was no longer a favor to Canada. The United States had a massive interest in this case. While Nelly and Joey stressed about the American sleeper, Doug chimed in.

"What about the train plot?"

Doug cared about the American sleeper, but it was his job to protect Canada. He had an active cell planning an attack. I didn't blame him, but that was my first whiff that I was now working for two competing masters. The Canadians wanted Chiheb and Jaser. We wanted the sleeper.

I told him the train attack was scheduled for December. We had time.

"I'll get more details about the plot tomorrow," I said. "We're meeting for prayers in the morning."

At dawn, I joined Chiheb for the day's first prayer. Even with Chiheb right next to me, I asked Allah for help finding the American sleeper and protecting innocent men, women, and children. I needed His strength and wisdom to stay the course. After prayers, we agreed to sleep a few more hours before meeting Jaser at the mosque. We drove over in silence. Both of us were tired after the long drive and late night.

From the outside, the mosque looked like a house. Inside, all of the non-load-bearing walls had been knocked down, and rugs and pillows were set out on the floor.

Jaser wasn't there. We prayed with the rest of the group and then went back to the car. An Afghan man flagged us down before we left. He introduced himself as Waleed. He was dressed in the same camouflage jacket worn by Osama bin Laden. His beard was thick but he didn't have a mustache. At a glance, he looked like someone dressed in a terrorist Halloween costume. It would have looked comical, except he was serious.

"Hello, dear brothers," he said. "I hear you are in from out of town. I am a good friend of Raed. He is running late. I'd love to take you out to breakfast."

Chiheb agreed immediately. He seemed taken with the young Afghan. Waleed climbed into the back of the car and we drove to Tim Hortons, essentially the Canadians' version of Dunkin' Donuts. Jaser called me while we ate.

"Brother, I'm so sorry," he said. "I overslept. I just got out of the shower. Where are you guys? Still at the mosque?"

"No," I said. "We met a friend of yours. Waleed."

"Yes, what a great brother," Jaser said. "Why don't you guys come to my house?"

"Great, can we get you anything?" I asked.

"No, I'm fine."

Then he paused a beat.

"Get me a tea," he said.

I ordered him a tea and we headed back to his house. He met us in the driveway.

"Why don't you leave your phones in the car," Jaser said. "There is no reason to bring them in."

Chiheb and I put our phones in the center console.

Jaser took Waleed's phone and removed the battery. We sat around the table. Jaser started talking from Qutb's script. But he never took it over the line. It was all talk. He knew what he could and couldn't say. The whole speech came off polished. Practiced. I'd seen this before. I called it "the Imam Complex." Jaser liked to talk about jihad and quote Qutb, but he wasn't interested in getting his hands dirty. After an hour, Jaser said he had to go to work. He put his arm around me as we walked to the door.

"Come with me, brother," Jaser said as we left the house.

Chiheb and Waleed walked behind us. They were becoming fast friends. It was clear Chiheb still dreamt of fighting in Afghanistan, and Waleed represented everything he wanted to be.

"Brother, why don't you leave Chiheb with me today, since you have a long day," he said.

I had told Jaser about my plans to see a few properties with a real estate agent.

"That's fine," I said, welcoming a chance to get away from him. "You guys haven't seen each other in a while."

Jaser smiled.

"I have to go into the office, and he can come with me," he said.

Jaser was a taxi dispatcher. They could speak freely in the office, since it was Saturday and only he was on duty.

"Yeah, that sounds great," I said.

"Let's shoot for dinner tonight," Jaser said.

"Done. That sounds great. See you guys later."

As I drove off, I called Joey.

"I can't go back to the hotel," I said. "They think I'm going to look at properties. Got a place I could hole up? I need to get some sleep."

Joey sent me the address of a new hotel. Joey, Kenny, and Nelly met me an hour later with Doug and the other Canadians. The Americans wanted to know about the sleeper. Nelly, Kenny, and Joey took turns asking me the same questions and getting the same answers. I still didn't know the sleeper's identity, his location, or if he was operational.

The Canadians were focused on the train plot and my dinner with Jaser and Waleed. They wanted to know if I thought the mosque was radical, if Waleed was part of the attack, and where I planned to have dinner with them so we could set up surveillance. After the debrief, I watched as everyone jumped on their phones. The cacophony of conversations made it impossible to sleep, so Joey and I went into the other room and started to plan the night's operation.

The plan was to pick up Jaser and Chiheb for dinner around 7:00 P.M. I was in the car heading to Jaser's house when he called and switched the location. A few minutes later they switched it again. I was on edge. What was going on? Were they onto me?

I called Joey.

"Get every surveillance body off the street," I said. "If I get burned because of surveillance, I'm going to kill somebody. Tell them to let me do my job."

Joey didn't like leaving me without backup.

"We need to make sure—" Joey said, hoping to change my mind. I cut him off.

"I will do everything in my power to keep you posted," I said. "But shut it down."

I had no choice. Chiheb was my lifeline to both the Canadian cell and the American sleeper. I was either walking into an ambush or they were ready to cut me in on the plot. I knew how to defend myself, but I was more concerned about getting burned because of some RCMP agent. I'd never be able to forgive myself.

Before I could confirm dinner at the third location, my phone pinged. It was a text from Jaser. He wanted to meet at Waleed's house. Before I could respond, my phone rang.

"Brother, did you get the address?" Jaser said.

"Yeah, what's with all the cloak-and-dagger stuff?"

"We don't want to go out," he said. "We'd rather have a more private dinner."

"Alright, on my way."

Waleed's house was in an upper-middle-class neighborhood in southern Toronto. The four-bedroom colonial style house sat on a cul-de-sac. I pulled up to the house and parked facing out toward the exit of the cul-de-sac. The streets were dark, lit by an occasional streetlight. I stayed in the shadows until I reached the walkway leading to the front door.

It was a cool fall night and I thrust my hands into the pockets of my peacoat. I could hear someone shuffling to the door after my second knock.

"Brother Tamer?" an older Afghan man said after he cracked open the door.

"Yes," I said, my eyes looking past him into the house.

"Come on in," he said with a smile.

I stepped into the foyer and kicked off my shoes. There was a pile of men's shoes next to the door. I tried to count the pairs, but the old man motioned for me to follow him down the main hall.

Everything was dark inside the house. The smell of food cooking hung in the air. I could hear the sounds of pots and pans banging around deeper in the house. Something moved in my peripheral vision. A woman's hand drew a drapery closed, but I could just make out a counter and some bowls used for cooking before the room got darker.

The Afghan stopped at a door near the kitchen and opened it. A wooden staircase led to the basement. The Afghan held the door open and urged me to go down first. I smiled and hesitated for a second. I really didn't want to go into the basement. The Afghan smiled. Another beat and things were going to get awkward. I started down the steps.

The Afghan shut the door behind us as I walked down the stairs. The basement was finished and well lit. Oriental rugs covered the floor, and posters showing off various sites of the Middle East hung on the wall. A bar near the staircase was stocked with water and fruit. As I got to the last step, I could hear Chiheb talking. He was sitting at a large picnic table with Jaser and Waleed. The tabletop was covered with a cloth and plates of lamb, shrimp, and hummus. Everything was home cooked and looked delicious.

I started to calm down immediately. Chiheb stood up to greet me. Everyone had a smile. They were waiting for me. I took a seat near the corner and everyone started to eat. Before I could get more than a few bites, Waleed and the Afghan—his father—started asking me about my business.

"What do you do?"

"Real estate," I said.

"Is it commercial or residential?"

Before I finished an answer there was another question. A half hour into dinner and I'd only had a few bites. By now, the main course of stewed meat and rice with raisins was served.

Between answers, I started to look for the exit. The staircase was the only way in or out. Going around the room, I figured the old Afghan would be the last one I'd kill. I'd start with Waleed. He was in good shape and would give me a fight. Then probably Jaser and Chiheb in that order.

But with each question I got more comfortable. There was no malice, at least toward me. It was clear they believed the legend and were curious. I was something new. Jaser, Waleed, and his family lived in isolation. An insular community of Muslims who didn't fit in with their neighbors.

But I was a Muslim brother who spoke English like an American. I was very successful. I had money, my own business, and yet I still had the same values as they did. They were tired of talking to one another. My presence at dinner injected new topics of conversation. I was the entertainment.

After dinner, we prayed. Jaser led this time. When it was over, I pulled him aside. I still had to win him over and knew the best way to do it. Stroke his ego.

"Brother, you have an amazing Quranic voice," I said. "It just takes me over."

I wasn't lying. His delivery was flawless. He never hesitated. He never stammered. Jaser's eyes lit up after the compliment. He pulled out his phone and let me listen to recordings of him reciting other prayers as we ate dessert. When everyone was done, Jaser pulled me aside.

"I'd like to take a walk with you," he said.

"Sounds great," I said. "It's a beautiful night."

Waleed volunteered to walk us out. Jaser was wearing a brown leather jacket. As I buttoned up my peacoat, I asked Chiheb if he had a coat.

"It's cold out here," I said.

Chiheb had only a button-down shirt and jeans. Waleed took off his camouflage jacket and handed it to Chiheb. He refused it until Waleed insisted Chiheb take it.

"Brother, it's a gift from me, it's a gift from me," Waleed said.

"But it's a big gift," Chiheb said, trying to hand the jacket back to Waleed.

He was afraid this was Waleed's only jacket.

"Brother, I have another jacket," he said. "I have so many. I need to get rid of them."

Finally, Chiheb pulled the jacket on, and I could tell he loved wearing it. In his mind he looked like the Sheikh, Osama bin Laden. I thanked Waleed and his father for the hospitality and started for the door. Just before we walked outside, Jaser stopped us.

"Keep your phones in the car and walk in the middle of the street," Jaser said.

By walking in the middle of the street, no one could overhear our conversation and we could spot surveillance. We left the house and walked down the middle of the road. Chiheb was on my right. Jaser on my left.

A few minutes into the walk, I spotted a couple walking a dog. They were trying not to look at us. When Jaser spotted them, they turned and walked in the opposite direction. Jaser kept watching them until they disappeared. It wasn't RCMP. It had to be CSIS. They were keeping tabs on us.

Once we were alone, Chiheb started the conversation.

"The issue is that we would like to tell you what we are planning, me and Raed," he said. "Because me and Raed, we have some plan . . . But of course we need someone to protect our back."

"Of course," I said.

"And this person who protects our back should be someone who is in a very good position, high position. He has the ability to manage the situation by distance. The ability to deviate the attention of the security services."

"Staying careful," I said.

"You understand?"

"I understand," I said.

Chiheb said Canada and America have armies in the Middle East.

"These armies are taking control of our land and they are spreading corruption on the Earth," he said. "They are spreading evil, they are spreading, you know, adultery, they are spreading alcohol, you understand? They are spreading Christianity. So it's our mission to fight those countries that have harmed us. The military power comes from the money power. Because those people who are supporting those evil governments are making war in our land, our home, our lands. So it's our duty to break their economic resources. To make trouble in their homes."

"Destroy their homes, because they are destroying our homes," I said.

Chiheb nodded his head yes.

"An eye for an eye and a tooth . . ." Jaser said.

"A tooth for a tooth," Chiheb said, finishing his thought.

"And the oppressor is who started it," Jaser said.

Chiheb thanked me for supporting the brothers overseas with my profits, but said this time was different.

"This is your time now," Chiheb said. "This is your time and your opportunity to not only support our brothers by money, but also by action."

Chiheb again laid out how they were going to do the attack. Having talked to Jaser about it at the taxi office, he was pretending to tell me for the first time. The whole time Jaser was silent. In order to prove the conspiracy, I needed him to talk. I needed to bring out the Imam in him.

"It's brilliant in its simplicity, but how does that serve our purpose as far as letting the world know?" I asked about the plot. "The important thing is to let the nonbelievers understand. Am I right? To let them know that this will keep happening—we can strike you whenever we want. But they're just gonna think it's an accident. But actually, it's an act of war. You understand, *habibi*?"

Chiheb started to answer. Shielding Jaser, I grabbed Chiheb's arm and squeezed it. He stopped talking and looked down. Jaser stepped in to fill the silence.

"I got the question for you answered," Jaser said.

He and Chiheb told me about the video.

"Because we want to make sure that they understand that as long as they're over there, their people will not feel safe on this side," Jaser said.

At first, I had feared the dinner might be a trap, but now I was the one setting the trap—and Jaser walked right into it.

"God almighty says fight their leaders," Jaser said.

He wanted to launch a string of sniper attacks targeting Canada's leaders. Chiheb was puzzled. How would we get near their leaders? They live in "castles," as he put it. They were protected, but Jaser said local leaders gave public speeches and attended parades. His example was a recent gay pride parade.

"The reason why is because they feel safe," he said. "Bunch of faggots. You know what I mean? Who's gonna attack them? They're just like them. Okay. That's when we hit them. This is the plan."

I stayed silent. Jaser and Chiheb were both committed to carrying out a terrorist attack.

"They feel safe," Jaser said. "We're gonna change all that."

CHAPTER 14

The Christian Burial Speech

Chiheb had to piss.

I could see him squirming in his seat as I drove east back to Montreal. We had spent the last two hours drinking tea and talking with Jaser at Denison Park next to the Humber River.

After our walk the night before, I'd agreed to meet with him before our drive home. Jaser's Imam Complex was in full swing. He agreed to the train plot, but he was more focused on his own sniper attack. It turned out Chiheb was annoyed by Jaser's rants. The train plot was sent from the brothers overseas. It was the priority, but every time it came up Jaser changed the subject. Jaser didn't want to take orders from overseas, from brothers hiding in caves who had no idea about Canada.

He became emotional at one point and shed a tear.

"Islam is a very powerful weapon, okay, and if it's in the right hands, you can bulldoze the whole world," he said. "And the beauty of Islam is that even the ruler or the president or the Caliph who is ruling himself, he submitted to the law of Allah."

It was the first time I saw the cracks in their relationship.

After the meeting, Chiheb and I drove back to Montreal. There were no bathrooms at the park, and we both climbed into the car with full bladders. I watched Chiheb fidget in his seat.

"Come on, we're gonna piss our pants," I said, laughing.

"My Lord," Chiheb said, a look of anguish on his face. "Allah, may Allah relieve me and relieve you. We should look for a washroom."

I searched my GPS for the closest gas station. It was uncomfortable for me. For Chiheb, it was a full-on crisis. One drop of urine on his skin or clothes and he'd be unclean. Making *wudu* wasn't enough. One drop of urine would send him careening off the path of Allah.

"Yeah," I said. "The first washroom I see. We'll stop, Allah willing, even a restaurant or whatever."

The closest one was a couple of miles off the highway. We both leapt out of the car. It took me a few minutes to go and wash up. Chiheb went in at the same time and didn't come out for forty-five minutes. He would urinate and then painstakingly make sure he didn't get any urine on himself. By the time he was done he sometimes had to urinate again. He was an extremist in every sense of the word. I sat in the car and waited. Thirty minutes was common, but this was a longer trip than usual. He looked distraught when he got back to the car.

"Tamer, I think I got some urine on my clothing," Chiheb said. "I had to go so bad that I barely made it."

"No worries," I said. "We'll figure it out."

I had to solve this or all conversation was done. He was already distraught and it would only get worse as we got closer to prayer. I got my phone and found a Gap a few miles away.

"We shouldn't waste money," Chiheb said when I told him where we were going.

"Don't worry," I said, putting the car in gear. "It's tax deductible."

Chiheb exhaled. He seemed relieved.

"God bless you, brother."

Chiheb picked out a pair of boxers, jeans, and a button-down shirt from the Gap. I paid and we went over to a nearby Marriott hotel. He went into the lobby bathroom to clean up. The Gap gave him an extra bag, so his urine-stained clothes wouldn't touch anything.

I walked over to the front desk.

"My friend and I would like to pray," I said. "Is there a place that is quiet that we could use so we don't have to pray outside?"

"Of course," the clerk said.

A few minutes later, I had the key to a banquet room. Chiheb came out an hour later wearing a smile and his new Gap clothes. Suburban dad with a jihadi beard.

"Brother, we have a place to pray," I said.

Once we got back to the car, my mind was stuck on my new mission: to find the American sleeper. The Canadian case, for all intents and purposes, was done. We had all the elements of a conspiracy. It would be nice to have one more overt act, like scouting the location or buying equipment, but it wasn't necessary.

I had everything I needed to convict Chiheb, but I wanted to give him the "Christian burial" speech. I was inspired by *Brewer v. Williams*, a 1977 United States Supreme Court case dealing with waiving the Sixth Amendment's right to counsel.

Robert Williams, who escaped from a mental hospital, kidnapped ten-year-old Pamela Powers on December 24, 1968, at the YMCA in Des Moines, Iowa. She was watching her brother in a wrestling tournament and left to use the bathroom. A fourteen-year-old boy saw Williams carrying something wrapped in a blanket through the lobby. He saw Powers's legs when Williams put her in the car. A warrant was issued and two days later Williams surrendered.

The Des Moines police drove 160 miles to Davenport to pick him up with a promise not to interrogate him without his lawyer present. Detectives knew Williams was deeply religious. Once they reached the highway heading back to Des Moines, the detective gave Williams what would later be called the "Christian burial speech."

> I want to give you something to think about while we're traveling down the road. . . . Number one, I want you to observe the weather conditions, it's raining, it's sleeting, it's freezing, driving is very treacherous, visibility is poor, it's going to be dark early this evening. They are predicting several inches of snow for tonight, and I feel that you yourself are the only person that knows where this little girl's body is, that you yourself have only been there once, and if you get a snow on top of it [sic] you yourself may be unable to find it. And, since we will be going right past the area on the way into Des Moines, I feel that we could stop and locate the body, that the parents of this little girl should be entitled to a Christian burial for the little girl who was snatched away from them on Christmas Eve and murdered. And I feel we should stop

and locate it on the way in rather than waiting until morning and trying to come back out after a snowstorm and possibly not being able to find it at all. . . . I do not want you to answer me. I don't want to discuss it any further. Just think about it as we're riding down the road.

Williams took the police to Powers's body on the way back.

My version of the speech was different. Basically, if Chiheb didn't waver and back out, then there was no defense for his actions. I didn't entrap him. He was plotting to murder hundreds of innocent people. I used this technique as a final nail in the coffin. I was looking to bury him using his own words.

"Okay, so look, thank God, you are a religious man and are more learned about our religion than the majority of Muslims I know," I said, starting the speech. "But I need to ask you something. I don't want you to think that I'm wavering here. I'm thinking ahead a bit. When the news breaks about what we've done, we will see that there were women and children who died. Are you sure this is considered halal? Is this what Allah wants?"

Chiheb turned in his seat to face me. This was serious. He started in English to make sure I understood. He had three proofs that condoned the attack.

"God almighty, He gave us the permission to eat dead animals, and to drink alcohol if you are close to death," Chiheb said. "But when you eat the dead meat or you drink the alcohol, you should do just what you need to survive; not more than that. That means don't fill your stomach. You just eat enough to keep you alive. Right?"

"Of course," I agreed.

His voice was measured and serious. Chiheb wasn't scolding me for doubting, but he wanted to crush any doubts.

"So what does this mean?" Chiheb said, settling into his lesson. "This means that you are allowed to do something haram if there is a necessity behind that haram. And when you do that haram, there are two conditions. You should not do this as you like to do. That means that when I do that haram, inside myself, I should have the feeling of not loving what I am doing. This is the first condition. Second, I should not exceed the necessity. Now please, brother, follow me on this point. If God almighty allows us to do that haram to save your life, what about saving your religion?"

Chiheb slapped his thigh and startled me.

"The necessity of saving religion is much higher than the necessity of saving your life. But God almighty, He allows you to do this haram for a lower level, which is the necessity to save your life. So what about the necessity to save the religion? So of course, you are more permissible to do that haram. This is one point."

For a second, I thought Chiheb might be turning. He admitted killing innocents was haram and that he shouldn't and couldn't like it, but he justified it.

"The second point, you know very well that all the civilian people who are living here, they are paying taxes. But also you know that those nonbelievers, they are attacking and killing our women and our children in our land. God almighty, He said that you should make aggression as they aggress you. You know aggression?"

"Do unto them as they've done to you," I said.

"So if they are killing our women and our children in our country, why don't we kill their women and their children in their country? And God almighty told us in the Quran to do to them as they are doing to you. So, this is the second proof. The first, you get the first, right?"

"The first one, yes," I said. "Of course."

"The necessity of . . ."

"Saving Islam," I said.

Saving Islam from him, was what I really meant. My job was to keep him talking. But in my mind I was arguing. This was not the religion my mother and father taught me. Islam wasn't a religion of violence and revenge. The Quran says he who slays a soul on earth shall be as if he had slain all of mankind, and he who saves a life shall be as if he had given life to all mankind.

"Saving religion, the necessity of saving religion is higher than the necessity of saving a life," he said. "But God, He allows you to do some haram. You understand?"

He was making sure I understood every point. This was jihad 101 and he wasn't sure why I needed to be told why our actions were justified.

"The second is that they are killing the women and children in our land. So why we don't do as they are doing? Now the third point, it's not from religion but it's a practical justification."

This I have to hear, I thought.

"You know very well that the nonbeliever is controlling our land. He's colonizing our land. Tens of years, right?"

"Yeah," I said. "Long time."

"One hundred, maybe more," Chiheb said.

I agreed in hopes he'd get to the point.

"Okay, so are we able to kick out the nonbeliever from our land with military organization? With a military army? Are you following? Do you get my question?"

"Meaning they have a big army," I said.

No Muslim army could kick the Western militaries out of the Middle East, Chiheb said. The brothers lack resources, technology, and equipment to resist. And when a Muslim nation does gain strength, the West destroys it.

"Look at Iran: Israel is preparing herself to send planes to destroy the nuclear factory," Chiheb said. "So this means that the nonbeliever is not allowing us to use technology. We are not able to kick out the army by fighting army between army. So, in that case, we are in the obligation to use other ways. Are you following me?"

"Absolutely," I said. "We have to fight the only way we can."

"The only way we can for the purpose to remove them, even when you find yourself obliged to do something haram," Chiheb said. "Are you following me?"

I felt his eyes on me.

"One hundred percent," I said.

"Are you following me?" he repeated.

This was the last time he wanted to talk about justifying the attacks.

"Amazing words," I said. "It's never gonna be an issue again. You explained it brilliantly. You said it perfectly. You are right on."

"So the first and the second, they are religious, the third is practical. You understand?"

"Of course," I said. "I'm thinking about the media and what is going to be said about us and everything else. They are going to call us terrorists and they will call us all kinds of bad things. They're gonna show pictures of the women and the babies that died, but they'll never show the pictures of the women and the children that are dying every day back home."

But what I was saying wasn't Islam, and I knew it. The Quran was very clear on the laws of war. A Muslim could only fight against other combatants. The Prophet Mohammed had clear rules. He instructed his soldiers it was forbidden to kill "any child, any woman, or any elder or sick person." Mutilation, scorched earth tactics, and destroying crops and villages were forbidden. The Prophet said nothing about terrorism, because there was only one way to wage war as a Muslim.

There was no question Chiheb wanted to commit an act of terrorism. He was convicted by his own words. My questions must have concerned Chiheb. A little while later, after we'd stopped talking about his proofs, he quizzed me.

"So, can you repeat the three points?"

"I will repeat them right now. Is this my test?"

Chiheb giggled.

"Because you failed your test when I asked you how many brothers you have, but I'm gonna pass my test."

Chiheb had three brothers. When I asked him about his family, he didn't include me as one of his brothers. I never let him forget.

"First proof, God almighty, He allows us in times of need, if we are this close to death, we're allowed to eat a dead animal or drink alcohol, just enough to save our lives. And to do that haram to save our life. Now imagine what God is going to allow in order for us to save our religion. Right?"

Chiheb smiled like a teacher happy with his pupil.

"Number two. Look at what they're doing to our women and children. For dozens of years, and years and years, they are killing our women and children nonstop. Right? So they're killing our women and children, we're gonna kill their women and children.

That's the second proof. And the third, which is what we just discussed . . ."

"Which is not religious, it's practical," Chiheb said.

"It's practical," I said. "They have occupied our land."

"And our brothers, they can't succeed right now," Chiheb said.

"They're winning some battles but they're losing some battles and they're not succeeding, but the point is, they are over there occupying our land. And they are a big military. For example, let's use Israel and the United States. Both of them have huge military armies. We can't get a military army to take our land back, so we have to use any means necessary, any means necessary to fight that evil. And the only way we can is this way."

I was getting into the act now.

"We're gonna have more success doing it this way," I said.

"Yeah," Chiheb said. "But don't forget that the nonbeliever, when he is in our land, he's taking more security procedures than he is in his land."

"Exactly," I said. "Because he feels comfortable here."

"They are ready for them over there," he said. "But here they are not ready for us."

"Can I ask you a question now?" I said.

"Yes," Chiheb said.

"How did I do on the test?"

"One point for you and zero points for me."

"I did well?"

"You are a good player."

"But you're a good teacher."

And convicted, I thought.

CHAPTER 15

Best of the Mujahideen

Back in Montreal, Chiheb wanted me to meet two like-minded brothers for dinner.

We met them at an Egyptian seafood restaurant not far from his apartment. The last two weeks had been a blur. I'd gone from relaxing on a beach in the Caribbean (well, trying to), to being embedded in an al Qaeda plot to derail a train in Canada, to trying to find an American sleeper cell.

It was September 11, 2012, and I was in no mood to be breaking bread with a terrorist. But I put on my best smile and tried to at least enjoy my food.

The two men were actual brothers from Tunisia. They arrived just as we got to the restaurant. Both were engineers who worked in Montreal. Typical Middle Eastern foreigners: young, educated, religious, and generous.

Over fish, Chiheb worked politics into the conversation when he could, but it was obvious that the brothers weren't interested. There were a few times when I was a little embarrassed for Chiheb as he tested their interpretations of hadiths and scolded them when their views were different from his. The brothers failed Chiheb's test.

I paid for dinner and we walked to the Cold Stone Creamery across the street for ice cream. The Tunisian brothers paid for dessert. As we were eating our ice cream, I was making fun of Chiheb about his hard-line views. He knew I was trying to placate the brothers and played along. We said our goodbyes and I drove Chiheb home.

"Those are good brothers," I said.

"But not like-minded," Chiheb said. "They are not like us."

"Few of us are like you, brother," I said as I stopped in front of his apartment building. "I am floored that you were actually trained by our elders, my brother. How did that happen? I'd love to hear that story."

From the beginning, something had bothered me about Chiheb. It didn't make sense that this goofy scientist with a Canadian visa ended up one step removed from the leader of al Qaeda in less than one year.

There was no doubt he wanted to kill Westerners. It never left his heart, even when it was the furthest thing from anyone's mind. But this dark center was hidden from view by a jovial scientist working to cure the world's deadliest diseases. He laughed like Baba Noel, the Arabic name for Santa Claus. It was hard to wrap my head around.

As we sat in front of his building, I wanted to know whether he was evil or someone overseas had turned him into a monster. Chiheb was happy to tell me the story. He was proud of his time in Iran.

When Chiheb got to Canada in 2008, he was lost. Everything

was foreign. He barely spoke the language. The weather was frigid and he recognized few customs. The order he found in the laboratory was absent in his daily life. Exiled from the daily rhythms of Montreal, his focus turned inward. He studied Islam, read the Bible and Torah. He was looking to bring order to the chaos of the real world. But it wasn't until he started to follow the war in Afghanistan that things crystalized.

"I researched their struggles in Afghanistan," he said. "I wanted to die on the battlefield with the mujahideen brothers."

In the spring of 2011, Chiheb emptied his bank account, bought a one-way ticket to Tehran, and planned to drive to Afghanistan.

"Buying a ticket to Kabul was too obvious," Chiheb told me.

"Why didn't you go to Pakistan?" I asked.

Most foreign fighters filtered in through the ratlines in Pakistan's tribal areas.

"Pakistan is a friend to the United States," Chiheb said. "Iran is not."

I still didn't know what pushed him to seek out the mujahideen, but I didn't press it. I wanted him to tell his story.

When he landed in Tehran, a cab driver at the airport befriended him. The cabbie was a Sunni Muslim, like Chiheb, which is a minority in Iran. Chiheb stayed at the cabbie's house for a few days. But his mind was still across the border in Afghanistan.

"I need to get to the border to cross into Afghanistan to help the brothers," Chiheb told the cabbie.

"No," the cabbie said. "Stop talking. That kind of talk will get you in trouble."

Chiheb pleaded for his help, and the cabbie hooked him up with a friend who was more sympathetic. Chiheb paid thousands of dollars for a ride to Zahedan, a town in southeastern Iran that bordered Afghanistan and Pakistan.

"I just told him to drive me as close to the border as possible," Chiheb said.

When they arrived in Zahedan, Chiheb and the driver stopped at a local mosque to pray.

"Everyone stared at us," Chiheb said.

Right after prayer, a couple of young men wanted to know who Chiheb was and why he was there.

"I told them I was passing through on my way to Afghanistan. I asked to speak to the Imam so I could get some guidance on crossing the border."

One of the young men got El Mofti, an old Iranian man in his late sixties. He limped out from the back of the mosque to meet Chiheb.

"Where is the easiest place to cross the border into Afghanistan?" Chiheb asked.

"Are you hungry?" El Mofti asked. "Come, I know a restaurant nearby where we can eat."

Chiheb thanked the driver and followed El Mofti to a restaurant. They took a table in the back and ate.

"I was completely truthful with him," Chiheb said. "I told him that I was ready to die for Allah and that it is my destiny to fight with the mujahideen in Afghanistan."

Chiheb found out later El Mofti had thought he was a spy, but his truthfulness at dinner changed the Imam's mind. El Mofti invited Chiheb to stay at his home.

"El Mofti kept telling me not to go to Afghanistan," Chiheb said. "I stayed at his house for a few days until I needed a new visa."

Chiheb got a cab and started his trek back to Tehran to renew his visa. On his way out, he realized he needed to change his Canadian dollars to Iranian rials. Chiheb stopped at the mosque to ask where he could change money. One of the young boys ran to the back and told El Mofti Chiheb was leaving.

"Don't go, brother," El Mofti told Chiheb. "There is someone I want you to meet. A very special guest."

Chiheb tried explaining that he was just going to get his visa renewed, but El Mofti shooed the cab away and he brought Chiheb back to his house.

"Don't worry about your visa," he told Chiheb.

That night, a tall Afghan wearing a black robe and a black turban came to El Mofti's house.

"The second I laid eyes on him, I knew I made the right choice," Chiheb said.

It was Abu Hamza. He spent the evening getting to know Chiheb.

"He tested me," Chiheb said. "Like I tested you."

"You passed?" I asked.

"Yes," Chiheb said. "Like you."

Chiheb spent almost a week at Abu Hamza's house. He learned al Qaeda's codes and how to send messages to the brothers overseas.

"I wanted to learn how to shoot," Chiheb said. "I wanted to be a soldier."

But Abu Hamza had other plans. Chiheb had a Canadian visa. He had access to the West.

"Your brilliant mind shouldn't be wasted on the battlefield," Abu Hamza said. "You will be the best of the mujahideen because you will be able to do Allah's work in the heart of the infidel's land."

Abu Hamza told Chiheb to go back to Canada and await further instructions. Chiheb spent almost a year working and studying in Montreal.

"My mother called me months later," he said. "She said strangers came to her house and introduced themselves as my new friends."

Al Qaeda was checking his story. Then in February 2012, Chiheb was instructed to return to Zahedan for his training. He bought a ticket and flew out the day after he got the e-mail. He stayed at Abu Hamza's house.

"Tell me about him, brother," I said.

"Abu Hamza was a general with the Taliban, but I was trained by a general in al Qaeda."

"Who is that?" I asked.

"El Massoul," he replied.

Abu Hamza drove Chiheb to the outskirts of the city to meet El Massoul, who dressed in a long white robe and wore a camouflage jacket like Osama bin Laden.

"It was the Sheikh's jacket," Chiheb said. "El Massoul wore it everywhere. Meeting him was the greatest moment of my life."

Chiheb lived with El Massoul for six weeks, where he learned about the train plot, how to recruit like-minded brothers, and how to resist torture.

"Resist torture?" I said. "Did they actually torture you?"

"No," Chiheb said. "El Massoul explained that it would be an honor to be tortured by the infidels in this life instead of the afterlife and to accept the pain. Because it will be nothing like the pain of hellfire."

"Was there any Islamic studies done during your training?" I asked.

"Not once," he said. "That's not what this training was about."

Of course not.

"El Massoul left for a few days, but promised to return before I went back to Canada," Chiheb said. "When he returned, he had a note for me."

It was handwritten in Arabic, Chiheb said.

"It said 'Focus on your studies and don't argue.'"

"What does that mean?" I asked.

"It's like what your uncle told you," Chiheb said. "Live amongst them, as them, to defeat them. Blend in using my work. The second part, I had to ask El Massoul. He told me it meant not to draw any attention to myself when I was finding good brothers."

"Is that how you found me?" I asked, hammering home the fact that he chose me.

"Yes. El Massoul told me that when you try to bring a brother along and he argues with you, try again. If he argues again, leave him. Don't fight with him."

"That's an amazing story, my brother," I said.

But Chiheb wasn't done. He took out his wallet. It was thick with notes, receipts, a small Quran.

"Tamer, that note that El Massoul gave me was from our Sheikh," Chiheb said.

He held up his wallet.

"I carry it everywhere with me."

He'd mentioned the note during our road trip to Toronto, but I didn't really understand its significance. The Sheikh was Ayman al-Zawahiri, the leader of al Qaeda. El Massoul was one of a handful of people on the planet who could meet with the Sheikh in person, Chiheb said.

"Are you kidding me? *Habibi,* you have a note directly from our Sheikh?" I said. *"Masha'Allah."*

Chiheb returned to Montreal soon after getting the note and continued his studies just like al-Zawahiri ordered. He also started working on the train plot. We met shortly thereafter.

"El Massoul told me to be ready by the end of the year," Chiheb said. "He will send me an e-mail with the code word to attack."

"What is the code?" I asked.

"Akbar."

CHAPTER 16

Pizza with Terrorists

I buttoned my peacoat when I got out of the taxi and watched as the Delta Hotel bellhop loaded my bags onto the cart.

It was late September 2012—ten days after my car trip with Chiheb—and I was back in Toronto to find a safe house and meet with Jaser.

Everything changed when we learned of the American sleeper. Chiheb was planning attacks across the border, but the RCMP was aware. We had our own Chiheb and had to find him.

This had become my only case. The FBI had other undercover agents take over my caseload. Progress on the case was briefed daily to the White House. My four-day babysitting mission had stretched into three months with no end in sight.

While we focused on the American sleeper, Canada wanted an airtight case and pushed me to get the plot's final details.

I called Jaser from my two-room suite. No answer. The RCMP

wanted me to spend some alone time with him. Take his temperature without Chiheb. They were concerned he was just following along.

Jaser had moved to Canada in 1993. His family was forced to leave the United Arab Emirates after his father refused to spy on the Palestinian refugees living there. Jaser, fifteen, arrived with his parents and two brothers—eleven-year-old Nabil and ten-year-old Shadi. His mother was pregnant with another boy. The Immigration and Refugee Board accepted Jaser's family into Canada under an old program that accepted stateless refugees.

While the family fought to stay in Canada, Jaser was convicted of fraud in 1997 and for threatening a pub manager in 1999. Ordered out of Canada, he was finally picked up in 2004 after Canadian immigration issued a warrant for his arrest. He was released from the Toronto West Detention Centre when officials couldn't find a country to deport him to. Being Palestinian, Jaser had no country.

He stayed out of trouble after that. Jaser married and started a limo company. He was pardoned in 2009 and received permanent resident status in 2012. When his limo company failed in 2011, he took a job driving special-education students and working customer service for a moving company. By the time I met him he'd gotten his job as a taxi dispatcher.

Jaser fit the profile of a petty criminal who was now sprinkling a little jihad on his activities. Disenfranchised, he wanted to lash out against the Jews and the government for stealing his country. Jaser was a cliché.

I unfolded two maps of the Toronto area and spread them out on the living room table. We still didn't know the target for sure. Was it the bridge they scouted over Labor Day or another one? Doug came up with the idea for the maps.

"If he sees them, maybe he can walk you through where they are potentially going to do this," Doug said in the briefing before I went to the hotel.

Worth a shot.

My cell phone rang about an hour later. It was Jaser. I told him I was in town and wanted to meet up. I could hear radio traffic in the background as he talked. He suggested we meet at the taxi dispatch office but reminded me that there was audio and video there so we couldn't discuss the plan.

"Why don't you come by the hotel?" I said.

We could have a late dinner and talk in private, I told him. Jaser agreed. I hung up and called Chiheb. He knew I was in Canada and I had promised to check in. When he found out Jaser was coming over, he got upset.

"Any discussion about the projects should be with all three of us," he said.

He was acting like a jealous girlfriend. He didn't want to be left out, but he was busy with his dissertation and couldn't leave.

I sensed some tension after the first trip, but it was clear Chiheb and Jaser were in a power struggle over who was the leader. There was no way Chiheb was going to let Jaser sap my resources with his plans. For now, the tension worked in my favor.

"I could get to Toronto Sunday," he said.

"Perfect, brother," I said. "We will pick you up then."

That gave me two days with Jaser. He arrived around nine o'clock. We prayed and then ordered room service. While we waited for our food, Jaser noticed the maps on the table and started to show me where he and Chiheb were thinking of derailing the train. It was a bridge south of Toronto near Lake Ontario. But he didn't think the plan was doable. There was no way to cut the rail in two hours, the time between trains. He wanted to do it his way. Jaser made a gesture with his hands, like a bomb.

"Boom," he said, hinting that the best way to derail the train was with explosives.

Dinner arrived—fish and risotto—and we talked about renting a safe house as we ate. I told him I had talked to a real estate agent and my company was ready to sign a lease for a condo north of Toronto. Jaser liked the area, but he was concerned my name would be on the lease. I assured him my name wouldn't appear on anything regarding the safe house.

The food was delicious. I picked up the plate of fish and offered him more before taking another sliver. He waved it off but kept eating the risotto.

"This rice is good," I said. "The rice is nice, right?"

"It's good, yeah," Jaser said. "It has a nice flavor to it."

"It's called risotto," I said. "Vegetable risotto."

"Yeah, it's pretty good," he said between spoonfuls. "Mind you, though, if I would make this risotto it would be creamier. And the rice would be cooked more."

I chuckled. That was such a Jaser comment. He was that kind of guy. Everything he did was better. This was his first taste of risotto, but he could make it better.

After dinner, he laid out his ideas. He wanted to train a sniper—likely from the household mosque where I met him on my first trip—and target Jewish businessmen, gays, and local leaders. He told me how we could inflict more damage than anyone in al Qaeda because he knew Canada and Toronto better.

"There is so much we can do," he said. "So much pain we can

inflict. Look at the Prophet, peace be upon him, all the wonderful things he did. He did all of that, but he didn't have a day job. I do, unfortunately, and if I didn't and I could focus on this, I think I can do . . ."

I stopped listening and looked at him. Did he just say if he didn't have a job he could be like the Prophet? A Muslim never compares anyone or anything to the Prophet, or any prophet for that matter. It was haram. But Jaser was as good as the Prophet, except he had to dispatch taxis.

It was getting late and Jaser wanted to go home to his wife. We planned to meet the following day. I told him about my plan to meet with a real estate agent to finalize the lease on a condo on Harrison Garden Boulevard in North York.

After Jaser left, I met the team at a nearby hotel suite. Frank answered the door. Nelly, Joey, and Doug were waiting in the living room.

"Good call with the maps," I told Doug as we talked about the meeting with Jaser.

"I know," Doug said, shrugging his shoulders and sniffing.

It stopped me in my tracks.

"Did you just sniff?"

Doug did it every time he was right or told a joke that made someone laugh. From that moment on, we called it the "Dougy Sniff."

As we talked through the next Jaser meeting, Frank filled us in on the layout of the condo. The living room had a couch and an easy chair with a table in the middle. The whole place was wired with microphones and cameras.

"Hey, Frank, tell me where the best cameras are," I said. "Where do you want them? I can throw my bag on the chair to make them sit on the couch, or if you'd rather have one of them in the chair?"

I was trying to figure out where I could sit to avoid the camera. It made life for their tech guys a little easier because they didn't have to pixilate my face. But Frank looked at me like I'd just asked him for a naked picture of his wife.

"You don't need to worry about any of that," he said.

"Excuse me?" I said.

"Don't worry about where they are. Just get them in there and we'll figure it out."

I looked at Joey and Nelly. Nelly shook his head. Joey cringed. He knew this was something he'd have to fix.

"Is this fucking guy for real?" I said. "Is he really not telling me where the cameras are? Frank, you know I'm a cop, right? I'm not a confidential informant or a source. I'm police just like you."

That was the big difference between how the Canadians and Americans ran their undercover programs. The Canadians kept their undercovers in the dark. American undercovers were in on everything behind the scenes. I wasn't used to working in the dark.

"No, I just meant don't worry about it. You have enough to think about," Frank said, realizing he'd hit a nerve.

"Fuck you," I said. "I don't want to know where your cameras are. It's your prosecution."

I left to put my bag back in my hotel room. I could hear Nelly behind me.

"You fucked up," he said to Frank.

Joey found me a few minutes later in my room. I was unpacking.

"Come on," he said. "I'll tell you where the cameras are."

"Don't worry about it," I said.

I wasn't interested.

"I was making an effort," I said. "I was trying to make their lives easier so they didn't have to redact me for hours and hours. If I sat in a chair and my face was obscured they could use the whole tape."

Their case. Their country. Their rules. But Joey told me where the cameras were anyway.

That night I picked up Jaser and took him to the condo. It had two bedrooms, a small kitchen, and a sitting room. In the foyer, Jaser noticed a fruit basket with a thank-you note from the real estate company. Next to the basket was the lease.

"Please enjoy this place on us," the thank-you note read. "We'd love to do business with you."

Jaser was intrigued with the lease and that my name was no-where on it. I told him my company got the condo for two months. I gave Jaser a quick tour. He approved of the place and looked forward to showing it to Chiheb.

Chiheb called Jaser from downtown the next day. He needed a ride to the condo after catching a carpool from Montreal to Toronto.

"I know where he is," Jaser said. "I'll go grab him."

I gave him the extra set of keys to the condo.

"I'll get dinner," I said.

There was a Pizza Pizza restaurant around the corner. I got two large pizzas with green peppers and onions and met them back at the condo.

Chiheb seemed happy to be in Toronto. I sensed he didn't like being out of the mix. We gathered around the table and started to eat. When the train plot came up, Chiheb mentioned their first recon trip. This was the Labor Day fishing trip. The bridge sat near

Lake Ontario. Both Jaser and Chiheb started to giggle. They were like two old college buddies telling stories from their glory days.

"We wanted, from the beginning, to get closer to the bridge," Chiheb said. "I mean, there was many trees, many trees. And it was some type of a mountain, very strong to walk . . ."

"Hard," Jaser said.

"Hard, is very hard. There is a lot of trees, a lot of insects, a lot of—" Chiheb said.

"I saw a frog this big," Jaser said, holding his hands about six inches apart.

"Oh my God, you're kidding me," I said, egging them on.

"That was a crazy place," Jaser said.

Jaser said they got lost in some thick grass that was ten feet high. Both made it sound like an expedition to the Amazon. The insects. The frogs. The brush. Finally, they stumbled onto the banks of the lake. Out in the distance was a boat. A young couple with big cameras was paddling nearby.

"We waved at them like this," Chiheb said, waving his hand over his head like he was trying to flag me down. "We would like to see the sea."

I started to laugh. He had tried to flag down the CSIS surveillance team. The same guys who had insisted Chiheb and Jaser were going fishing. I was having trouble keeping a straight face.

"He's calling them over to take us to the other side," Jaser said.

"No way," I said.

One of the agents put down his camera and waved back.

"They didn't understand," Jaser said. "They were just waving back, but they wouldn't move. So I was telling him maybe they're not in a good mood. That's why they wouldn't come."

Jaser and Chiheb fought their way back through the grass but got lost again.

"We ended up in somebody's backyard and they were out having a barbecue," Jaser said.

"Halal?" I said, laughing.

"You ask if it is halal, ask him what they said to us," Chiheb said. "Ask him what they said to us."

I looked at Jaser and then Chiheb.

"What?"

"'Why are those terrorists there?'" Jaser said.

"No they didn't," I said.

Chiheb couldn't keep a straight face as he tried to avoid my gaze. He started to laugh.

"I am testing you if you will get scared," he said.

"No, they were nice people," Jaser said.

"Ah, okay," I said. "What'd they say?"

"We talked to them for a while," Jaser said. "I gave them a copy of the Quran."

"They were thinking that we are camping, because many people come to this place, I mean for adventures," Chiheb said.

Despite getting lost twice, they saw enough of the bridge to look for another target. There were too many houses nearby. The terrain made it impossible to bring the equipment needed to cut the rail on the bridge.

Instead, they set their sights on a new, more isolated location near the U.S. border. The location fit the criteria set out by Chiheb from the start, but they only visited it at night. They needed pictures and video of the rails during the day.

"What do you think, we go visit soon?" Chiheb said to both of us.

This is what I was hoping, that they would ask me to scout the location with them. The final piece of evidence for the Canadian case. One more overt act for the conspiracy.

"What do you think, do you have work tomorrow?" Chiheb asked me.

"No," I said.

They wanted me to come because of my expertise in construction. We agreed to scout the new location the following morning.

Chiheb stayed at the condo for the night, since I already had a hotel room. I left with Jaser. The cold hit us as soon as we left the condo. Jaser zipped up his leather jacket. I left my peacoat open.

"You don't get cold?" he said, shivering. "I'm freezing."

"If you feel my skin, I'm hot," I said. "I'm always hot. When I'm at home, my wife goes to bed with two sweatshirts, sweatpants, socks, and sometimes even gloves."

Jaser laughed.

In legend, I am always married. It would be odd if I wasn't.

"I'm wearing no shirt and I'm on top of the covers. I have a tremendous amount of heat, I'm always very hot. Maybe because I'm Egyptian."

We got in the car. Jaser's smile was gone. He stared out the window. There was no energy to his movements. I noticed his mood changed when Chiheb started talking about the train plot.

"Something's on your mind. I want to know what you're thinking," I said. "Spell it out for me. You're the brains here, *habibi*. You can't hold back now."

Jaser just shook his head.

"Not brains, brother. You know, like I said to you, it seems to be too much work for a very small job."

"You think we should go bigger," I said.

"It's too small," he said, turning to look at me. "It's a big operation, we're setting up for a big operation and we end up doing something very tiny. The setup is nice, but the operation doesn't make sense."

I couldn't tell if Jaser didn't like the plan or didn't like that it wasn't his idea. He hated being one of the workers. My job was easy. Pay for equipment and supplies and upload the video. Jaser and Chiheb had to go out in December and cut the track. If he was going to get his hands dirty, it had to be for his plan. He wanted to do his sniper plot instead, but there was no way Chiheb would go for it.

Unless Jaser convinced me.

"Who are they?" he said about the people on the train. "Slaves. Really, just like you and me, workers. You know? Sheep. We don't want sheep. We want the wolf. We can get the wolf. Brother, we can get the wolf."

CHAPTER 17

The Bridge

Chiheb climbed into the passenger seat of my rental car the next morning. On the way to Jaser's apartment, I worked the American sleeper into the conversation.

"Do you think he would want to meet me eventually?" I asked.

"Without a doubt, without a doubt," Chiheb said. "I mean, once he talks with me."

"How do you make this meeting happen?" I asked. "Do you have to call someone? Do you have to send an e-mail because you don't have his number?"

"When I go back to Montreal I will start making contacts with the brothers, God willing, to make arrangements to make the plan for the meeting with the brother."

"Beautiful," I said.

Jaser was waiting for us and jumped into the front seat, forcing Chiheb into the back. Chiheb put up a fight, but Jaser insisted. He knew the way. Like a human GPS, he spent the whole drive barking out directions.

We were headed to the Highland Creek railway bridge in Scarborough. The Maple Leaf, a train line jointly operated by VIA rail—the Canadian train service—and Amtrak—the American rail service—travels over the bridge en route to Penn Station in New York.

We parked in a lot next to a water treatment facility. A trail ran near the train bridge. I saw a few bikers riding away from us as I got out of the car. Jaser had his leather jacket over his white robe, and Chiheb wore his bin Laden jacket. Both Chiheb and Jaser wore kufis, knit Muslim prayer hats. There was no mistaking we were Arabs.

Chiheb led the way as we walked toward the bridge. We cut through a thicket of trees and walked along the edge of the tracks. A commuter train heading toward Toronto passed us. I could feel the rumble of the cars in my chest.

"That was nowhere near the size of the target," Jaser said.

Soon, the steel bridge came into view. It was a one-hundred-foot drop off the bridge into very shallow water. A steel railing ran the length of both sides of the bridge. A footbridge ran underneath for pedestrians. Before we got on the bridge, I stopped Chiheb.

"Are you sure about the train schedule?" I said.

Once we were on the bridge, we were stuck. There was no place to go if the train came.

"Positive," he said.

There were two sets of tracks on the bridge separated by about four feet. Chiheb got on all fours to inspect the rail. The scientist in him took over. He looked at the attack like it was an experiment. He estimated the thickness of the rail and talked about the different ways we could cut it.

Blowtorch.

Jackhammer.

Jaser suggested a military-grade laser, which we all knew was impossible to get.

It was clear a blowtorch was never going to cut through the rail in time. Explosives were probably the only course of action, something Jaser had pointed out in an earlier discussion. Chiheb was thinking out loud as he tried to figure out if two hours was enough time to cut the rail. He was yelling out his ideas in Arabic.

"*Habibi,* lower your voice," Jaser said.

Chiheb ignored him.

"I'm talking in Arabic," he said. "No one knows what we're saying."

I looked back at Jaser. He was nervous we were drawing the attention of joggers and cyclists using the footbridge and nearby paths. Jaser was supposed to be videotaping the tracks with a small camera, but when he saw bikers or runners, he stuffed it into his pocket.

"What's wrong, Raed?" I asked. "There is something on your mind."

"There are many things on my mind," Jaser said.

"Talk to us, *habibi,*" I said.

"When I tell you there is someone looking at you, okay, you don't say to me it doesn't matter," Jaser said. "The devil sent him to spy on us."

"The devil sent him?" Chiheb said.

"Of course, who else sent him?" Jaser said, losing his patience a little.

Chiheb laughed.

"Praise God," he said.

"So why don't you take these things seriously?" Jaser asked. "In a serious way?"

"Because in my mind, what does this person know about our project?"

"Brother, it is not about him knowing or not knowing. Just the fact of collecting information for the devil."

Jaser said if we made a mistake and got caught because we didn't take the plot seriously then we were committing a sin.

"I don't need this kind of sin, man," Jaser said. "So take today's act as a lesson."

Chiheb was still on all fours looking at the rail. He waved me over. I climbed down next to him and put my hand on the rail. It was vibrating.

"Chiheb," I said. "Do you feel that?"

He ignored me.

I stood up. Jaser was frozen. We both saw the train at the same time. There was no outrunning it. I looked at both sets of tracks and then back at the train. There was nowhere to run, but the bridge was wide enough for two trains to pass. Our only chance was to get on the far side of the active track and hold on to the fence. But which set of tracks? We had to decide, because once the train reached the bridge it was too late.

I studied the pair of tracks. The south side of the tracks was close to the water. About 250 yards west of the bridge there was a bend. If the train made the bend and I saw tracks, it was on the north side. If I didn't see tracks, it was on the south side.

Jaser started hopping back and forth from each track. At my

feet, Chiheb was still talking about the rail. My eyes were fixed on the bend. The train started to turn and the tracks disappeared.

I grabbed Chiheb by the back of his jacket and headed for the north side of the bridge.

"Grab the rail," I said.

Jaser was already following me. I reached the cold metal railing and hooked my arm around it. Jaser was fixated on the train. He looked stiff and scared. Chiheb's face didn't change. If the train killed him, he believed Allah would reward him. I wasn't going to take that chance. I held on to the rail with both hands.

The train got louder as it approached. The thundering of the engine hit me in the chest. I pulled myself tighter to the rail. Wind whipped at my pant legs. It felt like the train was trying to drag me under its wheels. The shrill of the whistle hurt my ears as the engineer spotted us on the bridge. He was hanging out of the window. His face was a mix of shock and fear.

Our eyes locked.

What are you doing? the engineer's eyes asked.

A few seconds later, the train was gone. I let go of the railing.

"That's the target," Jaser said.

We climbed off the bridge and inspected underneath before walking back to the car. Jaser and I walked back the rest of the way in silence. My legs were a little wobbly as the adrenaline of almost getting hit by a train wore off.

Chiheb didn't stop talking about what needed to be done. He got into the front seat of the car and took out a pad of paper. I got behind the wheel and Jaser got in the backseat. Chiheb was unfazed by the train. Seeing the bridge and the train just energized him. He was already thinking of what had to be done. I was sliding the key into the ignition when Jaser spotted the police.

"There's police over there, brother, but they're just passing by," he said.

I checked the mirror. They weren't passing by. They were getting in position. I knew what a felony traffic stop looked like. My mouth went dry. These cops were just doing their jobs, but if they searched the car and found Chiheb's notebook or Jaser's video camera, we were cooked. The investigation was over. I looked over at Chiheb. He was still writing.

"Put it down, the police are coming to talk to us," I said.

He tossed the notebook faceup on the dashboard. I looked at Jaser in the rearview mirror. Sweat was beading on his brow. He looked tense. Scared. As the officers approached, he stuffed the video camera under the seat.

"Hi, sir," a male police officer said as he reached Chiheb's window. "How are you?"

He was dressed in a dark blue uniform. His hand rested near his belt, within reach of his holstered pistol.

"*As salamu alaikum*," Chiheb said.

"How are you?" the male officer said. "*Wa alaikum al salam*."

I was focused on the officer talking to Chiheb when I caught some movement out of my peripheral vision. A female officer was at my window. In the rearview mirror two police cars boxed us into the parking spot.

"So what happened was the driver of the train called in and said that he had to honk his horn to have you guys move out of the way," the male officer said. "That's why we're here."

"Yeah, we thought the pathway to get to the walkway was there," I said. "So we realized when we got there that this isn't . . ."

The officer's eyes scanned the car while I spoke.

"You're in the wrong area," he said, cutting me off.

I smiled.

"When we saw we were in the wrong area," I said. "We doubled back."

"What brings you down here?" he said, his gaze alternating between me and Chiheb.

"We're just sightseeing," I said.

The male officer asked for identification. He noticed Chiheb was from Montreal and I was from New York. We told him I was looking at real estate investments in the Toronto area.

"I'm trying to stay away from downtown but the condominiums are unbelievable down here," I said. "You guys seem to be the only country in the world that's not affected by this economy."

"I know, we're lucky," the male officer said. "Unless you walk into some of the condominiums that we have to deal with; then you'd think otherwise."

We all laughed. We made small talk for a while longer and then the officers left.

"Thanks for your cooperation, guys," the officer said, returning to his police car. "Have a nice day."

"All right, you too," I said.

"Peace upon you," he said.

"Upon you too," Chiheb said.

We waited for the police to leave. I let out a deep sigh and looked over at Chiheb. He was back to work making lists in his notebook.

The police stop didn't register with Chiheb. It was just an obstacle to overcome on the path of Allah.

"Damn them," I said. "As brother Raed said, the devil is always watching."

Jaser's nerves were shot. He was jumpy and his eyes darted between me and Chiheb.

"You guys are stupid, that's why," Jaser said. "You don't listen. Sorry, I'm very upset with you."

"Why?" I said.

"I told you to be serious about this. I told you the devil sends people to locate you. You don't listen."

"But thank God, we handled it," I said.

I looked over at Chiheb and shrugged.

"No, no, no, no," Jaser said. "This is okay, but we just compromised the location. So no worries, we just have to find another place. It's not a big deal, there's a lot of good places."

Chiheb stopped working.

"How would they make the connection?" Chiheb said.

"You're foolish," Jaser said. "And you should be happy and say, thank God that you have a brother like me who is telling you about your faults. You're very foolish."

"What does it mean, foolish?" Chiheb said, partly as a challenge and partly because he didn't know. "I don't understand."

"You're gonna make a video, okay, and then the video is not gonna be aired until after the train derails. Where? About two hundred meters, five hundred meters away from where three Arab guys, one from the States, one from Quebec, and one from Ontario, were found, you know, uh, hanging around and checking things out not too long before this happened. This is what they do. Now they have a piece of information. A piece of the puzzle. They're gonna put it in their database and when the right time comes, they're gonna connect one, two, three and they have our information. So this is what I'm talking about taking things seriously."

"But we said that we are just being tourists, we are seeing beautiful pictures," Chiheb said.

"And they probably bought it," I said. "If they didn't buy it, we would've been out of the car."

Jaser just shook his head. He wasn't going to take part in the attack unless we changed the location.

"You do things according to the reality that's on the ground," he said. "You don't do it according to how they do it back there. Do you see my point? There is a completely different set of scenarios and situations. So, if you wanna do this, fine, we can do it, but we're gonna do it our way, not their way. You see, because we're in Canada, we're not in Kandahar."

"Our mistake is that we didn't leave the place immediately," I said.

Jaser sighed.

"Yes. That was a mistake," he said. "We should've left as soon as we got to the car."

"We stay at the car like a stupid person," Chiheb said.

"It doesn't matter, nothing happened," I said, hoping to calm everyone down. "We're good."

The police stop was just the opening Jaser needed to change the plot. He asked Chiheb how long he had lived in Canada as I drove back to Toronto. Chiheb told him four years.

"Okay, that's all," Jaser said. "You've been busy studying."

"Yes," Chiheb said.

"I've been busy living. For twenty years. Okay? Who has more experience?"

"You of course," Chiheb said.

"Okay. Who knows how to hurt these people the most? You or me?"

Chiheb looked at me and then back at Jaser. I could see where Jaser was going, but I wasn't sure if Chiheb was tracking.

"You."

"That's it. Okay? Now . . ."

"But, this operation . . ." Chiheb said, realizing he'd fallen into Jaser's trap.

"This is an operation because they asked you to do something," Jaser said. "Okay? That's it. But we can do our own operation. Okay? And their operation, we could do, if it makes sense. If it's safe to do. Okay? But we can do our own operation. Now, if you want to talk about how to hurt these people the most—"

Chiheb cut him off.

"Now you are making the whole operation in question, right?"

The train attack was important to Chiheb and the brothers overseas because it proved al Qaeda could reach out from the battlefields of the Middle East and attack the homeland. The symbolism was almost more important than the attack. It empowered the brothers and terrified the nonbelievers.

Jaser said no, but no one in the car believed him.

"I'm telling you that they gave us a command to do something," Jaser said. "Okay? We're going to try to fulfill the command as we see fit. Not as they see fit, because they're not here. You are following me, right?"

"I am following you," Chiheb said.

"Okay. So we're trying to work things out according to what we know, what we see, and the reality on the ground. Now, at the same time, I can bring your attention to something that is even more relevant than a train. The train, we can continue to do, no problem, find another location, God willing, you never know."

Jaser was in Imam mode.

"These people, they only understand the language of two things. Death and money. That's it. You hurt them. You hit them where it really hurts. You take their lives. You take their wealth. You do these two, they will go crazy."

Jaser said the real target should be Jews living in Toronto, not a train full of sheep. But the people on the train were giving tax money to the governments killing the brothers overseas, Chiheb said. That justified their deaths.

"They are paying taxes, yes," Jaser said. "But do they mean to pay the tax for the government to go, are they giving the green light to the government to go and kill people? No."

"But they know that their government, they are killing . . ." Chiheb said.

Jaser was getting frustrated with Chiheb.

"They don't know, brother, they don't know, you think they follow the news like you? Okay? They are sheep. The whole thing in their head, I gotta pay the mortgage payment, I use my Visa to buy milk, oh, I gotta pay my Visa bill, what are you talking about, man? Get a hold of yourself. Okay? Stop being so dramatic. Dramatic doesn't do anything for Islam. You are becoming a problem more than an asset."

I pretended to listen. This wasn't my first jihadi bitch fight. The biggest misconception about radical Islam is that everyone agrees. To most Westerners, Islamic terrorists are a bunch of bearded brown guys with one worldview. But a jihadi from Saudi Arabia likely has a totally different grievance than one from Iran or Syria. The only unifying idea is the perversion of Islam.

Chiheb sat stone-faced for a few minutes as his mind tried to grind out a response.

"Raed, we are obeying our elders," he said. "They ask us to do this kind of operation. They know better than us."

"They know better than us over there," Jaser said. "Not here."

"Can I ask you guys something?" I said, trying to defuse the situation. "Why can't we do both?"

Chiheb grabbed my lifeline.

"We do both," he said. "I agree with him. I never say no, but my question, how?"

This was what Jaser and I had talked about in the car the night before. If he brought up killing Jews, he had to have a plan or Chiheb would never accept it. Chiheb needed to know the process, how Jaser could accomplish the plot. Otherwise, it was too abstract. Too wishful thinking to merit debate.

"Brother, listen to me," Jaser said. "Why are you asking me how now? I'm sitting in the car right now, just been interrogated by the police."

"He can come up with a plan," I said, hoping to end the debate.

"You can come back with a plan?" Chiheb said.

He was skeptical.

"Brother, I can come up with a better plan than anybody else in this city," Jaser said. "I know this city inside and out." He said his plan was far easier and cheaper than derailing a train. It took only one gun and a bullet.

"If you kill one hundred people, it's more effective than if you kill one or two people," Chiheb said. "And after that you are arrested or killed even."

It was a circular argument. No one was going to win, because they were both too stubborn to admit both plots were stupid. There was no way two men could cut the rail in two hours. We didn't have the expertise or the equipment. Explosives would work, but they didn't have access to any. Jaser's attack was no better than a mugging and would likely lead to the assassin's death. It was time to put a stop to the fighting. It was counterproductive to the case.

"We live to fight another day and we do more," I said. "I think we all agree they need to be killed, especially because of how safe they think they are, but we have to have a plan to do it so we can continue. If we shoot them or kill them with a knife, or walk up to them in Tim Hortons, there are witnesses. We're done. It's over. Sure, we got one of them or two of them. But why not kill them all, and then when the next head of the snake comes up, we kill him too, because we're not arrested and we're not dead yet."

Chiheb looked at Jaser.

"You understand?" he asked.

"Do you know how hard it is for mujahideen to be in the Western world?" I said. "They fucking hate us. So we have to use our heads. You both have beautiful minds. You both are saying the exact same thing."

"But different way," Chiheb said.

"We all have the same goals," I said. "We just have to organize."

Chiheb was very clear. The location was changing. The target was not. We shouldn't be scared of going to jail or dying for God. That was what we wanted.

"Answer me this question, Raed," Chiheb said. "Why do you care about all of this stuff and the only thing that is the most important thing you didn't care about it?"

It was a challenge. Chiheb was calling Jaser out for being scared. For being unwilling to sacrifice for Allah. I looked into the rearview mirror at Jaser.

"Because Allah doesn't want us to do the operation," Jaser said. "Yeah, don't play that game with me, man."

"If God don't want us to do the operation, why those police they didn't arrest us?" Chiheb said.

The reason was simple, according to Chiheb. Allah protected us from being searched because He wanted us to succeed. I marveled at how Chiheb could twist Allah's will into anything he wanted it to be.

"I don't know if God wants us to do the operation," Chiheb said. "But what I know is that we have to fight those disbelievers. This is what I know. But I think, Raed, you now are a little bit scared about what's happened today."

"Yeah yeah, I'm very scared," Jaser said.

I could tell he was being sarcastic. No doubt the police spooked him. He didn't want to get arrested doing the train plot. It wasn't worth the risk to him. But he also didn't want to get lectured by Chiheb.

"He is joking," I said.

We dropped off Jaser at his house and drove over to the mosque, where we prayed with Waleed. Jaser said he would meet us there.

"My feeling is that he is not afraid, but he feels that you are . . ." I paused, trying to find the right word as we drove toward the mosque.

"Careless?" Chiheb said.

"He wants to do something, but he wants to do it on a much bigger scale," I said. "Meaning in his mind this isn't big enough."

"It's not big enough?" Chiheb said. "If he has another plan, show it to us. He's comparing himself with the brothers? Our brothers? They are sleeping on the ground. In the mountains with the animals. No way, don't say to me any kind of this bullshit things."

"No, you're right," I said.

"I don't want to be harsh with him," Chiheb said.

We were at a crossroads. Jaser or Chiheb. It was a split-second decision, but an easy one. Chiheb had the world to offer me. Jaser didn't. Jaser wanted to kill Jews on the street. But he had no access to the brothers overseas or the American sleeper. I was never going to walk away from the guy who could get me to him.

"I know, I know," I said. "But I can tell it bothered you, and it bothered me because he said they don't know here like we know here."

Then I sealed the deal.

"If we did something with the train and the projects you're talking about, this will be in the news and they will say, 'Oh my God, what did the mujahideen say?'" I said. "They said, 'Get out of our country or we will hit you in your home.' Which is better, this or a Jew died because someone killed him? He is Palestinian *habibi* and for a Palestinian brother, his heart is in the right spot. He hates the Jews to an unbelievable degree, like us. But he has extra hate for the Jews, right? That's why his thinking is such, we can kill the Canadians, we can kill those people, yes, but let's kill the Jews. My opinion is, it would be better after we meet the brother in America, he may tell us. He will be able to tell us do X, Y, and Z or stay with the plan. He will tell us. What do you think?"

"The brother may benefit us, the sleeper," Chiheb said. "But do you think what happened today has an effect on our operation as a whole?"

"No," I said.

"There is nothing," Chiheb said, just making sure the train plot was still on track.

"Nothing," I said as we reached the mosque to pray.

We were partners now and we were going to derail a train.

CHAPTER 18

Team Chiheb

Joey paced in front of the flat-screen television in the living room. Every few steps, he paused like he was trying to figure out a way around an invisible barrier. Nelly tried to talk to him, but Joey held out his hand like any noise would knock a good idea out of his head. He started to pace again. With each step, Joey puzzled through our latest problem.

The Canadians weren't happy that I'd sided with Chiheb. They wanted me to play both sides. But that wasn't an option. It was clear Jaser and Chiheb were on diverging paths, and I had to make a choice.

"We need the American sleeper," I said. "We need the intel from overseas. We need everything that is in that brain."

We were meeting at a hotel suite in Toronto. In a few hours, I had to take Chiheb to the bus station.

"Let the Toronto guys worry about Jaser," I said. "Sorry, Doug. But we've got to focus on Chiheb."

Doug shrugged. He understood what his bosses wanted but also saw my logic.

"I would have done the same thing," he said.

The debriefs after each day were intimate affairs. Joey made sure the core team of Nelly, Kenny, and Johnny were always there. Doug was the Canadian representation. Every now and then if the situation was serious, Joey invited one or two RCMP bosses, but that was it.

I usually got to the safe house first to collect my thoughts. I put a pinch of snuff in my lip and just bullshitted with the guys. When I was ready—sometimes right away, sometimes I needed more time to come down—I went over the day's meeting in minute detail. Nelly and Johnny took notes. Joey just listened. When I was done, they peppered me with questions. After the debrief, Nelly and Kenny sent the highlights to executive management in New York and FBI Headquarters in Washington. Doug briefed his people. Joey paced and we started strategizing for the next meeting.

"Dougy, we have to stick with Chiheb. If the situation presents itself, we'll reengage with Jaser," Joey said.

Joey looked at me.

"As for you, make sure Chiheb knows Tamer is with him," Joey said. "Leave no doubt."

The threat was under control and that was the main concern. Chiheb was convinced, after inspecting the track, another brother was needed to help. No way two guys could cut the rail in two hours, which meant there was no way the plot would be ready in December. Plus, Chiheb and Jaser were under arrest. They just didn't know it yet. The only play was to stay with Chiheb for the intelligence in his head, and his potential connection to the sleeper.

I left to pick up Chiheb around 7:30 P.M. The condo didn't have

Internet, so I offered to let him use my hotel room. He met me in the lobby and we headed to pick up Jaser. Chiheb's bus left at nine o'clock. As we drove, I asked him about his work.

"So you will be a doctor?" I asked.

"Yes," he said. "I am not looking for money or looking for PhD. I am just looking for the PhD because it is good for our projects. You understand?"

"Of course," I said.

"I mean if I am a doctor or a professor, who will catch me?"

"Nobody," I said. "No one is going to look at a doctor." Not true, but it made sense to him. I asked about the safe house. Did he approve? It was a chance to pull Chiheb closer.

"I worked for a week with these idiots in order not to have my name or your name on it, because I know this is what I do," I said, talking about the condo lease. "To protect us. That's my job. You said to me, Tamer, we need you to protect us. Right?"

"Yes."

"I'll give you guys the key. I am in America and you guys are here in Canada, use it. Use the computer, if you need phones, if you need tablets, anything. Just ask me for it. Before you are done asking, you will have it. Whatever you need from me, I will give it to you right away. Because I need us to be on the same page. But he will start talking back and forth, saying, let's do the sniper thing and he wants to do this and he wants to do that. Come on, this is a joke."

Chiheb was still upset after our trip to the train bridge. "We need to focus and be on the same page," I said.

"And maybe while you are focusing on the sniper he comes up with another plan," Chiheb said, laughing.

"Exactly," I said.

Jaser was waiting outside when we arrived. He got into the back and we drove to the bus station. I found a parking spot and we started talking more about the train plot. Chiheb wanted to be ready when El Massoul sent the code word to attack. But Jaser wanted to delay.

"There's always wisdom in patience," he said.

Chiheb let out a long sigh.

"You see?" Jaser said. "So for me rushing into something just because you want to do it, for the sheer fact that you want to do something, doesn't make any sense."

Jaser told us he prayed *salat il Istakhara* after our visit to the bridge. It is a specific prayer asking Allah for guidance.

"I said if this is good for us in this life and the next, He will make it happen," Jaser said. "If not, then no."

But Chiheb saw Jaser's prayer as the move of a coward unwilling to commit to the path of God.

"No, this feeling that you have, Raed, is coming from the devil," he said.

"The devil?"

Chiheb nodded.

"The devil wants you to leave the project."

"I'm not leaving the project, *habibi*," Jaser said. "But we have to be extra careful."

"No, of course I agree with you," Chiheb said.

"Yeah, you agree with me, I tell you I cannot do anything any-more in this operation because you see, unlike you, for me I am very well known in the city of Toronto, okay," Jaser said. "Thank Allah I have no record. I have no problem. But I am very well known in other ways, you see."

"So what's the point?" Chiheb said. "You are scared that you go to jail?"

"Scared of going to jail?" Jaser said. "You are the one who's worried, not me."

"No, I am not worried," Chiheb said. "If I go—"

"We want to live for another day," Jaser said.

"If I go to jail, I don't care," Chiheb said. "If I die, I don't care."

"Why are you talking like this?" Jaser said. "This is not the right time for this. You have to watch what you're saying. You are just not very professional, *habibi*."

Chiheb bristled at the "professional" comment. He was trained by al Qaeda. Jaser had no training.

"So this means that you are scared that you go to jail, right?"

"It's not about jail," Jaser said. "It's about success. There's a difference."

"But I don't care about my security," Chiheb said. "I care about the security of the operation."

I could see the anger on Jaser's face.

"I cannot help you," he said. "Get somebody else. That's what I'm telling you. I cannot help you. That's what I am trying to explain to you. For me personally, it's no good for me. It's compromised, for me. But, I mean, there's many other things we can do in this lovely place, you know."

"Okay then," I said.

I was happy to be done with Jaser. Now I could focus on Chiheb full-time. But Chiheb wasn't going to let him go without a rebuke. It was clear to Chiheb that Jaser was no longer a good Muslim. His true colors were exposed. He cared more about this world and that was haram.

"This is your obligation," Chiheb said. "You are scared that you go to jail, no problem. But I can say to you one thing, if you are scared about entering jail and you are not scared about Allah and your obligation in front of Allah, I say to you, we don't need a person who will do this behavior. We want someone who isn't scared about anything except Allah."

"Praise the Prophet, *habibi*," I said.

I was trying to calm Chiheb down.

"Okay, *habibi*, no problem," Jaser said. "I cannot work with you. You are very rash."

Chiheb was getting worked up.

"Our women, they are raped," he said, his voice almost a scream. "They are raped. They are raped in jail."

"It doesn't do anything yelling and screaming," Jaser said. "Yelling and screaming doesn't work."

Jaser's eyes shot from Chiheb in the passenger seat to the window and back. He was searching for a way to calm Chiheb.

"Do you want that your sister is raped?" Chiheb said.

Chiheb's eyes were dark as he turned to face Jaser.

He radiated hate and anger.

"Pay attention," Jaser said. "Yelling and screaming does not work. Go ahead, go in the street, yelling and screaming, what is it going to do?"

I scanned the street to see if anyone was looking at us after Chiheb's screaming.

"Relax, relax," I said.

They both sat in the car, arms folded, with scowls on their faces.

"We'll clean this up, Allah willing," I said. "The most important thing is to understand we're going to have disagreements. We're going to have arguments. Right now let's just chill out."

Chiheb kept trying to interrupt me.

"Tamer?"

"Yes, *habibi*," I said.

"Tamer," Chiheb said. "We will go search for another believer, okay?"

"Listen, *habibi*, don't talk that way," I said.

"You see, this is the extreme ideology," Jaser said. "That's why I can't work with you, brother."

Jaser didn't mean jihad. He was objecting to the way Chiheb planned the attack.

"No," Chiheb said. "We don't want someone who stops our project. We want to go forward. We want someone who wants to give his blood to Allah."

I couldn't take much more of this.

"Listen, let's get you on the bus, so you don't miss the bus," I said.

All three of us left the car. We found the bus and I bought Chiheb a sandwich and drink. As we walked, Chiheb seemed anxious.

"He wants to work with you," Chiheb said. "I hope that he will not tell you another plan and ask you to leave the project."

I shook my head and put my hand on Chiheb's shoulder.

"We are all brothers here," I said. "I'm leaving my home constantly to come visit my brothers because I feel like I have a purpose, thank Allah. I'm being careful. I'm practicing everything that you guys have taught me from the beginning, and I am trying to do right and then we have one bad day, does that mean we're going to lose focus? Do you think that the brothers who are dying over there daily, what do you think they would do, with an opportunity that we have? This is what I am thinking."

I thought Chiheb was going to hug me.

"They are not seeing police like we see today," Chiheb said, happy to be compared to the brothers overseas. "They are seeing missiles. They are seeing bombs. He just sees three police and he becomes scared."

I looked at Jaser. He just glared at us.

"I don't think that's his issue," I said. "I think he's thinking about the success of the operation."

Jaser shrugged.

"You are too aggressive," he said to Chiheb. "I can't work with you."

Chiheb's bus boarded just before nine. Jaser and I waited until it left. On the way back to his house, Jaser tried to explain why he was out.

"It's too much work," he said. "It's for nothing. At the end, they're going to downplay it. Train derailment, whoop-de-do?"

Jaser was stung by Chiheb's accusations of not being a true Muslim. He spent half the ride proving himself to me using the Quran.

"I need to look right and left before I cross the street," Jaser said. "If I don't look right and left, a car is going to hit me. And especially if I didn't look at the traffic light to see if it's green or red. Allah says do not lead yourselves into destruction, do not go with your own hands into destruction."

Before he got out of the car, Jaser returned the thousand dollars I gave him to buy a new video camera to shoot the message after the attack. He promised to get me a plan for his sniper attack and his plan to build a training compound. But I think we both knew it would never come to be.

It was now just me and Chiheb.

CHAPTER 19

The Responsible One

It was Eid al-Adha, or the Sacrifice Feast, and I was back in Montreal to spend it with Chiheb.

Since the American sleeper revelation, we wanted to get him a visa so he could visit the United States. The goal was to get him to New York in hopes he could facilitate a meeting with the sleeper. I flew up to Canada to take him to Ottawa to get his visa paperwork.

I arrived in Montreal a few days before the holiday, the second of two Eid holidays. The better-known Eid al-Fitr celebrates the end of Ramadan, the month of dawn-to-sunset fasting. Eid al-Adha celebrates Abraham, who almost sacrificed his son for Allah, and signifies a Muslim's submission to God's will. The morning of Eid al-Adha, Muslims sacrifice a lamb. The meat is split among family, friends, and the poor.

A few days before Eid al-Adha, I took Chiheb to an Islamic butcher shop to buy a few lambs. Two for me. One for Chiheb. The butcher shop was at the back of a small supermarket with produce and dry goods. The meat was stored in refrigerated glass cases in the back. One of the butchers—a Muslim—met us at the counter.

"We'd like three lambs for Eid," Chiheb said. "One for me and two for my friend. Do we sacrifice them here?"

The butcher took out his pad and started to take the order.

"Sorry," he said. "Canadian law kicked in this year. You're not allowed to slaughter it yourself. It has to be done by a licensed butcher."

Chiheb looked at me and shook his head. The lambs aren't just slaughtered and eaten. The slaughter is an integral part of the celebration. A good Muslim makes his own sacrifice.

"That is not right," he said, placing both hands on the counter and leaning into his argument. "There are prayers. It is something that I need to do."

"Sorry, that's the law, but you still get your credit from God," the butcher said, smiling. "Your hands are tied. You have to respect the laws of the country you live in."

The butcher sounded like my father, I thought. God would understand, and even the Prophet Mohammed said to follow the laws of the land where you live. We were still fulfilling our obligation. But Chiheb was upset. He looked at me, urging me to protest. I looked away.

"Fine," Chiheb said. "Do you have a piece of paper and a pen?"

The butcher gave up his pad and pen. Chiheb wrote out the prayer that is said when the lamb's neck is cut. He wrote it in Arabic first. Then he wrote it in English and tore the sheet off the pad.

"May Allah force you to do this," Chiheb said. "Make sure you give this to the Imam. Have him recite this Quranic verse while you are slaughtering the lambs."

The butcher looked at me. *Is this guy for real?* his face said. I looked back at the butcher with my best *Please take the paper* face.

"Of course," the butcher said, folding the page up and sliding it into his apron's pocket.

For the rest of the day, I had to listen to Chiheb complain about the butcher and Canada's laws. Another grievance on a long list.

Nelly and Kenny worked with the State Department to get the visa approved; otherwise Chiheb had no chance, given all that law enforcement already had on him. But it was my job to go through the motions. That meant getting the paperwork from the American Embassy. Chiheb knew a Tunisian in Ottawa, so we planned to meet him for dinner and take his temperature on our way there.

We met his friend at a Chinese buffet on the outskirts of Ottawa around 9:00 P.M. When we got there, the restaurant was deserted. The food on the buffet looked like it had sat all day under heat lamps. It was near closing, but the staff was happy to have a few more paying customers.

Over spring rolls and General Tso's chicken, Chiheb ranted about the West and its war on Islam. His friend didn't join in, but admitted he was thinking of moving to Saudi Arabia because he wanted to live in an Islamic country. That didn't make him a jihadist. I scratched him off the list by the end of dinner.

This was normal since Jaser left the plot. Chiheb dragged me into meetings with like-minded brothers ready to help. But most of them were just lost souls having trouble coping with a foreign culture or angry about what they saw in the news. No different from Americans angry at Washington. Conversations got heated. There was real anger. But no one—Muslim or American—was about to derail a train over it. Anytime a Muslim expresses any anger they get stamped a terrorist. But what is the difference between a devout Muslim who doesn't drink and a Mormon who doesn't? Nothing. Same God. Different name. It was easy for non-Muslims to confuse a devout Muslim with Chiheb. But I knew different. Chiheb was a perversion who believed that God wanted him to kill in His name. His friend just wanted to live in a Muslim culture.

On the drive back from Ottawa, we talked about Chiheb's recruiting. He hadn't found another like-minded brother since we met.

"What made you trust me and know I was who I claimed to be?" he asked.

Chiheb was being polite, because what he really wanted to talk about was why he trusted me. But it would be rude not to ask me first.

"No disrespect, brother, but if you recall correctly, I pushed you away," I said.

He started to laugh and smile and rub his beard.

"I do remember that," he said. "That was very telling for me."

"But I could tell every single hadith, every single passage of the Quran you interpreted, the way you saw the world was exactly how I saw the world," I said. "Exactly the way my uncle taught me Islam. I saw me in you. I saw my uncle in you. I saw a true mujahid in you. But as happy as I was, I couldn't trust you. I'd just met you. I believe in fatalism but I had to be sure."

He laughed.

"That is exactly right," he said.

He was smiling, his eyes bright and happy remembering our trip to San Jose. It made me sad. He and Tamer were friends. He'd found a like-minded brother, but he'd also found a friend. Someone to share meals with and talk with in a country so foreign to him. Al Qaeda used his isolation, his awkward social skills, and his naiveté to brainwash him. Part of me wished I could save him. Clean his mind of their filth.

"So, I ask you, brother," I said. "What about me?"

"Your interpretation of certain hadiths led me to believe you were a true brother," Chiheb said. "The fact that you pushed me away led me to believe you weren't government. But what really did it for me that week was that night at the Moroccan restaurant. Do you remember that night?"

In my head, I couldn't stop thinking about his face when he saw all the booze on the bar or the belly dancer.

"Remind me," I said.

"Every test I put you through was good," he said. "But it wasn't until we were at that restaurant when you told me about your mother and how it turned you. How it brought you back to Islam. You cried that night. There was no way a government operative could fake that. I knew that night that you were a true brother."

He was right. I wasn't faking. Even though I'd twisted some of the details to appeal to Chiheb, the foundation of the story was true. My mother's death was a defining moment in my life. Losing her was a pain I'd never felt before. But driving back to Montreal from Ottawa, I realized my mother was a hero. She made me into the man I am and armed me with a story that allowed me to infiltrate this evil and stop it. I was following through with her dying wish to use what she taught me about Islam to do good in this world.

"Speaking of true brothers, tell me about the brothers in Iran," I said. "El Massoul is a brother like us, right?"

FBI Headquarters was after me to get more on Chiheb's training in Iran. In the past I acted in awe of El Massoul and the brothers in Iran. But on this trip, I flipped it. I downplayed him, prompting Chiheb to defend him.

"No, no, no," Chiheb said. "He was like a son to Sheikh Osama. He has been with him since he was a boy."

I urged Chiheb on with "Oh, dear brothers" and *Masha'Allah*. But in my mind, I was puzzled. How did we miss bin Laden's protégé? We had to know him.

"Tell me more about El Massoul," I said. "I'm fascinated."

Chiheb told me he had a bus company. He owned thirteen buses and his twenty-six-year-old son was in an Iranian prison. But El Massoul was proud because every single morning the entire prison was awakened by his son's call to prayer. El Massoul's son had a beautiful Quranic voice.

"How old is he, brother?"

Chiheb said he was around forty-six or forty-seven. He had wild salt-and-pepper hair and a scar under his left eye.

"I looked at it every day," Chiheb said. "I wanted to ask him if that was from him being a mujahid."

These nuggets didn't seem like much at first glance. But to our intelligence analysts, these bits of conversation—the buses, the son, the scar—were bread crumbs to El Massoul.

On our way back from Ottawa, I dropped off Chiheb at his lab in Montreal. The plan was for him to get some work done and we would meet up for dinner later that night. The lab was located in an industrial part of town, and as we drove up to the campus, I started to hear some static coming from the dashboard.

Chiheb noticed it too.

"Tamer, what is that sound?" he said.

Chiheb feared technology because he assumed it allowed the government to listen to us.

"No idea," I said as I fiddled with the radio.

The static stopped and I could hear Nelly and Doug talking. They were in a surveillance car nearby. Somehow, the signals got crossed and the receiver became the transmitter. Chiheb's eyes went from the radio directly to the GPS unit in the middle of the dashboard. It was the only logical explanation. I smacked the GPS unit as I pulled in front of his lab.

"This stupid thing has been acting up," I said as I yanked it off its mount.

"You should replace that one," Chiheb said as he grabbed his bag. "I will call you when I'm done, brother."

I tossed the GPS into the passenger seat and drove back to the safe house. I was angry when I arrived. I wasn't sure if this technical glitch had just fucked up the case.

"Kenny, are you fucking kidding me right now?"

Kenny was checking the transmitter.

"This doesn't make any sense," he said. "It's new tech but that's obviously not supposed to happen."

"You think it was the electrical lines?" Doug said. "It's a very industrial area."

But why it happened didn't matter anymore.

"Get rid of it," I said. "I never want to see that thing again. And tell Headquarters never to use that in the field."

Joey pulled me aside before the debrief.

"What was his reaction?" Joey said.

"I blamed it on the GPS," I said. "We could only hear them for a few seconds."

Joey started pacing.

"Did he buy it?"

I shrugged.

"I don't know," I said. "I think so."

Joey wasn't convinced. He looked nervous.

I hadn't eaten all day. I ordered a feast—Caesar salad, French onion soup, pizza, poutine (French fries with gravy and mozzarella) burgers, and pitchers of iced tea with lime. We spread the food out on the table and started to work. Topic number one was El Massoul.

Nelly grabbed my MacBook.

"What's the password?" he said.

"King Tut," I said, as Joey paced in front of me. "There is no way we don't know who this guy is. I feel like I'm at the point I could give him a photo lineup and ask him which one he is."

Joey laughed.

"You could probably show him your badge and he wouldn't believe you're government," Joey said.

I heard Nelly typing. A few seconds later, he spun my laptop around so I could see the screen. He was on the FBI's Rewards for Justice page. He scrolled through the Wanted photos.

"I bet you it's one of these guys," he said, pointing to a group of photos. "He has to be in the five-million-dollar range if he is that close to bin Laden."

Joey was looking over my shoulder.

"Why don't you just show him this website?" Nelly said.

Everyone was silent. I looked at Nelly and then Joey.

"You know what?" Joey said. "Why not?"

It wasn't a bad idea, I thought. Our relationship was solid. But why would I be on that website?

Joey started pacing again.

"Tamer likes to search for different brothers that he reveres," Joey said. "He came across the site and looks at it sometimes. It's like an affirmation."

"And next time I'm sitting with him, I'll surf over to the site," I said.

The plan was to grab dinner with Chiheb, pick up the meat from the butcher shop, and then go back to his apartment so I could show him the website. After the debrief, I got a call from Chiheb. Everyone knew it was my undercover phone, so Doug muted the TV and Joey put his hand up, signaling everyone to be quiet.

"*Salamu alaikum,*" Chiheb said. "I am home now."

"*Wa alaikum al salam,*" I said. "How was your day, brother?"

"*Al hamdul'Allah,*" he said, meaning "thank God."

"Where do you feel like having dinner tonight? When will you be ready?"

"It doesn't matter," he said. "Come and pick me up when you are ready, *insha'Allah.*"

I hung up the phone. Something was wrong. I told the team that I was going to pick him up later and go to dinner. Doug un-muted the TV and everyone jumped back into their conversations. Joey pulled me into the bedroom because he'd noticed the look on my face.

"What's going on?" he said.

"I don't know," I said. "He sounded off."

"Listen to me," Joey said. "Do not look at him like the Arab Santa Claus. He is a mujahid that would cut your throat in a heartbeat if he suspected you were government. You know how he feels about munafiqeen."

"I know."

"Do you want a weapon?"

"No."

"Then remember your training. Grab whatever you can and defend yourself," Joey said as he grabbed a pen from the dresser and held it like a knife.

"I'm good, brother."

I went back to my room to get changed and left for Chiheb's apartment. As I climbed into the car, I saw the concern on Joey's face. He had been in dangerous situations before and recognized the potential danger of the meeting. It was his job to protect me, but his nerves were getting the better of him. But I was confident we weren't burned. Call it a gut feeling, but I knew the guy. There was something bothering him, but it wasn't me.

I arrived around eight o'clock. It was October 26, 2012, the last day of Eid al-Adha, and we were headed to dinner before picking up our meat at the market.

Chiheb was standing in the foyer of the apartment building speaking with a woman when I arrived. He didn't notice that I was there, so I parked and waited. After a few minutes, I brought him his Eid gifts—a box of dates and a prayer rug provided to me by the RCMP. Chiheb let me into the foyer.

"*Eid Mubarak* [Blessed Eid]," I said.

Chiheb took the gifts and thanked me. I ignored the woman and started for the door.

"I'll wait in the car," I said. "Take your time. We're in no rush."

He finally got in the car, and I studied him as I drove off. I found a seafood restaurant on my phone while I was waiting that wasn't too far away. He barely spoke during the ride to the restaurant. My instincts were right. There was definitely something bothering him. I knew I had to address it.

"How was your day, *habibi*?" I asked, trying to fill the silence.

"*Al hamdul'Allah*," he said, trying to smile.

I got lost on the way to the restaurant. I was a little preoccupied and couldn't use the GPS anymore. We decided to try a Turkish restaurant downtown, but I could tell it was Americanized and probably had an open bar. I considered pushing him to look the other way so we could eat, but something was already bothering him.

I pulled over and turned to face him. Joey's warnings echoed in my head. I didn't want him to attack me while I drove.

"Talk to me, brother," I said. "I know you. Something is bothering you."

Chiheb forced another smile and crossed his hands between his legs.

"Tamer, you know me better than I know myself."

Right then and there I relaxed. This wasn't going to be about the equipment malfunction. His body language spoke volumes. He was embarrassed about something.

"What happened?"

"Today in the office, she was laughing and joking with a man in our group," he said. "She was doing it very loud so I could hear them."

It was girl trouble again. The Jordanian was talking to another man. Thank God. The wire glitch was forgotten.

"Tamer, you won't believe, she touches his arm when she is laughing," he said, looking like he was about to cry.

"Oh no, *habibi*. What did you do?"

"I waited until he left and then I talked to her," he said.

"What did you say?"

"I told her that what she is doing is against Allah. She is not married to him and she shouldn't be touching another man."

I felt bad for this poor girl.

"What did she say?"

"She got very upset. She was yelling at me and told me none of your business. She shut the door of her office very hard."

"I'm so sorry, Chiheb," I said. "I can tell how much this is bothering you. But now you have your answer, right?"

"I think she did this because she knows I will see. I don't want to be part of her doing haram. I have to forget her. May Allah forgive her."

Chiheb's phone rang, ending the conversation. One of his colleagues was calling to wish him *Eid Mubarak*. Chiheb asked his colleague if he knew of any good halal restaurants nearby. He told Chiheb about Château Kabab on Rue Guy in downtown Montreal. We got a table and had a long dinner. No jihad this time. We talked a little more about the Jordanian girl instead. I managed to shoot a text to Joey during dinner because I knew he was worried.

"All good. Just girl trouble."

After dinner, we got ice cream at Tim Hortons. While we were eating, Chiheb called Jaser to wish him *Eid Mubarak*. It was a short call. Polite but not warm. Chiheb had no respect for Jaser any longer.

"We don't discuss projects," Chiheb said after hanging up. "If I said anything, Raed would hang up. He is fearful of the police. Any true believer should not be worried about jail or death. It would be an honor to die for Allah; why wouldn't it be an honor to go to jail for Allah?"

Jaser was now munafiqeen.

It was close to midnight when we arrived at the market to pick up our lambs. The shop was busy because of the holiday.

"Sorry, guys, crazy day," the butcher said. "It's going to be another thirty minutes. I'm working on it now."

I suggested we go back to my car to wait. I fired up my mobile hotspot. Chiheb opened his laptop and showed me some jihadi sites that posted videos of attacks. I got my MacBook from the back seat.

"Brother, you don't mind if I check my e-mail?" I asked.

I logged on to my e-mail and then pulled up the Rewards for Justice website. The plan was to wait until we got back to his apartment, but I couldn't.

"By the grace of God," I said as I scrolled down the website.

He was talking about one of the jihadi websites, but stopped when he saw my screen.

"What's that, brother?"

My MacBook was on my lap in the driver's side. I turned the screen so he could see it better.

"These are the true brothers, just like you were discussing with me," I said. "I saw this on TV. All the brothers wanted by the Americans are on this website. I wanted to see who these brothers were."

He tilted his head and moved it so he could see the whole screen as I scrolled through the photos. I started reading about Sheikh Ayman al-Zawahiri. He pointed out one of the Pakistani individuals as I scrolled.

"By the grace of God, I know that brother," he said. "I met that brother when I was in Iran. He is helping the Taliban."

"These are the brothers—" I started to say when Chiheb gasped.

He snatched the MacBook off my lap. The screen smashed into the steering wheel as he pulled it into his lap. He tried to scroll up but didn't know how to use a MacBook.

"Tell me what you're trying to do," I said, concerned that he was going to damage my computer. "Relax. What do you need?"

"Go back up, go back up," he said, half handing it back, but clutching it at the same time.

I showed him how to scroll with both fingers. Seconds later, the picture of a barrel-chested man with a mane of thick, wild hair and a bushy beard with no mustache filled the screen.

"Tamer, that's him," Chiheb said. "Brother, that's him."

"That's who?"

"El Massoul. That is the brother I spent six weeks with."

"You're kidding me," I said.

We zoomed in on the picture and I saw the scar under his left eye.

"That's his face," Chiheb said. "Those are his eyes. That is his scar. That's definitely him."

According to Chiheb, El Massoul was Muhammad ar-Rahayyal, one of four terrorists who took part in the 1986 hijacking of Pan Am Flight 73 in Pakistan. After a sixteen-hour standoff, ar-Rahayyal and the others opened fire, killing at least twenty passengers and injuring more than one hundred. Pakistani security forces arrested ar-Rahayyal. He was released from prison in January 2008. The hijackers were added to the FBI's Most Wanted list in 2009 after they were indicted in federal court for the murder of U.S. nationals outside the United States.

As I read his bio, Chiheb agreed with everything until we got to his nationality. The website said he was Palestinian and hiding in a Middle Eastern country.

"He's not Palestinian," Chiheb said. "Every Palestinian speaks Arabic. El Massoul only speaks Farsi and Dari. He doesn't speak Arabic well."

Chiheb said he still had the crazy hair, but he had aged since the photo was taken. The image on the website was from 2000. I checked ar-Rahayyal's date of birth. It checked out. Every single thing checked out. Without him knowing, Chiheb gave us El Massoul. Nelly's idea panned out. Before we moved on, I checked the reward. Five million. Nelly nailed it.

After finding ar-Rahayyal, we were looking at other pictures when Chiheb suddenly had a solemn look on his face.

"Brother, what's wrong?" I said.

"Nothing."

"Talk to me. You seem upset."

He sighed and stroked his beard. He paused for a full thirty seconds.

"I wish I was on that list," he said.

His words hit me like a punch. He wanted to be on a list of murderers. Of men who brainwashed the young with an ideology of hate. He revered these men like bin Laden, who would send their followers to the grave for an ideology they refused to fight for themselves. Ar-Rahayyal wasn't any different. He didn't care if Chiheb lived or died as long as the attack was a success. He was safe in Iran, hiding in the shadows and sending others to die. His jihad was one of safety, if not comfort.

But I wasn't me. I was Tamer. I had to bite back my words as I put my arm on his shoulder.

"God willing, one day, we will be at the top of that list with Sheikh Ayman," I said. "We will be wanted for twenty-five million."

He smiled.

"God willing."

CHAPTER 20

The Radicalizer

Chiheb was under surveillance twenty-four hours a day. We knew his friends. We knew his family. So, when a friend of Chiheb's in Quebec City popped up on our radar, we were puzzled.

Who was this guy? How did he fit into the picture? Why hadn't Chiheb brought him up?

The Canadians wouldn't tell me his name. All they would tell me is that I should consider going to Quebec City and hinted that there may be something or someone of interest there. Nelly told me the friend's name: Ahmed Abassi.

"Why are you going up to Quebec City?" Nelly said, as we strategized a reason to get me in front of Abassi.

"Ski rentals," Doug said. "Tamer wants to invest in some ski houses."

I liked it. It was October 2012 and Tamer wanted to see some properties before winter. Since we needed help for the train plot, I pushed Chiheb to get us in front of as many like-minded brothers as he could.

"Are there any brothers for us to meet with up there?" I said after he agreed to come with me to Quebec City.

Chiheb grimaced and looked away. He had someone, but didn't want to say.

"What are you not telling me?" I asked.

"There is a brother," Chiheb said. "He is the brother that got me on this path."

That was something that had bothered me since Chiheb told me about his training. It was never clear why Chiheb chose radical Islam. Now I had the chance to meet the man who put him on the path. But something was wrong.

"Tell me," I said.

"It is sort of complicated."

"Come on, brother," I said. "Talk to me. Let's meet him."

"I gave Ahmed two thousand dollars for one semester of his school and he never paid me back," Chiheb said. "He can never go to his grave in debt."

Chiheb didn't care about the money. It was haram to not pay your debts.

"Clearly, money matters," I said. "In the grand scheme of things, maybe it is time to forgive and forget. You're telling me he is a like-minded brother. Not only that, he is the like-minded brother that started you on this path. I'd love to meet him."

"He is Tunisian like me," Chiheb said. "He is my age. Very smart. Very religious."

"Is he like us?"

"He is a mujahideen brother," Chiheb said.

Abassi was studying engineering at Laval University in Quebec City. He met Chiheb at a conference. Two Tunisians far from home. It was Abassi who taught Chiheb jihad was part of every Muslim's duty.

"E-mail him," I said. "Tell him you're here with an Egyptian-American brother, a like-minded brother, and we're traveling up to Quebec City because I have business there. Tell him I am a dear friend and you'd love him to meet us for dinner."

Chiheb typed while I spoke. About an hour later, we got a response, which he shared with me.

"I'd love to host you, dear brother," Abassi wrote. "Let me know when you'll be here. I'll make sure I am here so we can go to dinner."

I was sure Chiheb was exaggerating Abassi's intentions. But Abassi was the only person Chiheb ever described as a "mujahideen brother."

I picked up Chiheb at his apartment around eleven thirty in the morning and we headed for Quebec City. We met Abassi for dinner after looking at rental properties all day.

Abassi was tall and thin with a neatly trimmed beard, no mustache, and close-cropped hair. There was a confidence, swagger even, like he knew he was good-looking. Both his English and his Arabic were flawless. He also spoke French fluently. I studied his face after he got into the back of the car. His glasses hid his eyes, but his eyebrows poked up above the lenses. They were shaped like devil horns.

We ate at a halal restaurant on a quiet cobblestone side street near Parliament Hill. We ordered at the counter and ate at one of the many wooden tables. I covered the table with hummus, tabouleh, bread, stuffed grape leaves. We each got an entrée. I got the kofta with rice and salad. Abassi and Chiheb had grilled kebobs.

Most of dinner was small talk about my work, ski houses, and properties in the area. Abassi was recently engaged and I bought him baklava to celebrate. After dinner, we went for coffee at a nearby shop. On the way, we passed the Parliament Building, the meeting place of Quebec's National Assembly. The 125 elected representatives serve as the legislative body for the Province of Quebec. The Parliament Building—constructed between 1877 and 1886—reminded me of Philadelphia's City Hall with its frontal clock tower.

"That would be a great place for an attack," Chiheb said, looking at me.

Chiheb let out an uncomfortable giggle looking for affirmation, but I didn't say anything. My focus was on Abassi. He didn't flinch. Didn't smile. Didn't turn his head to even look at the building.

"No, no, no," Abassi said. "Don't talk that way."

All through dinner Abassi was very guarded, especially when talk veered toward the war in the Middle East or some of Chiheb's extreme interpretations of the Quran. He was savvier and more disciplined than Chiheb. This guy had the right rhetoric, but he stopped short every time. He knew how to run to the line and stop.

Usually I make the target earn my point of radicalization, but I didn't have time for the slow play. I wanted him to know he had an audience ready to listen. We were talking about the war in Syria over tea when I brought up my uncle.

"I have an uncle in Egypt that put me back on the path," I said. "I wanted to go home. I was done with America, but he told me to stay. To live amongst them, as them, to defeat them."

Chiheb had a big smile as I talked.

"Oh, God bless him," Chiheb said. "If you only knew the things he did."

I knew Chiheb would echo my legend and give me the bona fides to be believable to Abassi. I watched Abassi closely. He had a look. A twinkle of recognition in his eye. It was like I hit a chord with him. He looked at Chiheb and then at me. There was no doubt he got the gist. And he liked it. But he said nothing. Then, as we walked back to the car, my phone buzzed. It was Joey.

"Wrap it up. Everything is okay."

My mind jumped to all the worst-case scenarios. Was my father sick? My sister? I had trouble concentrating on the mission. Abassi asked if we'd like to stay up late, but I declined.

"You know what, if we're getting up early to leave, we're going to get going," I said.

I exchanged e-mail addresses and phone numbers with Abassi and promised to call next time I was in town. I dropped off Chiheb at his hotel room and joined the team at the safe house. I was barely through the door when I confronted Joey.

"What's wrong?"

"We need to get a flight back," he said. "There is a hurricane coming."

"We live in New York, bro," I said. "There are no hurricanes there."

"There is one coming," Joey said.

Fox News was on the TV. A reporter was standing on the Jersey Shore talking about how Superstorm Sandy was bearing down on the East Coast.

I texted Chiheb and told him we had to go early because I had to get back to New York to check on my properties before the storm. He agreed to meet at eight for the drive back to Montreal.

"Another dead end?" Nelly said as we sat down to debrief the Abassi meeting.

"No, actually, there is something there," I said. "I can't put my finger on it. He is very good. Not good enough. But very good at disguising things. Something is in those eyes. In that head. It was on the tip of his tongue."

I explained to the team how I dropped my uncle into the conversation.

"Let him chew on that shit," I said. "He'll be thinking about my uncle until we meet again."

"Yeah, exactly," Joey said. "Let's see where it takes us. Let him come to you."

We finished the debrief after midnight and I got a few hours of sleep before meeting Chiheb. We were on the road back to Montreal when Chiheb brought up the project again. He still wanted to derail the train on Christmas, but he needed help.

"Your job is to get back and continue on with your work and do what you are doing," he told me, meaning raising money for the brothers.

"Look, you got the hardest part of your job out of the way," I said. "The funding and access to America, you have it. You have that done."

"You're absolutely right. Now I just have to get the true believers with us, and I will find them," Chiheb said. "Even if this means I have to go to where the munafiqeen are, I will go to all the mosques in Montreal to find the true believers."

"Did you hear from the brothers overseas?" I said, anxious to get the American sleeper meeting set.

Chiheb shook his head no.

"Sometimes it takes a week," he said. "I told them it was urgent."

"Good," I said. "God willing, they will contact you soon."

"God willing," Chiheb said.

I took a sip of my coffee.

"I got an e-mail about the apartment in Toronto," I said. "Do we want to let it go?"

"Could we hold it for a little bit longer?" Chiheb asked.

He was holding out hope that he could recruit another like-minded brother in time.

"Yeah, listen, I could call him back and tell him to hold it for a month. I can probably hold it to the end of November, early December," I said.

"That would be great, and tell him I promise I will have an answer by then," Chiheb said. "Listen, the only place we can do this project, and this project has to happen, is in Toronto. There's no other place to have a possible location as far as this particular project."

"No worries, no problem," I said. "We'll hold it for another month, and we'll go that route. Keep me posted on the brothers."

"Yes, brother," Chiheb said. "You'll be with me every step of the way."

I dropped off Chiheb at his apartment in Montreal before lunch and raced to the airport. The team was waiting for me at the terminal. Every flight was canceled.

"What do we do?" I said to Nelly.

"Shit, we've got to go," he said, looking at his phone. "The storm is hitting tonight. Fuck it. Let's rent a car."

Nelly got a minivan and I jumped in the back. Nelly drove with Joey in the front. Kenny was in the back with me. Joey gathered up our passports as we approached the border.

The Border Patrol agent leaned into the window and took our stack of passports. He shuffled through them like they were a deck of cards. Nelly, Joey, and Kenny all had diplomatic passports with brown covers. Mine was a tourist passport with a blue cover. The border agent looked at Nelly and then into the back of the van at me with my long jihadi beard.

"You know what?" he said. "I don't want to know. Welcome home, guys. Have a safe trip."

"Thanks, bro," Nelly said, smiling at him.

Nelly took the passports and crossed the border. We all waited until the window was up before everyone started laughing.

"That dude had no idea what he was looking at," Joey said. "For all he knew, we just snatched your ass."

We stopped at McDonald's just over the border and I jumped behind the wheel. Fueled on cheap hamburgers and snuff, I drove south like my hair was on fire. We arrived in New York in five hours. I got to my house an hour before the storm hit. Rain was lashing my windshield as I drove the last mile. Three hours later, the power went out for three weeks.

Back in Canada, both Chiheb and Abassi watched the coverage of the storm and flooded my phone with text messages of encouragement. Abassi seemed especially anxious to develop a relationship with me.

The Canadians decided to fly me back to Quebec City in mid-November 2012. This time they didn't want Chiheb there. They wanted me to take Abassi's temperature alone. But without Chiheb, I couldn't record the conversation. Under Canadian law, we could record only when a target of the investigation—Chiheb or Jaser—was present.

I sent Chiheb and Abassi an e-mail telling them I was coming up to Canada. Chiheb volunteered to catch the bus to Quebec City, but I waved him off. I told him I had business and I'd come down to Montreal after I was done.

Abassi responded right away to my e-mail.

"I look forward to hosting you," he said.

We agreed to meet for dinner. Before I left the hotel, I met with the team to go over a game plan.

"My intention tonight is to simply develop my relationship," I said. "We can eventually draw out what his true intentions are."

Joey agreed.

"Don't go down any roads unless he does," he said. "Let him guide the discussion. The Canadians just want you to gauge his religious ideology and his beliefs."

Back at my hotel, I called Abassi's cell phone but got a recording. I fired up my MacBook and sent him an e-mail.

"Are you still free for dinner tonight?" I wrote. "I tried your cell phone but it was out of service."

He responded four minutes later. "Where? How are you?"

I was about to click "reply" when my phone rang. I didn't recognize the number.

"Tamer, Ahmed," Abassi said. "I am so sorry. My cell phone ran out of minutes."

"No problem, brother," I said.

"What are your plans? What are you doing up here?"

I closed my laptop and sat back in my chair.

"Still looking at the ski houses," I said. "But I'm free for dinner. Say around seven or eight?"

"That is great," Abassi said.

"I'd like to take you out," I said. "Think of a good restaurant that we'd both enjoy."

"No problem," Abassi said. "I'll be ready. You just let me know when you're ready."

"E-mail me your address and I'll pick you up."

His e-mail arrived a minute after we hung up. A short while later, he called me from his cell phone to let me know he got more minutes. He called me again at six thirty.

"Dinner's getting cold," he said, chuckling. "What's going on? Are you ready? What's up?"

He sounded anxious.

"Yeah, I'm good, brother," I said. "I'm wrapping up with the Realtor now and I should be leaving here in about half an hour."

"Great, call me when you leave."

I arrived at his house around seven. He was standing outside waiting. It looked like he was holding a parking spot. When he saw me, he waved me over. I rolled down my window.

"Park here," he said.

"Come on, brother, let's not waste time parking and getting out of the car," I said. "Let's get to the restaurant."

"We're at the restaurant," Abassi said. "You're coming to my home. I prepared dinner for us."

This wasn't a social dinner. He wanted privacy.

I locked the car and followed him into the lobby. He lived on the second floor in a small but quaint apartment. I stepped into the foyer. The kitchen was to the left. It was small with a little table in the middle of the laminate floor. A bedroom was to the right of the front door, and the bathroom was straight back. Unlike Chiheb's place, Abassi had a 52-inch LCD screen TV hooked up to a laptop.

Nearby, I saw two other laptops. Al Jazeera news was streaming on the television, and the table in the kitchen was crowded with Middle Eastern dishes.

"My wife cooked," he said. "She teaches Mondays. She is usually out late."

"Okay," I said.

There were pictures of her and her family on the wall. We sat down at the kitchen table and started to eat. Abassi told me about his family. He was the youngest of seven children. His mother and father still lived in Tunisia. Talk soon turned to my meetings in Quebec City. I told him about some condos I was considering and how I hoped to make money renting them out as vacation properties. Abassi seemed impressed. I was setting the stage for another glimpse up my skirt.

"Everything I do is to make money for the brothers and the cause," I said.

Abassi let that go, but it was clear he understood what I was saying. He wanted to talk. The meal. The private setting. It felt like I was being recruited.

"I wasn't as religious as I should have been until my mother died," I said. "My uncle changed my life."

"This *Dunya* doesn't matter," Abassi said.

They were the exact words Chiheb said on the flight to San Jose. But I almost laughed when Abassi said them. Muslims are encouraged to not focus on earthly concerns and possessions. A Muslim's focus should be on the afterlife and earning a place in paradise, which is why Chiheb shared a small, cramped apartment, slept on a used mattress, and never wasted anything. Abassi didn't take it as far as Chiheb.

"Chiheb speaks very, very highly of you, more than anyone," Abassi said. "He said that he loves you more than anybody."

"That's very nice," I said. "I appreciate that."

"Everything happens for a reason; look what's happening in to-day's day and age. Allah has turned everything against the evildoers in America. Climate, the weather, other governments, politics, every single thing in this world hates America. Look at all that's happened with the natural disasters; it's a sign from God that their time is coming. Look at all the wars that they're starting in our lands. It wasn't just with the Muslim people. Look at what they did in Vietnam. And we're defeating them. We are going to defeat them. Their defeat is imminent."

Abassi was starting to sound like Chiheb. I wished I was record-ing his rant.

"Look what nine-eleven did to that country. It literally destroyed their economy. They've yet to recover and they're not going to re-cover. It's only going to get worse for them. The big, bad, evil per-son, the United States, was toppled by one man: Osama bin Laden."

Abassi's eyes changed with the mention of bin Laden. There was a reverence as he spoke. He told me a story about how in Tunisia they chanted his name to remind President Obama that one man could topple the United States.

I sat in stunned silence. On the surface he looked and acted like a mainstream Muslim, but he was of the same mind as Chiheb. But Abassi was more cunning. He was doing the same thing I was do-ing. Giving a little, testing the waters, and then going a little further.

Unlike Chiheb, who hated all infidels, Abassi's hatred was centered on the United States. At this point, he couldn't say one sentence that wasn't damning the United States or revering bin

Laden. His wife called shortly after dinner and interrupted his rant. He took the call right in front of me. I'd invited him to New York earlier in the evening to reciprocate his hospitality, and he was excited to tell her. They were traveling to Tunisia in January for about four to five weeks, but maybe when they returned we could meet in New York, he told her.

After he hung up, Abassi started to talk about studying nuclear engineering. He was close to completing his master's degree.

"If Iran had a truly Islamic regime, I would go over there in a heartbeat and study and learn with their nuclear program," Abassi said. "That would be the best way to help the brothers in the long term with jihad."

I'd sat in front of a lot of wannabe terrorists, but this was different. Abassi wasn't just talk. He was selling his knowledge to me because Tamer was the jihad lottery. Win him over and he'll throw money at your plots.

"You know, you can buy anything on the black market," he said. "You can buy bombs, you can buy chemicals cheaply and very easily. Anything you want, right? And you need the brains to operate behind that. But none of that matters if you don't have money. You need money for jihad. The brothers overseas need money for their jihad. You think they could fight the Israelis without money? No. Money is needed for all jihad. Jihad is *fard* [obligatory]. It is Islam's sixth pillar, even though all of the fake Muslims won't acknowledge it. There are a million brothers out there. You could put a gun in their hands, they can go wage jihad. But without money, you don't have jihad. That's what's rare."

Abassi was painting a picture for me. It was almost comical because it was the same technique we use in the FBI. We paint a picture for the bad guy and let him connect the dots. It's extremely cunning. He was preying on my emotions. He was putting it all out there without specifically saying, "I need your money to buy chemicals to build a bomb."

It was time for me to go. I wasn't recording this conversation. I didn't want to go down this road unless I could record it.

"Brother, I don't want to hold you up, I know your wife will be home soon," I said. "I'm getting up early and I'm leaving tomorrow to go to Montreal. I have some business there and I want to meet with brother Chiheb before I fly back to New York. Brother, it was so great to see you, I look forward to seeing you again."

He insisted I stay longer, but I resisted. As I got into the car, I let out a sigh of relief. I'd met many people who claimed to be mujahideen, but this guy scared the shit out of me. It was more of a gut reaction. He didn't say anything overt. He just painted pictures in my head. Bomb making. Exploding nuclear reactors. I knew it wouldn't take long to tease out his full intentions.

Back at the safe house, I was fired up. Joey told me to take my time with my notes so I could capture the conversation. Abassi was dangerous and he wanted to make sure the Canadians understood.

But I had doubts about my decision to cut the meeting short. I pulled Joey aside.

"I made the right call there, right?" I said.

"You absolutely made the right call," Joey said. "You walking away at that point only makes him more eager to tell you the next time."

"There is no doubt this guy is bad," I said. "We need to record our next meeting."

I told Doug and his bosses Abassi was the real deal. The Canadians promised to file a warrant with the court so I could record my next meeting with Abassi. With Abassi done, Doug and the Canadians wanted to talk about a new development.

Chiheb had signed up for a conference in Singapore the week before Christmas, and the Canadian government was going to arrest him at the airport.

The case was over.

We couldn't stop them from locking him up. The Canadians couldn't afford to let him out of the country. Plus, the case was eating up their manpower. They had enough evidence to convict. It was time to wrap it up.

But we had more work to do.

Doug wouldn't look me in the eye as his bosses delivered the news. I did the math. We had three weeks to get something on the American sleeper.

Joey started to pace after the Canadian bosses left. Suddenly, he stopped.

"What is the only thing that will stop him from going to Singapore?"

"Jihad," I said. "Helping the brothers."

Joey shook his head.

"Helping *you* help the brothers."

"I'm not tracking," I said.

"Follow me on this," Joey said, starting to pace again.

"Your uncle needs you," he said. "The banks are all fucked up after the Arab Spring. They can't get money and he needs cash."

I looked at Nelly. He had a smile on his face.

"Yeah," I said. "So I'm putting a delivery of cash together for the brothers . . ."

"Pitch it to him tomorrow in Montreal," Joey said. "Tell him you need him in New York at the same time as the conference. The Canadians can't arrest him in New York, and we'll invite them down to watch the operation."

"That is brilliant," I said.

"You need Chiheb's help with the delivery," Joey said.

"He'll do whatever you need, especially since you're helping the brothers."

CHAPTER 21

Spitting in the Eyes of God

I parked my rental car in front of Chiheb's apartment. I'd made the drive to his house so often I didn't even use the GPS. The streets of Montreal were comfortable. I fished out my BlackBerry and scrolled through my contacts until I reached Chiheb's name. He answered after a few rings.

"I'm in front of your house," I said.

It sounded like he was outside. I could hear him walking.

"I just finished praying and I'm walking out of the mosque downtown," he said. "Let me give you an address so you can come pick us up."

I heard some other voices in the background. *Us?* I thought.

"Chiheb, who are you with?"

"I'm with a good brother that I met at the mosque," he said. "I think you should meet him."

I was silent for a minute. I had to talk about Singapore and there was no way I was going to do that with a stranger present. I didn't have time for Chiheb's recruiting tonight. He was spending time in the mosques looking for a replacement for Jaser.

"Listen, get a phone number from him," I said. "Tell him you'll call him later tonight. We need to meet alone to talk about some things first."

"Yes," Chiheb said. "Yes. Okay."

He gave me the address of the mosque and I picked him up. We went to a nearby Tim Hortons. He ordered a hot chocolate. I got a tea. We went back to the car. Chiheb blew on his hot chocolate as I talked about my meeting with Abassi.

"He said a few things that caught my attention," I said.

"He didn't ask you for money, did he?" Chiheb asked.

"No, no," I said. "Not at all. He just talked to me about his degree and how he knew chemicals and how with that knowledge he could make anything blow up. He also told me it was our duty to do jihad. What do you need more than manpower for jihad? You need money."

Chiheb shrugged.

"Of course you do," he said. "Everybody knows that."

"Well, it caught my attention," I said. "It sounded like he's got some thoughts."

"Yeah, well, does he have a plan?"

"We didn't go that far," I said. "I didn't go that far because as much as I feel like you're right—he seems like a good brother—I don't know him and I can't trust him like that yet. I just can't seem to bring myself to go there with him just yet."

Chiheb turned to face me to make sure I understood what he was saying.

"No, listen. He is a true mujahideen. But he doesn't want to do anything right now. I bet he is going to want you to pay for his PhD and get him through so that long-term he'll be able to help the brothers. But you're supposed to be doing projects along with what you're doing, your everyday work. You should run them parallel."

"Okay," I said. "We'll get back to that once I talk to him again."

I told Chiheb I was headed back to Quebec City in February to finish my conversation with Abassi.

"Listen, brother," I said, trying to sound serious. "I need a favor. You know what's going on with my uncle and everything. He's over in Cairo and he's helping the brothers."

"*Masha'Allah*," Chiheb said. "May God protect him."

I set my tea in the cup holder and turned to face Chiheb. It was important I sold this pitch. If we couldn't get Chiheb to abandon his trip to Singapore, our case was sunk. We'd never identify the American sleeper.

"He needs money," I said. "The banks are screwed up because of the Arab Spring and he needs cash."

Chiheb had a look on his face that said whatever I needed he would provide.

"No, no," I said. "I've got the money. I have it. I'll put it together. But he's sending a brother, a Palestinian brother, over from Egypt to the United States. A brother that I know and he's a trustworthy brother. He's good. But we're talking about a lot of money that we're going to hide inside a suitcase. That kind of money sometimes . . ."

I paused for a second, building up the tension, the gravity of our mission. I wanted him to come to me. Chiheb finished my sentence.

"The devil can come in," he said.

"That's why I need you," I said. "I can put a million dollars in cash with you. I'd leave. I'd come back and it would be a million dollars plus ten thousand. That's the way you work."

Chiheb laughed.

"You're right, brother," he said. "I'm as loyal as you think I am."

"I trust you with my life, let alone my money."

"Absolutely," Chiheb said.

I told him the Palestinian brother was coming to New York in mid-December to pick up the cash. Right when Chiheb was supposed to be in Singapore.

"Are you okay with everything? Your schedule?"

Chiheb looked concerned, like he was weighing his options.

"Well, there was this Singapore trip," he said.

"What's going on with that?"

"Don't worry about it," he said, sipping his hot chocolate. "It's no big deal."

"Well, tell me about it. What's the thought? What were you going to do?"

"I want to go there because it's not just for work," Chiheb said. "It's great for work, but it's also for religious purposes. Look at how I met you when I went on my last conference. But also there's a lot of good brothers over there in Singapore and I was hoping to maybe make some contacts over there."

But we both knew getting money to the brothers was more important.

"Did you pay? Did you buy a ticket or anything?"

"No, no," Chiheb said. "I didn't book anything yet."

But I could still tell he was hesitating.

"What?"

"Nothing," he said.

"What?" I asked again.

"Well, there was the registration fee, but don't worry about that."

"How much was it?"

"Don't worry about it."

"Tell me."

"Three hundred dollars."

I smiled as I imagined handing Doug the receipt. The Canadians were going to reimburse him.

"Do you have a receipt?"

"Yes."

"Great. Here's what you do. See if you can get your money back. If you can, great. If you can't, don't worry about it. Give me the receipt when you come to the States, when you come to New York, give it to me. We'll put it on your trip. We'll write it off."

"You can do that? That's wonderful. That's great."

"Listen, brother," I said. "I'm sorry about the conference. I really appreciate the help. I hate to ask."

Chiheb put his hand on my shoulder.

"Don't be sorry," he said. "It doesn't matter what I have going on. It doesn't matter. If you say you need me, I will be there."

"Thank you," I said. "Now go ahead and get your visa. Do it for a week. Until December 22. You still have the address, the name of the airport, location, my information, everything?"

"Yes," he said. "I'll e-mail the embassy tomorrow."

"How do you feel about eventually inviting Ahmed to New York?"

We both knew that Abassi was going to Tunisia to celebrate his wedding at the end of December. I wanted to get in front of him in Quebec City, get his true colors on tape, and then arrest him in New York.

Chiheb looked up like he was thinking for a second.

"Hear me out," I said. "You're not sure if he's about money or if he's about jihad. You say he's a mujahid."

"Yes," Chiheb said. "He's one hundred percent mujahideen. But I'm afraid that he has some money things as well."

We were back to the loaned money.

"Okay," I said. "Let's put him to the test. We fly him to New York, we have him stay at a nice place, we have him go out with us, see the sights, and then the three of us sit down together. And then you do your thing. You put him to the test."

I could just make out Chiheb's smile in the thick hair of his beard as he let out a deep chuckle like he was Baba Noel.

"We're putting him to the test so we'll see whether he's about the money or jihad," he said.

"Exactly," I said. "Don't give me an answer now. Think about it. If you want to do it, we do it. If you don't, we don't need him. I need you right now. I don't need him."

I could see Chiheb's pride swell.

"Wouldn't it be great if we can get everything lined up with the American sleeper by the time you get to the States?" I said.

"Yes," he said. "I just sent an e-mail a few days ago asking Abu Hamza for the phone number for El Massoul."

"Why don't you let Abu Hamza know you're going to be in the United States to meet with a brother and that you could call him from there," I said. "We'll get a secure phone of some sort."

"I'm not so sure about secure phones, and I can never tell him where I'm going," Chiheb said.

"What do you mean?"

"I'm under orders," he said. "El Massoul said I'm never allowed to tell anyone, even Abu Hamza, where I am or where I'm going. That's rule number one."

"Alright," I said. "So that's out."

Chiheb said the delay was getting in touch with El Massoul. Only Abu Hamza could do it, and El Massoul was still in Afghanistan.

"They are both traveling," Chiheb said. "I'm patient. I'm trying to be patient. We'll give it some more time."

"Okay," I said.

There was nothing else I could do that night. I was happy with my Singapore victory.

"Tell me about this brother you met," I said.

"I met him yesterday," he said. "His name is Mohammed. We met at the mosque. He is from Tunisia too."

Chiheb wanted me to meet him and test him. Mohammed was a promising lead, but I shook my head when he was finished.

"You know what, I don't want to meet this guy," I said. "Why don't you go ahead and meet him. Figure it out yourself. If you feel like this is someone worth talking to, we'll move forward. If not, then there's really no reason for me to meet him, right?"

"Yeah," Chiheb said, his shoulders slumped in disappointment. "You're right."

Chiheb called Mohammed and canceled. I could hear Mohammed on the line questioning Chiheb.

"Why don't you want to meet me?" he said.

I tried to ignore the conversation, but something was nagging me about Mohammed. On the off chance that I might be missing something, I reached out and touched Chiheb's arm. Chiheb asked Mohammed to hold on and covered the phone.

"Tell him we'll meet him," I said. "Where's he at?"

We picked him up near the mosque and went to a Turkish restaurant downtown. Mohammed was a large man with a beer belly. Something was off with him from the minute he got into the back of the car. He always seemed to have something on the tip of his tongue.

We kept the conversation light. Current events. Islam, but not the heavy stuff. Small talk about our families. I kept my eyes locked on Mohammed throughout dinner. He was always trying to say the right thing. He was constantly thinking. Nothing was natural. I could see it in his eyes. His mind was working through the conversation, always looking for a gap to draw out information. He was either a wannabe jihadi or an informant. In the car afterward, Chiheb wanted to know my impression.

"There's something there," I said. "I don't know what it is, but there's something there. That's your job to vet him."

We both were perplexed and quiet because we couldn't figure out his deal.

"One thing I know for sure is he's fat," I said.

Chiheb chuckled. "Yes, he is fat."

We never brought him up again. I dropped off Chiheb at his apartment. Before he got out, I gave him a hug and thanked him again for coming to New York.

"I can't thank you enough," I told Chiheb. "I'll get the paperwork together. Let me know when your visa comes in. Brother, do you need anything? Can we stop at a food store so I can stock up your fridge?"

"No, brother," Chiheb said. "I am eating. I am praying. I am sleeping. I have all that I need."

I drove back to the safe house. The more I thought about

Mohammed, the angrier I got. I was convinced he was an informant, likely put in place by CSIS to keep tabs on the case. This was the second time they'd gotten in the way. The first was the dog walkers who interrupted my talk with Jaser and Chiheb in Toronto.

But this was worse.

Mohammed wasn't a good informant. He didn't actively listen. He tried to steer the conversation. Everything came out forced. We were lucky Chiheb was so desperate for help that he wasn't picking up the tells. I slammed the safe house door shut and slumped into a chair. Nelly looked at Joey and Doug.

"He didn't go for the New York trip?" Joey said.

"No, he is on board," I said. "That worked beautifully."

"What's wrong then?"

I pulled my jacket off and put in a pinch of snuff.

"Fucking CSIS," I said.

"What?" Nelly said. "They had surveillance out there again?"

"No," I said. "The guy I had dinner with tonight is a fucking informant. His body language sucked. He was trying to give us his legend, which was full of holes. Everything was a lie. All he wanted to do was bring the conversation back to jihad. You better call CSIS. This shit has to stop."

Joey looked at Doug and Nelly. Both men hung their heads. No one wanted to look at me.

"Well, the cat's out of the bag," Joey said.

"Calm down, brother," Doug said. "He's not CSIS."

I looked at Joey.

"Don't look at me."

"That was our call," Doug said. "Chiheb was in the mosque talking jihad and this guy walked into our office and said he had information about a terrorist. We interviewed him to keep him from knowing we had an ongoing op. We signed him up but we didn't think you'd meet him. We didn't want to tell you about him so it wouldn't cloud your judgment."

"That motherfucker knew who I was?" I said.

"No, we didn't tell him shit," Doug said. "As a matter of fact, he just called his handler with his assessment. He said you were an evil fuck and we should let the Americans know you're a real terrorist and Chiheb is a danger to everything and everyone. His assessment was spot-on. But we didn't tell him anything."

I understood why they didn't tell me. Under Canadian rules they couldn't. I flew home the next day. Chiheb's New York trip was paramount; that was where I had to be focused. At this point, the team was convinced if we identified the American sleeper, the Canadians couldn't shut us down.

But Chiheb still confused me. He was a bad guy when he was in jihadi mode. But that wasn't all the time. I'd spent so much time with him when he wasn't talking about murder every minute. I knew how much he liked the Jordanian girl in his office. I admired his willingness to help me. That kind of selflessness you don't see very often. I saw him as a human and not just a target. I wished there was a way to keep him from throwing the switch. A way for him to keep his deep, hearty laugh. Keep him in Baba Noel mode. Abassi and El Massoul had poisoned him. I knew he was going to jail and that was where he belonged. But I wondered if we could bring him back to true Islam.

It was Thanksgiving week and I wasn't going to see my father, a tradition we'd held since my mother passed away. I called him as I drove home from the airport.

"How was your trip?" my father asked.

He knew I worked undercover for the FBI.

"It was alright," I said.

"What's wrong?"

He heard it in my voice.

"You know what?" I said. "It just weighs on you."

"I know you can't talk about what it is you do, but if there is anything you want to talk about generally, I'm here for you," my father said.

"Let me ask you something."

"Sure," he said.

I still had Chiheb on my mind. The question of if he could be saved was nagging me. As a Muslim, I wanted to know if it was my duty to try to save his soul. I was stepping out of my cop mind-set when I called my father. I was searching for guidance in the same religion Chiheb perverted. I couldn't go to an Imam, but I could ask my father. I knew few non-Imams who understood the Quran better.

"When someone misinterprets our religion," I said. "When someone is so far gone and uses Islam as a weapon to kill, but that is their only bad fault, is there anything redeemable? Is there anything that can fix that person? Bring that person back to being a true Muslim?"

I heard my father let out a sigh. He was thinking. Searching his memory of the Quran and his experiences. It was a question all Muslims struggle with. Islam is what makes me who I am. So, how do I identify with the same faith as a small group of mass murderers? Being a Muslim didn't make us villains.

"Listen, it has been my experience that it is very rare when someone is so taken by hatred and evil that they've reached the point where they are using God and Islam to take another soul, any soul, even a military soul," my father said. "That person is far gone. Nothing you say or do will bring them back. But the only advice I can give you is to be sure that person is at that point."

In my head, I was thinking about the Christian burial speech. How Chiheb had laid out his justifications for killing men, women, and children in the name of Allah.

"And if I am sure they are at that point?" I asked.

"If that is the case, it is your duty as a Muslim and as an American to not only stop them but stop them dead in their tracks and make an example of them," my father said. "That is not Islam. That is not anything resembling Islam. That is an evil that needs to be wiped off our planet."

As my father was explaining things to me, I became Chiheb. I argued his justifications for the attack, testing my father's assertions. Each time my father shut it down.

"What you are describing is a warped rationalization," he said when I was finished. "It is human. The Quran is from Allah. When you try to change what is black and white, that is human. That is haram. The Prophet said to you, peace be upon him, this is Islam. These are the rules of Islam. These are the rules of war in Islam. No innocent person can be killed. Women and children of your enemy are off-limits. Even the men of your enemy who are not fighting are off-limits. Never to be touched. The only people of your enemy that you are allowed to kill during times of war are the combatants. That is black and white in the Quran. Anyone who colors outside those lines is spitting in the eyes of God. Anytime you change the meaning of Islam, it is a complete desecration of the religion."

Just hearing my father say that gave me the affirmation I needed. I never doubted my actions. I wasn't seeing things in Chiheb's way. I just saw the human side of a monster, and I didn't want to abandon Chiheb if he could be saved.

But I knew he couldn't.

My father was right. Chiheb was gone.

CHAPTER 22

Operation Happy New Year

Chiheb was due into New York in a week and FBI Headquarters wanted to talk about the plan.

They called a meeting at the joint operations center in midtown Manhattan. I sat next to Nelly at the conference table and stared at a wintry, cold Hudson River. Ari, the assistant special agent in charge of counterterrorism in New York, went over the plan. The Canadians agreed to let him travel. Doug and two of his bosses were scheduled to arrive the day before Chiheb to monitor the operation. The embassy in Ottawa granted his visa on our request, and his flight was booked. The last hurdle was the money. We needed to show Chiheb the cash or the ruse wasn't going to work.

Joey waited until the end of the meeting to spring it on Ari.

"By the way, we're going to need two hundred thousand in cash to show the bad guy," Joey said.

There was a pause as Ari chewed on the request.

"We're not going to put that kind of money in this guy's hands," Ari said. "There's no way."

Ari was worried Chiheb was going to steal it, but we assured him Chiheb would never be alone with the money. And even if he was, it would still be safe.

"You don't need to worry, because that money is safer with him than anyone in this building," I said.

Ari cocked his head in disbelief. He was used to dealing with criminals, not terrorists.

"Listen," I said. "He is not a criminal. I understand what he is doing is criminal. But he believes this money is going to help his cause. He would die before anyone touched it, let alone spent it. I'll make you a bet. Not only will he protect that money, I bet he finds a way to add whatever he has in his pocket to it."

Ari just shook his head.

"You're out of your mind," he said.

I shrugged.

"Gentlemen's bet, then," I said.

"No," he said. "Put your money where your mouth is. Twenty bucks."

I held out my hand.

"You're on."

We shook on it and then Ari turned to Joey.

"Approved," he said.

As we walked out of the conference room, Joey patted me on the back.

"Good job," he said. "And it only cost you twenty bucks."

"I think he just made a sucker bet," I said.

Nelly nodded his head in agreement.

"I think you're right."

The day before Chiheb's arrival, I met with Osman, a new undercover officer. I'd planned to use Yasser, my Palestinian buddy whom I traveled overseas with to meet the Sheikh, but he wasn't available.

Osman grew up in the Midwest and joined the FBI right out of college. Prior to the undercover school, he was saddled to a desk. This was one of his first chances to go undercover as the courier sent by my uncle. We met in Brooklyn at a Buffalo Wild Wings near the Brooklyn Nets arena. We ordered lunch and we talked about Chiheb. I warned him to steer clear of religion. Osman is a devout Muslim and had trouble bending his religion to fit into the jihad ideology.

"Listen, this guy is hard-core," I said. "Watch yourself. For the sake of this investigation, you can't let him know you're a true Muslim. You need to be a like-minded brother."

"No problem," he said.

"Do not correct him," I said.

"No problem."

"You're the courier," I said. "You just arrived from Egypt. My uncle sent you to bring back a suitcase."

"The money?" Osman said.

"Yeah," I said, putting down my iced tea glass. "But you don't know what you're carrying. You're just here to get a suitcase and take it back to the brothers."

Osman smiled.

"No problem," he said.

"Good, I'll call you in a few days and set up the meeting with the target."

I kept in touch with Abassi via e-mail. He was still in Quebec City. But he was getting ready to fly to Tunisia. I wanted to firm up plans to meet again. Abassi suggested that we meet the first week in February back at his apartment to finish our conversation.

"Mark it down," I wrote to Abassi. "I will be up there for business and I'd love to meet for dinner, dear brother."

"I can't wait, brother," Abassi wrote back. "We have a lot to discuss."

But first I had to pick up Chiheb. His flight landed at LaGuardia Airport around four fifteen in the afternoon on December 15, 2012. I met him outside the terminal. I could see his smile through the scruff of his beard. He threw his arms around me in a bear hug.

"Good to see you, brother," I said.

"God be praised, how are you, brother?" Chiheb said.

"I'm well," I said, walking him toward the car.

I put his bag into the back of my Mercedes C300. I purposely chose the smaller sedan because I wanted to have a nice car, but not too flashy and certainly not wasteful. I took the Grand Central Parkway to Interstate 278 to the Manhattan Bridge. We were headed for lower Manhattan. Chiheb was staying at one of my rental properties next door to Ground Zero. It was not done on purpose. It was the only apartment the FBI could get on short notice. As I drove, we talked about Abassi. Chiheb had come around a bit and saw some value in meeting with him.

"He is for real," Chiheb said. "Raed is gone and we need to see what he can do to help us."

"We need to talk about that," I said. "That first week in February I'm going back up there to talk to him. I think we should do that together."

That was my backup plan if the Canadians didn't file the paperwork to get a wire for Abassi. If Chiheb was in the room I could record. Chiheb agreed and then changed the subject to the American sleeper.

"I got great news from Abu Hamza," Chiheb said. "Our dear brother is back from Afghanistan, but he is now in Syria helping the brothers."

I was annoyed.

"You're here for a week, brother," I said. "We need to set this meeting up ASAP."

"I have a number," Chiheb said. "We can try calling him tomorrow."

After dinner, we went back to Chiheb's apartment and made several calls to the number. None went through. We didn't have the correct country code. I promised to figure out the right one and left Chiheb to pray.

The next day we planned to go to dinner near my apartment in midtown, but not before we went over the plan for the money and courier.

"My uncle sent his best friend's nephew instead of the Palestinian brother," I said. "He is good. He is just a little green and gets a little nervous."

I set the stage for Osman to be nervous on his first major undercover operation.

"Do you trust him?" Chiheb said.

"I do," I said. "I trust his family. His heart is in the right place. He is a good Muslim brother. He is just like us."

If I trusted him, so did Chiheb.

"Here is how it is going to work," I said, quickly moving to the next topic. "This is the way we've done it in the past. We have a guy in customs in Cairo . . ."

"Is he your guy?" Chiheb said.

"My uncle's guy," I said. "My uncle will be there waiting to receive the package, because we've lost money in the past and this can't be lost."

"Okay, what is the plan for us?"

I told Chiheb about my baggage handler at JFK—another FBI undercover—who would make sure the suitcase got on the plane.

"I need you to help me pack the suitcase and make sure Osman doesn't know what is in it," I said. "All he knows is he has to deliver the suitcase. You're going to help me hide the money."

"Perfect," Chiheb said, content with being one of the trusted brothers in the operation.

"We'll count the money once I get it," I said. "You need to watch over it until it gets to the airport."

"With my life," Chiheb said.

He would never question why I needed his help, especially when it was for the cause.

"You're another set of eyes," I said. "I'm trusting you. The brothers are trusting you with the money. We have to deliver it."

I told Chiheb that Osman was around for dinner if he wanted to meet him. We planned to go to the Palm, a steakhouse on West Fiftieth Street. It was only a few doors down from my apartment.

Chiheb hesitated.

"I don't know about dinner," he said.

I didn't blame him. He wanted to talk with Tamer more and not waste time on a courier. I was happy, because I wasn't sure how Osman would do over a long dinner.

"Once we're done with dinner, I'll text him and he can have dessert," I said.

"Okay," Chiheb said.

We got to the Palm around eight. One of the waiters remembered me from past visits and greeted me warmly. He was Egyptian and spoke Arabic. I purposely got to know him prior to Chiheb's arrival in an effort to show Chiheb that I was a regular at a restaurant near my apartment.

Chiheb studied the menu.

"Have the lobster, brother," I said.

He put down his menu.

"I've never had it before."

"You'll love it," I said, ordering him the whole lobster.

There was no way he could eat the whole thing. It was my solution to waste not, want not. I couldn't have him scooping food off of a plate again. The lobster arrived on a white plate. It was bright red and wisps of steam rose from its shell. Chiheb slid the lobster bib over his head as I showed him how to crack the claws and pull the meat out with a little silver fork.

He smiled as he chewed.

"It's good," I said. "Right?"

"*Masha'Allah*," he said. "It is wonderful."

Between bites of my lobster, I watched Chiheb crack open the tail and another claw. By the end of the meal, he was rooting through the pieces of shell to make sure he got every morsel of lobster meat. As the waiter cleared the table, Chiheb grabbed the butter from the bread basket. He held it in his left hand at an angle and started to spoon it into his mouth with two fingers from his right hand.

"You know that's butter, right?" I said.

Chiheb looked at me and then went back to eating it.

"Thank God," he said.

I understood the idea of not wasting food, but now he was eating butter. I took out my phone and sent a message to Osman.

"Come now."

Osman was nervous when he arrived. He wouldn't sit down until I motioned to the empty chair. Chiheb didn't take his eyes off him. The Arab Santa was gone. I had flashbacks to our flight from Houston to San Jose. Chiheb ran through the hadiths, listening closely to Osman's interpretations. When I could, I answered or guided the conversation away from Osman so all he had to do was agree. By the end of dessert, I was exhausted.

"We'll see you tomorrow at my apartment," I said. "I'll call you when we're ready."

"Great," Osman said, shaking my hand and Chiheb's before leaving the restaurant.

As Osman walked out, I looked at Chiheb.

"What do you think?"

"He is a little nervous," Chiheb said.

"I know he is," I said.

"May Allah protect us," he said.

I paid the check and we walked out to the curb. I didn't want to go back to the apartment and have the same conversations over again. Times Square was only a few blocks away and it wasn't too cold.

"Want to go walk this off? I'll show you Times Square."

We started down the street toward the massive video screens.

Chiheb was silent as the lights of Times Square got brighter. We joined the crowd heading toward the pedestrian plaza. Neon illuminated signs and "zipper" news crawls surrounded us. I let it wash over him.

"That's where the ball drops?" Chiheb said, getting his bearings from the countless movies and shows filmed there.

Times Square was crowded with shoppers getting ready for Christmas. Chiheb kept his eyes up at the buildings and the neon. I watched as several times he cocked his ear, picking out some of the languages spoken around us. We stopped near a McDonald's and he started to scan the tops of the buildings.

"This is the center of the universe of the West," he said. "What a brilliant place to have an operation. Operation Happy New Year."

I pretended not to hear as we walked back to the parking garage.

"We'll need multiple bombs," he said. "The best-case scenario would be vehicles, but the security could be tight around New Year's Eve."

I looked over at him as we drove down Eleventh Avenue toward his apartment.

"It's two weeks away," I said.

"Not this year," he said. "Next year. It will take some time. I'm going to have a job for you. Can you come here for New Year's Eve?"

"Sure," I said. "I live here."

"You need to take pictures from an elevated location," he said. "Show me what the security looks like."

"Okay," I said.

I stopped listening before we reached Canal Street. At his apartment, we tried El Massoul's number again, this time with the correct country code. But a recording told us it was disconnected. Frustrated, I told Chiheb I was tired. I suggested that he reach out to Abu Hamza again and figure something out, because we were running out of time.

I picked up my peacoat off the couch.

"We've got a lot of work tomorrow," I said. "I'll pick you up in the morning."

When Chiheb got into the car the next morning, he started quizzing me about who was getting the money.

"Are you sure this money is going to the mujahideen and not the munafiqeen?"

"Absolutely," I said.

"Who is it going to exactly?"

"Al Qaeda in the Arabian Peninsula," I said.

"Not Hamas."

"No," I said.

The divisions among groups like al Qaeda, ISIS, and Hamas are stark. They all use radical Islamic teachings to brainwash their followers, but that is where the commonality stops. Each group has its own goals. Hamas is a Palestinian Sunni-Islamic group whose primary target is Israel. Al Qaeda in the Arabian Peninsula is a franchise of al Qaeda based in Yemen whose primary target is the United States. All the groups compete for the same pool of recruits. Chiheb was recruited into al Qaeda and didn't want to support a competing group.

"I have five thousand dollars in my checking account," Chiheb said after I convinced him the money was going to a group he supported. "I want to give half of it to the brothers."

"Chiheb, I'm sending two hundred thousand dollars," I said. "All due respect, that is plenty."

"Are you telling me I can't do this?" he asked, an edge in his voice. "This is for Allah. I have to. I have an opportunity to send money."

I shook my head. I didn't care that he was about to give the American government money. I just didn't want to add anything to the plan.

"That's too much," I said, turning into the parking garage of my apartment building.

"I insist," he said. "Don't stop me from getting this credit from Allah."

"Okay," I said, closing my door and heading for the elevator. "How are you going to get the money?"

After an hour on the phone with his bank in Montreal, Chiheb withdrew slightly more than a thousand dollars from an ATM across the street, because that was the most they would allow him to take out in one day. We wrapped it up with my two hundred thousand. When we were done counting and wrapping it in bundles, Chiheb took out a twenty-dollar Canadian note and added it to the pile. That was all the money he had in his wallet.

The suitcase had a hidden compartment in the base and we packed the money inside. I called Osman to come pick it up and ordered a pizza for lunch. While we waited for the pizza to arrive, Chiheb watched as Osman transferred his clothes from his suitcase into the one with the money. Before lunch, we prayed. Chiheb acted as the Imam. Osman and I removed our shoes. Chiheb kept his on as he recited the call to prayer.

"He's got his shoes on," Osman whispered to me.

To a mainstream Muslim, that was frowned upon. But to a mujahid, it was accepted. I shot him a look like I wanted to strangle him. No religion talk.

After prayer, we sat around the table and ate pizza. Chiheb laid out his rationalization for killing innocent people. Osman flinched at each interpretation. I could tell he wanted to argue. Finally, Osman had enough.

"Time out," he said.

Osman started questioning everything. He broke cover and stumped Chiheb using my father's rationale. Chiheb had no answer for why his views violated the Prophet's rules of war. I was proud of Osman as a Muslim. But at that moment, I wanted to smash his face. *Shut it the fuck down and finish the operation,* I thought as the conversation got heated.

"Alright, guys, we've got to get going," I said, breaking up the argument.

Chiheb shot me a look like he wanted to talk. I gathered up the pizza boxes.

"Hey, Osman, can you take these pizza boxes to the trash chute?" I said.

Chiheb pulled me aside after he left.

"What's up?" I said, knowing damn well what the problem was.

"Are you sure you trust this guy?" he said. "Can he be trusted?"

Chiheb wanted to know how Osman, who clearly believed in mainstream Islam and was possibly munafiqeen, was chosen for such an important job.

"He is young and naive," I said. "He is on his way. Just like the brothers you introduced me to in Montreal. He is close. He is being converted. He is a good soldier right now, but he is still confused by the munafiqeen mind-set. He is okay. Trust me."

Chiheb didn't say anything at first.

"I don't trust him," he said as he waved his finger in my face. "May Allah watch over us."

Chiheb sat down on the couch as I put the last of the dishes in the sink.

"He probably couldn't find the trash chute," I said, hoping to catch Osman before he came back to the apartment. "I'll be right back."

I grabbed my key and met Osman in the hall.

"No more religion talk," I said.

"I'm sorry," he said.

He looked down at his shoes and started to explain his actions when I gave him a throat-slash gesture. I was still wired.

"Okay," he said. "Okay."

"It's time for us to go," I said. "Got it? Silent ride to the airport."

Osman and Chiheb avoided each other as we rode down the elevator. A car driven by another FBI agent was waiting to take us to the airport. The (FBI) baggage handler met us at the terminal so Chiheb could see him.

"Wait with the car," I told Chiheb. "I'll get Osman checked in and be right back."

The next morning, I called Chiheb and told him the money arrived safely and my uncle was taking it to the Sinai Peninsula to give to the brothers. Chiheb was fired up after being challenged by Osman. I spent hours listening to him rail against everything. It was six hours of hate.

By dinner, I'd had my fill. All I wanted was to identify the American sleeper. But Chiheb was focused on Operation Happy New Year. The U.S. attorney was ecstatic. He had listened to the previous day's recordings and knew we already had a strong case against Chiheb. He'd gifted us by putting his own money in the suitcase and verbally earmarking it for a specific terrorist group. Now he was planning an attack on American soil, and the U.S. attorney wanted audio. I did my best to stay plugged in, but it got harder as each hour passed.

By the time I reached his apartment after dinner, I was fried. I parked around the corner and we walked the half block to the front door. The building sat next to the entrance to the 9/11 memorial. One World Trade Center towered above us. Chiheb stopped and looked up at the building. He slid his arm over my shoulder and pulled me close.

"Tamer, this town needs another nine-eleven. And we're going to give it to them," he said, rubbing his beard. "Come upstairs. I want to tell you about Operation Happy New Year."

I saw red.

I could feel a pen in my jacket pocket. Every fiber of my being wanted to grab it and jam it into Chiheb's eye. I wanted him off the face of the earth. He died in my mind that night. Any concern I had for the human inside that monster was gone. I shoved him away. He looked at me funny.

"You know what, brother, I'm not feeling good tonight," I said, turning back toward the car. "It might be something I ate."

"Are you okay?" Chiheb asked, not sure how to read my body language.

I started to walk away.

"Just an upset stomach," I said. "See you tomorrow."

I got to the safe house on the west side first and sat by the window. I left the lights off. I felt like I had let everyone down. It was my job to separate my personal feelings from the goals of the investigation. My anger was turning to shame. I was not a professional undercover that night.

Joey arrived a few minutes later.

"Can I turn the light on?" Joey said.

"Sure."

"Are you okay?" Joey asked.

"I fucked up, bud."

"No you didn't," he said, failing to be convincing.

"I fucked up. I know I fucked up. Are they losing their shit?"

Joey shifted in his seat.

Everyone in the operations center was listening in on our conversations. A known terrorist was about to lay out a plot to attack the United States and I walked away. I found out later the U.S. attorney listening to the wire lost his shit. He should have. I failed.

"Fuck them," Joey said. "Are you okay?"

"Yeah, I will be."

Joey pulled out a tin of Copenhagen Long Cut Straight.

"Put a pinch in," he said, switching off the light. He sat in silence for the better part of an hour as I collected myself. I didn't want to talk about the case anymore. I didn't want to talk about killing people. I didn't want to be fake.

I finally pulled the wad of Copenhagen out and looked at Joey.

"Tell them they'll have everything they need tomorrow morning."

CHAPTER 23

High Five

I called Chiheb first thing in the morning.

"I'm coming over with breakfast," I said.

"How are you feeling?"

"Feeling great," I said as I headed out of my apartment.

I stopped and picked up some bagels and drove downtown to his apartment. We sat around the coffee table in the living room eating as he explained Operation Happy New Year.

"There needs to be three explosions at different points of a triangle," Chiheb said, looking at his computer.

A Google map of Times Square filled the screen. The plan was to hide the bombs in parked cars.

"They have to be set off between five and ten seconds apart," he said. "As one explosion detonates, people will run away from it. That is when the other explosion will take place. Maximum destruction, maximum fatalities if you do it that way."

I chewed and listened. If he had said that last night, he'd be dead and I'd be up on murder charges. A decent night's sleep saved his life.

"I need you to spend some time there," Chiheb said, leaning back in his chair and taking a bite of his breakfast. "Take video and pictures. Learn the security procedures. What do the police do if you leave a car unattended? Checkpoints and things like that so that we can accurately plan the attack."

I nodded.

"I'll e-mail you the pictures," I said.

"No e-mail. Put them on a flash drive."

"Okay," I said. "I'll have them in February when I come up to meet with Ahmed."

"We'll do it in a year," Chiheb said. "We're going to need hotel rooms nearby so we can see down onto the street. We can set off the bombs from there."

All of this came from one walk through Times Square. The bumbling professor persona was just a façade, and I fell for it, even going so far as talking to my father about saving him. This plot showed Chiheb's true nature. This was his idea, not the brothers'. He was thinking for himself. Forget the train plot. This one scared me because he was using his training. No e-mail. Figuring out security and getting access to Times Square. While in its infancy, this plot seemed more doable than the train plot. I never said it, but this is what Jaser told us to do from the start.

Chiheb's flight left later that day. He was flying back to Montreal and then getting a ride to Toronto. His lease was up at his apartment in Montreal, so I offered him the safe house in Toronto.

"They let me have it for a few more months," I said. "It's yours if you want it."

"Thank you, brother," he said.

I took out an envelope from my backpack and put it on the table. There was five hundred dollars in cash in it.

"What is this?" Chiheb asked.

"For your visa and conference registration," I said. "Thank you for coming down here, brother. I needed you and you gave up everything to come."

Chiheb smiled and rubbed his beard. His eyes lit up as he talked.

"Look at what Allah is doing for us now," he said. "We just sent two hundred thousand dollars to the mujahideen overseas. I was able to give a little bit and look what is happening now. I got five hundred back from you. My apartment lease was up and you give me a place to stay. Your business is doing so well, *Masha'Allah*, God has paid us back already."

Just after New Year's Day, Joey got a call from the Canadians. They wanted me to fly to Toronto and meet with Chiheb.

I balked.

"I'm not getting on a plane," I said. "I'm not being a dick, but what the fuck are we going to gain from me hanging out with Chiheb? Nothing. There is no imminent threat. I don't understand."

Chiheb wasn't going to do anything without me.

"They need to re-up the wire," Joey said.

Every thirty days prosecutors had to prove to the court that a wiretap was still warranted. They had to show significant progress in the investigation, which was simple when you have a terrorist like Chiheb.

"Bullshit," I said. "They have everything from the New York trip. What more do they want?"

"I know, it doesn't make sense to me either," Joey said. "But that's what they are saying. Maybe Canadian courts are different."

"But they haven't been for the last several months," I said. "There is something going on. If it made one iota of sense to me, I'd be on the next fucking flight out. You know that. But it doesn't make sense. It doesn't. We're not going to acquiesce to this bullshit."

"Fine," Joey said. "I'll go back and tell them."

The Canadians backed off and I stayed in New York. Nelly, Joey, and the team flew to Toronto instead to discuss strategy. Joey called me after the meeting.

"Looks like all the cards are on the table now," Joey said.

"What happened?"

"They revoked Abassi's visa," Joey said.

"Are you fucking kidding me?"

I'm convinced that when I told the Canadians Abassi was a bad guy, they decided to pull his visa. They didn't want this case to drag on any longer. But now we had problems. Abassi wasn't just a loose end; he was a threat to the United States. Revoking his visa didn't protect us. And sooner or later Chiheb was going to find out. This might tip him off to the whole investigation.

"Do I need to come up?"

"Don't come up right now," Joey said. "We're coming back. We'll have a meeting and figure it all out back in New York."

A day later we were all sitting around the conference table overlooking the Hudson. Abassi didn't know his visa was revoked, but when he found out, we planned to invite him to New York instead. Ari wanted to make sure it was worth the effort.

"Is this guy the real deal?" Ari said to me.

Nelly walked Ari through my first meeting with Abassi. We talked through how he flirted with the line, talking about jihad one second and then his nuclear engineering degree the next. He was painting a picture for me to connect the dots. Abassi had Chiheb's brains and beliefs, but he knew how to blend in with the West. He kept his true nature hidden.

"He scares me more than Chiheb," I said when we were done presenting the evidence.

"Enough said," Ari said. "Get it done."

As I was leaving, Ari stopped me. He had a twenty-dollar bill.

"You were right," he said.

I took the cash with a smile.

A few days later, Nelly called me. He and Kenny were getting Abassi cleared to enter the United States.

"Listen, they're breaking my balls," Nelly said. "They want you to reach out to Abassi. They want you to invite him to the States."

"Nelly, do you know what I'm going to say to you right now?"

"I know exactly what you're going to say," he said.

"Tell me what I'm going to say."

"It's going to stink," Nelly said. "It's going to look weird if you call him right now on the heels of his visa getting revoked. All of a sudden he is hearing from you with an invite to New York."

I laughed.

"I couldn't have said it better myself. Tell them I'm not making the call. I'm not sending an e-mail. Trust the technique. Believe me when I tell you, the second he finds out his visa was revoked, I'm going to be his first call."

I got a call from Abassi three days later. He was about to return to Canada when the Canadian Consulate in Tunisia informed him his visa was revoked.

"You won't believe this," he said, his voice sullen and defeated. "I just put my wife on a plane. I couldn't get on the plane. It is haram for her to travel alone, but she had to get back. She had her work and studies."

"What happened?" I asked, acting surprised. "Are you okay, brother?"

"I have no idea," he said, his voice cracking. "They are just telling me my visa was revoked."

"Oh no," I said. "Brother, I already booked my flight to Toronto because I was going to visit Chiheb. We were going to fly out to visit you."

"I know," he said. "I was looking forward to that. They messed my life up. And my brother got into an accident. He is in a coma."

There was real pain in his voice.

"Ahmed, I don't know what to say," I said. "I am praying for you and your family."

I could hear him sniffle as he tried to regain his composure.

"Thank you, Tamer," he said. "It means a lot that I have a friend in you."

I offered to send him money and medicine for his brother and told him to call me if he needed anything. I resisted the urge to invite him to New York. That would seem scripted. But he knew I wanted to help him. The seed was planted.

The next day, I flew to Toronto to babysit Chiheb. The trip was planned and it would be weird if I canceled it. I got to Toronto on February 9 and went straight to the condo on Harrison Garden

Boulevard in North York. When I told Chiheb about Abassi, he dismissed his troubles.

"He shouldn't have gone to Tunisia in the first place," he said. "What a waste of time. He deserves what is happening to him. He did not have to go there. Look what happened. You see what we do? We send two hundred thousand dollars to the brothers and Allah opens doors for us. He goes there to waste time and Allah shuts doors for him. It's amazing."

His rant ended as soon as I took out the thumb drive.

"I have pictures from Times Square," I said. "I was able to get on the rooftop. A friend let me shoot some photos from where CNN was broadcasting."

In reality, the New York City Police Department gave me behind-the-scenes access to the ball drop.

As he looked at the images, Abassi came up again. After visiting the tracks with Jaser, Chiheb was convinced the only way to derail the train was with explosives. We also needed someone to build the bombs for Operation Happy New Year. Abassi gave us that capability.

"What if we bring Abassi to New York?" I said. "We'll vet him in New York, see if he is like-minded, and you can test him."

It was an idea I'd pitched a few months before. Chiheb stopped clicking through the pictures and looked at me.

"For one month," Chiheb said. "One-month visa and no more."

Chiheb started to rub his beard.

"Do it so it is the same time of my two conferences," Chiheb said. "I have a conference in Philadelphia in late March, and then I have to be in San Francisco in early April. Between the conferences we will see if he is truly ready."

"Okay," I said. "I'll invite him next time he contacts me."

I walked into the kitchen to get some water. I was tired of talking about the plots.

The next night we planned to meet Waleed, Jaser's Afghan friend, for dinner. Chiheb said he was close to joining the cell to help with the train plot. The hope was that dinner with us would seal it. Chiheb called him.

Chiheb hung up the phone and looked at me.

"No answer again," he said.

"And you're sure he is like-minded?" I said.

Chiheb nodded.

"Yes," he said. "We had the tax talk and everything. He was ashamed that he still paid his taxes."

"Try him again," I said. "If he doesn't answer, let's just go have dinner."

While Chiheb called again, I did a Yelp search. Waleed never answered. I suspect Jaser told him to stop talking to Chiheb, but I wasn't sure.

"How about the Lobster Trap for dinner?" I said.

"I am expert now," Chiheb said.

It was a Tuesday and the restaurant wasn't crowded. It resembled an old fish house inside. The waitress, a bubbly college student with auburn hair and a smile that made you fall in love with her, brought us both whole lobsters. For whatever reason, Chiheb was normal that night. It wasn't jihadi talk. He'd gotten that out of his system at the condo.

The waitress was joking with us all night. Chiheb's plate was a pile of broken shells by the end of dinner. He got every morsel.

"Wow," she said as she cleared Chiheb's plate. "This lobster didn't stand a chance."

Chiheb smiled.

"I've been traveling the world eating lobsters with my brother," he said. "I am expert now."

We all started laughing.

"You the man," she said, putting her hand up to give Chiheb a high five.

He didn't move except for his fading smile.

"High five?" she said, smiling at him.

His eyes got dark and the jihadi returned.

"No, no, no," he said, turning away from her. "I cannot touch you. You are not my wife."

There he is, I thought.

Her smile turned. She wasn't mad, more embarrassed. She wasn't sure what to do.

"We'll take the check," I said, breaking the tension.

She turned and walked back to the serving station. She left the check on the table without a word and disappeared. I left her a generous tip and we left.

Back home, I sent Abassi an invite to New York via e-mail. Chiheb's blessing was all the cover I needed.

"Why don't you come here? I'll have my lawyers look into your situation. At least you'll be closer to your wife if you come. Maybe she can visit you here. I'll take care of you. You can stay at one of my apartments."

Abassi's response was almost immediate.

"I don't know what to say," he wrote. "I really appreciate it."

Abassi was on his way.

CHAPTER 24

The Sixth Pillar

I merged onto Interstate 95 heading south toward Philadelphia.

It was March 2013. Chiheb had landed at JFK a few hours before, and I was driving him to his conference in Philadelphia. Something was different from the moment I picked him up at the airport. He was quiet. Focused.

"I tried to get an earlier flight," he said as we left New York behind. "But the woman at the American Airlines ticket counter told me I couldn't."

I turned to look at him. He was staring at the highway in front of me.

"Why?" I asked.

"I am flagged," Chiheb said, turning to look at me. "That is what she told me. I could only fly on the ticket I had."

"Really," I said. "That's weird."

Shit. Shit. Shit. Think fast.

"You know what?" I said. "It's because you're an Arab. I'm always getting hassled by security. It's happened to me even with an American passport."

Chiheb shook his head.

"No matter," he said. "Even if they are watching they don't know anything. We are going to need explosives. It is the only way we can complete the work on the train in time."

Enter Abassi. I mentioned he was arriving at the end of the week.

"I hope he knows how lucky he is to have a brother like you," Chiheb said.

"It's not about the recognition or the money," I said. "I just want to make sure he is a like-minded brother."

"He is like-minded," Chiheb said.

"How do you know?" I asked.

"I knew when we met," Chiheb said. "It was a conference like I am going to now. We met the first day and he watched as I left the sessions to pray. He stopped me the second day at lunchtime."

"Why?" I asked. "Didn't he pray too?"

Chiheb tipped his head back like he was watching his memories play out on the roof of the car.

"Yes, of course," Chiheb said. "But he told me, 'Brother, you're leaving this conference to pray, but you're leaving out the most important pillar. That's jihad. It's obligatory. Don't you think for a second you are a true Muslim if you are not following every single pillar and every single obligation Allah has put on you.'"

"Allah bless him," I said. "He is wise."

But there is no sixth pillar. Islam has only five pillars. The first is Shahada—the declaration of faith. There is only one God and Mohammed is his messenger. The second pillar—Salat—requires

Muslims to pray five times a day. The third pillar—Zakat, or charity—requires a Muslim to be charitable, and the fourth is Sawm, fasting during Ramadan. The last pillar is Hajj, the pilgrimage to Mecca for Muslims who are able to do it. Islam's pillars have the same theme: peace, submission, helping the less fortunate.

"Yes," he said. "That night we talked about Sheikh Osama and the brothers overseas. Ahmed talked about how much he admired Mohammed Atta. He wanted to wage jihad too once he finished his studies."

"And now he is almost done," I said. "We have operations for him now."

"Yes," Chiheb said. "But after that conference, I couldn't wait. I didn't care about my studies. That's why I went to Iran. That's why I wanted to fight in Afghanistan. Ahmed showed me the way, but El Massoul showed me how to do jihad. But I fear he loves this world too much. We will test him. It will be a surprise that I am here too."

"I Skyped with Abassi last week," I said. "I told him you're coming and we'd all meet in New York."

Chiheb sighed.

"It's no secret," Chiheb said. "I just didn't feel there was a need to say anything. He is coming here for a reason and that reason is to find out if he is ready to help now."

I had planned to prep Chiheb to recruit Abassi on the ride to Philadelphia, but it was the opposite. He was getting me ready.

"I have two projects—one in the United States and one in Canada—that need attention," Chiheb said. "We need his skills. He can do whatever he wants long-term. But I need explosives for Operation Happy New Year and Operation Fishing."

"And we need to meet the American sleeper," I said. "Have you heard from El Massoul?"

Chiheb looked away.

"No," he said. "I sent a message before I left but got nothing back. They are very careful. We must be patient."

I had already burned through all of my patience. The Canadians had pulled Abassi's visa. The ticket agent had told Chiheb he was flagged. It was only a matter of time before the Canadians or FBI management decided the case was over.

I slapped the wheel in frustration. Chiheb looked at me.

"How many of our brothers have died in the last year?" I said, a hint of anger in my voice. "How many infidels? It's too lopsided. They need to know what an amazing job you've done. It would take anyone else years to accomplish what you've done in so little time. Think about it. You've got the money. You've got like-minded brothers. You're the greatest cell leader they've ever sent over, and they're taking their time responding. We're ready. We've got another operation. You have access to the United States. You can do anything and everything. Money is no object. And they can't respond to an e-mail because they are busy fighting in Syria? In Afghanistan?"

"You're right, brother," Chiheb said.

I wanted him to think al Qaeda was failing him.

"You are our leader," I said. "You have the brains. You have the bomb maker. The money. We need direction now more than ever."

I let that sink in a bit. Chiheb's body language changed. He sat up in his seat. He stopped fidgeting.

"How ironic is it that your brother here is the money guy and the man who trained you happens to be their financier?" I said. "Don't you think we should meet or talk or something? Don't you think you should find a way to connect us? Don't you think he needs to know you have a Tamer?"

"You are absolutely right," Chiheb said. "I will send a strong message to Abu Hamza tonight."

I took Chiheb right to his hotel outside of Philadelphia. As he waited to check in, he took out an envelope and tried to hand it to me. I wanted to get it on tape, so I scanned the hotel and spotted some security guards standing near the front desk.

"Hold up," I said, nodding toward the security guards.

Chiheb slid the envelope back into his bag. When we got to his room, he took it out and handed it to me. I opened it and saw a thick stack of American one-hundred-dollar bills.

"It is three thousand dollars," he said. "I want it to go to the brothers in Mali if Uncle Ibrahim can get it there. If not, he can have it for our brothers."

The French intervention in Mali was in the news.

"May Allah bless you," I said. "I will send it to him with my next shipment."

I knew not to argue with him anymore. I took a mobile phone out of my backpack and handed it to him.

"I wasn't sure if your phone worked in the United States, so I got you one," I said. "My number is programmed in. So is Ahmed's. I got him a phone too."

"Thank you, brother," Chiheb said, putting the phone on the bureau.

We prayed and then I gathered my things to leave. I had to get back to New York. Chiheb walked me to the door.

"Make Ahmed comfortable when he arrives, but don't talk about the projects until I arrive on Thursday," he said.

"Of course," I said. "Do you need anything else before I head back to New York?"

Chiheb gave me a hug.

"No, brother," he said. "I'm eating. I'm sleeping. I'm praying. I have everything I need."

Back in New York, Nelly and the team were tracking Abassi as he left Tunisia for Paris. After a layover there, he got on a plane to New York. His flight landed around eight in the evening, but he didn't emerge from customs until close to ten. He looked tired. His shoulders slumped and his eyes were dead. He barely had enough energy to shuffle his feet forward.

I greeted him with a hug and ushered him to my waiting Mercedes. He climbed into the passenger side while I put his suitcase in the back. When I climbed into the driver's seat, he was riffling through the glove box. He shut it and ran his hands over the visor and poked his fingers in the air vents.

"What's wrong?" I said.

"They are listening," he said. "They are watching me."

"Who?"

"The Canadians," he said. "The Americans. Everyone."

"Be calm, brother," I said.

Abassi ignored me. The confident man I met in Quebec City was a distant memory.

"They interviewed me at every stop," he said. "Security guards checked my bags over and over again. In Paris, the Americans almost didn't let me on the plane."

"It has happened to me," I said. "They are always looking at us because we're Arabs."

"No, this was different," Abassi said. "A woman in Paris said I wasn't going anywhere until she spoke to someone in Washington."

"How do you know?"

"I know," he said. "I overheard. Be careful of everything and everyone."

All day his wife was texting me from Quebec City asking if he had arrived. I promised to call her as soon as he did. I dialed her number on his new cell phone. I wasn't about to hand him a phone cold. His wife gave me a reason to offer it to him.

"Someone wants to talk to you," I said as the phone rang. "It's your wife. She has been texting me and calling me."

He took the phone and relaxed when he heard her voice.

"I'm good," he said. "I'm just so tired."

When he went to hand the phone back, I told him to keep it.

"It's yours, brother," I said. "I got one for you and Chiheb from my company while you're here in the States."

Abassi looked at the phone for a second and then slipped it into his pocket.

"My number and Chiheb's number are already programmed," I said. "So is your wife's. Feel free to call her when you want."

"May Allah reward you for your good deeds," he said.

He sat in silence as we drove into Manhattan. If he was impressed with the scenery, he didn't show it. His eyes darted between looking out of the windshield and looking for microphones in the car.

"I still don't understand what happened with your visa," I said, trying to get him to talk.

"It's a long story," Abassi said. "We'll get into that when we get back to the house."

He was still angry.

"It is haram for her to travel alone," he said. "But she had to go. She is almost done with her studies. She had to return."

"You had no choice," I said. "I almost left this country for good after my mother died, but my uncle convinced me to stay. But that is a story for another time. You're tired. We can talk later."

I got him settled in the same apartment building near Ground Zero where Chiheb stayed and left him to sleep off his jet lag.

"I will come by tomorrow," I said. "I'll take you out to a nice dinner."

Chiheb called me the next day. I was on my way to pick up Abassi.

"Talk to him about the projects, but don't give him any money," he said. "Remember, he is a good brother. He can be trusted, but what is important is he wants to help with our projects."

"Okay," I said. "Do you need me to set up a ride back to New York?"

"No," he said. "I met an Iranian brother that will be traveling to New York on Thursday. He offered me a ride."

I stifled a laugh. It wasn't a coincidence that Chiheb tried to contact El Massoul in Iran when he got to Philadelphia and magically an Iranian was available to drive him to New York. It wasn't the FBI. I guess someone else was keeping tabs on him too.

"Fine," I said. "See you Thursday."

It was prayer time when I arrived at Abassi's apartment. I did the call and Abassi led the prayers. When we were done, Abassi asked me about my mother and uncle.

"What did you mean that you almost weren't going to be in this country?" he asked. "What happened?"

I tried to divert the conversation because I didn't feel that he was ready for my point of radicalization, but he wasn't having it. It was clear he wasn't going to dinner until we talked about it. I told him how my mother got sick and the doctors failed her. It was a vanilla version of the story. I didn't get emotional like with Chiheb, because it was clear Abassi wasn't interested in the details. He was interrogating me. Several times he stopped me and we went back over the details.

When I was done, he opened up a bit more. We read from the Quran and a sura about the seven levels of heaven and how a Muslim can never truly understand the beauty of paradise. From time to time, Allah sent down jinns to watch and listen to Muslims. These jinns watch everyone, but they can never know what the true believers are up to because they are the ones on the path of Allah. I learned the sura as a kid growing up. It warned Muslims the devil was always around us and tempting us and that the true believers would never give in to temptation. But Abassi got another message from it.

"Tamer, as we sit here on the floor, between you and me right now, there are millions and millions of bacteria like the jinns all around us," he said. "We can't see them, but we know they're there. We need to take precautions to protect ourselves from these germs, but they won't alter our course."

In his version, the jinns were the American government. He was warning me to be careful. We were getting back to the guy I met in Canada. As we were leaving the apartment, he stopped just out front and stared at the construction of One World Trade Center towering above us.

"Tamer, I can't believe my apartment is only a few meters away from Ground Zero," he said.

I could see his body language change. He no longer slumped. It was like he got energy from being so close to al Qaeda's major attack. It was sickening.

"It's been over ten years," I said. "They're still rebuilding."

"I'd really like to see the memorial and spend some time there," he said.

I shrugged but didn't say anything. That was the last place in the world I wanted to take him.

Dinner was uneventful except that with each passing hour the old Abassi started to come back. When a well-dressed woman in a dress walked by the table, he turned away and shook his head. As we were leaving, a man with liquor on his breath bumped into us. The man apologized, but I heard Abassi mumble "I ask the magnificent Allah's forgiveness" as he passed.

We drove back to my apartment near Times Square. It was too cold to walk. I let the ride pass in silence. His eyes were fixed on all the lights and sounds. Unlike Chiheb, he didn't see evil. He just saw the grandeur of New York and he liked it.

I made tea at my apartment while he looked around. I handed him a cup as he admired a picture of the Kaaba hanging on the wall. Muslims pray facing the Kaaba, a square building that sits in the middle of Al-Masjid al-Haram mosque in Mecca. It is considered the "House of Allah" and one of Islam's most sacred sites.

"My wife's parents have the same picture in their house in Tunisia," Abassi said.

He scrolled through his phone to show me a photo. As he was scrolling through the pictures, he paused. A strange look came over his face.

"Are you looking at some wedding pictures?"

"You won't believe what I'm looking at," he said.

I leaned over and he showed me his phone. It was a picture of bin Laden. The terrorist leader was bathed in an angelic light.

"There was a poster in Quebec City years ago," Abassi said. "Some French author said he must die. I contemplated finding that author and killing him. I took a photo of the poster to always remind me."

I was happy that everyone listening to our conversation in the command center heard him idolize Osama bin Laden. This was the Abassi I'd met in Quebec City. This was the guy I'd warned the Canadians about. He was warming up just in time for Chiheb to arrive the next day.

The FBI got Chiheb an apartment in the same building as Abassi. After a dinner at the Palm—Chiheb had the lobster—we went back to my apartment in midtown to talk. Chiheb asked me to take out my passport. He wanted to show it to Abassi.

"Look at my passport," Chiheb said, putting it on the table between us. "Look when I was in Iran."

Abassi picked up his passport and looked at the entry stamps. Chiheb nodded at me to show him my passport.

"Look at Tamer's now," Chiheb said. "He was in the Middle East at the same time. He was there helping the brothers. I was there training. It was Allah's will that we were both there."

Abassi handed us our passports back.

"That is who we are," Chiheb said.

"*Masha'Allah*," Abassi said.

But he wasn't all that impressed. It was more of a *so what?*

The next night Chiheb laid out both plots. He wanted Abassi to make the bombs. But Abassi stayed silent. He let Chiheb talk but didn't agree to help. He was still spooked. The clock was ticking. If the Abassi I met in Quebec City didn't fully reveal himself, we didn't have a case.

CHAPTER 25

Eyes of Allah

Abassi invited us to his apartment the next day. He wanted to talk. For the past several days he and Chiheb had been in a constant fight. Chiheb thought Abassi was of true mind and heart for the cause, but didn't agree with waiting. He had orders from overseas and wanted to act. But when I got to Abassi's apartment, something was different.

"You're a scientist," Abassi told Chiheb. "You work with hazardous materials. You work with deadly diseases. You can get some. We can grow it in our own lab. Take it to a reservoir and put the virus in the water. It will mutate and grow on its own. They'll drink it and we'll have thousands of dead Americans."

The Abassi I met in Quebec City finally had arrived. Even Chiheb was impressed. But it was the way Abassi explained the plot. He laid it out like someone sharing a cookie recipe. It was no big deal to either of them, and I sat there pretending to be impressed, but I was sick to my stomach.

"Look what I can come up with in a couple of days," Abassi said. "Imagine if we take our time what we could accomplish."

I realized we were at an impasse. Both wanted to kill Americans but disagreed how. I needed a change of scenery, so after dinner I took them to a small hookah bar on the east side near New York University. The scene was pretty mellow. There were a few students studying. A group was sitting at one table smoking hookah. We found a table near the back and ordered tea and baklava.

Abassi sat on a bench with his back to the wall. His legs were crossed and he wagged his foot up and down as he spoke. Abassi was holding court and looked very comfortable as we smoked and talked.

Chiheb was at the head of the table to his right. He was leaning forward like some anxious freak. He didn't smoke. The hookah bar wasn't on the path of Allah. In his mind, we were wasting time.

I was half listening to Abassi as I smoked.

"The U.S. government can never outsmart me," Abassi said, taking a long pull off the hookah and sending a stream of smoke into the air above his head. "I know the FBI is always watching."

He was looking at me as he spoke. I put a puzzled look on my face. Was he suggesting that I might be an informant for the FBI? I was exhausted with all the fighting between him and Chiheb. I needed to put Abassi on the defensive.

"Are you kidding me right now?" I said, keeping my voice measured but stern. "Is this your way of telling me that you are an informant for the FBI?"

I looked around the hookah bar like FBI agents were lurking around every corner. Abassi didn't know what to say. Chiheb looked at me with a puzzled expression. This was the first time he'd seen me this upset. I let the weird energy crackle between us.

Then I snapped.

"Do you have any idea how important my company is to the Muslim Ummah?" I said, staring at Abassi. "Are you trying to tell me that you are bringing them to my door?"

Chiheb tried to interrupt me.

"Tamer . . ."

The other patrons started to notice our table. I kept my gaze locked on Abassi as I put my hand up for Chiheb to stop talking. Abassi uncrossed his legs and put both feet on the floor.

"Tamer, that's not at all what I was saying," he said, lowering his voice. "I would never—"

I stood up and smashed the small tea glass against the wall. I heard someone behind me gasp. Abassi and Chiheb recoiled as I threw a hundred-dollar bill on the table.

"Find your own way home," I said.

This was my last-ditch effort to turn the tables on him. I wasn't sure if it would work, but we were out of options.

I stormed out of the hookah bar and climbed into my car. Chiheb called my cell phone before I arrived at the safe house.

"I'm sorry," I said.

"Don't worry, brother," he said. "I understand. We took a cab home. Ahmed was upset."

"Are you sure about him?" I said. "I don't know if he is a like-minded brother."

"He is," Chiheb said. "But he isn't worth it."

Chiheb wanted to break ties with Abassi, but I still had work to do with him. We didn't have enough to charge him. I couldn't cut him loose.

"Okay," I said. "I know you have work to do for school. I'll spend some time with him tomorrow morning. I will call you after."

The team met me at a hotel suite in midtown. As I told them what happened in the hookah bar, Abassi called me several times. I ignored the calls.

"You should answer it," Nelly said after the third call.

I refused. I wanted him to sweat it out. He was isolated in a strange city. His benefactor just rejected him. Any reunion with his wife felt remote. He was freaking out.

Joey smirked when Abassi called again.

"I love the play," Joey said. "Let him stew in it a bit more."

After the fifth call, I answered. I could hear the fear in Abassi's voice as he apologized. He asked me to come by his apartment to talk. I met him outside the building. He got into the passenger seat and apologized.

"Put yourself in my place," he said. "A few months ago, I was finishing up my doctorate and getting married. My life was perfect. Then Canada takes away my visa. I'm away from my wife. I don't know if I will get my degree. My brother is dying. The FBI almost doesn't let me come to New York. I have no idea what is happening and didn't know who I could trust."

He reassured me over and over that he would never betray me to the FBI, because then he would have to answer to Allah.

"Only Allah knows what is truly in a man's heart," he said.

But even his apology felt like a threat.

The next day, I brought breakfast to his apartment. He was wide awake and working on both laptops. He ignored the breakfast and ushered me over to the computers. On the screens were scientific journals and stories about Mohammed Atta. Abassi was studying the engineering behind how the steel in the World Trade Center towers melted. He talked about jet fuel and melting points. Most of it went over my head.

"The brilliance of that attack was in its simplicity," Abassi said.

Abassi wanted to top it. Chiheb's plans weren't big enough.

"We could do much bigger things that would truly make a difference," he said.

I wanted to foster his excitement and keep him on track, so I asked him if he still wanted to go see Ground Zero. I had resisted in the past, but he refused to let it go. I ran it by FBI executive management. They refused at first but finally gave me the green light after the New York police commissioner's office got on board.

Abassi stopped talking and smiled. He looked like a kid who was just told he was going to Disney World.

"Right now?" he said.

"Let's go."

As we walked through the memorial, a profound sense of loss came over me. It was my first time and I had to hold back tears. I had lost friends, and I didn't want to be there with him. The other tourists had solemn looks on their faces. But as Abassi looked at each plaque detailing the attack, a different look came over his face. It wasn't a smile. It was pride.

My tears turned to rage. I felt the same emotions and feelings I had when Chiheb put his arm around me and told me New York needed another 9/11. But I didn't have time to be unprofessional.

Abassi walked over to the two pools where the towers once stood and looked at all the names engraved on them. He then looked up to the sky as if he was imagining where the towers once stood. In his mind's eye, he could see the planes and the fire. He couldn't hide his smile now. He handed me his phone and asked me to take a picture of him in front of the pools. I handed the phone back to him.

"I don't think we're allowed to take pictures here," I said.

Abassi looked around the memorial.

"They're taking pictures," he said, pointing out some tourists snapping photos with their phones.

I needed this moment to be over, so I didn't argue and snapped a picture. I later told Nelly that he needed to delete that image after we locked Abassi up.

I went into the bathroom as soon as we got back to his apartment. I threw some water on my face and gathered myself. When I came out, he couldn't control his excitement.

"I was part of a study group in Tunisia," he said. "It was during the Arab Spring. One of the brothers from the group is here."

"In New York?" I said.

"Yes," Abassi said. "He is a taxi driver but he is visiting family back in Tunisia. Another is studying in Atlanta. I haven't been able to reach them, but I did talk to a brother studying computer science in Las Vegas."

Abassi had a contact with al Nusra—an al Qaeda offshoot—in Jordan. He wanted to stay in the United States to restart the study group. The underground groups were breeding grounds for dissent in the Middle East, but Abassi wanted this one to be a terrorist cell.

"I will need a visa," he said. "And we can get all of the like-minded brothers together. I will live here, pretending to work for your company while I prepare the attacks."

I left his apartment with a promise to return and take him to dinner. I went over to the operations center so that I could meet with Ari and the team. Nelly and I had an *I told you so* look on our faces when we all sat down to review my conversations with Abassi.

The assistant U.S. attorney didn't share our look.

"He didn't break any laws," he said after we were done laying out the evidence. "His thoughts and opinions, no matter how disgusting, aren't illegal. He hasn't met any elements of any crime. You have more work to do."

I was exhausted. The last place I wanted to be was back at his apartment. Then I got a call from Chiheb. He was done working and wanted me to meet him at Abassi's apartment, where he had spent most of the afternoon. Abassi went into the kitchen to make tea for us when I arrived. As he left the room, Chiheb leaned over and whispered to me.

"I got all of the scientific knowledge that I needed from him," he said. "We are good now."

The conversations must have provided Chiheb with enough details that he thought we didn't need Abassi's expertise anymore. Nothing Abassi said was going to convince Chiheb to work with him.

But I needed him to talk. I needed Abassi to commit to a terrorist act and make an overt act toward it. We had his intentions on tape, but I needed more for a charge.

"Please let him speak," I said. "Then we'll make a determination together."

Abassi returned and we gave him the pulpit. I was having Jaser flashbacks. Abassi began his sermon by explaining the religious justification for committing jihad. Chiheb made comments but let

Abassi speak for the most part. When Abassi said we were three travelers so our prayers could be shortened, Chiheb interrupted.

"Tamer is not a traveler," he said. "This is his home."

When you're traveling, you can combine your prayers and they are shortened.

"Would you please just let the man finish his thought process?" I said, staring down Chiheb. "Let him talk, Chiheb. Stop interrupting and nitpicking every single thing he says. You're harping on shit that we don't need to talk about right now."

Chiheb sat back in his chair and folded his arms.

"Fine," he said. "I will just sit here and not say anything."

Abassi took a sip of tea. He had my undivided attention and knew it.

"You see?" Abassi said. "That's what I'm talking about."

Abassi had pages of notes, but he skipped to point seven after Chiheb's outburst.

"How can we do these projects and expect not to get killed or arrested with irrational behavior like this?" Abassi said, staring at Chiheb. "If you don't tone it down we all will get captured or killed before our work is done."

Abassi waved me over to the laptops set up on the desk. How to build a bomb, how to deliver weapons of mass destruction, how to commit mass killings on U.S. soil.

Everyone was quiet.

"I need to evaluate Chiheb's orders in an effort to coordinate our efforts," he said.

It was an olive branch to Chiheb. By now it was midnight, and I told them I had a meeting tomorrow. Really I just wanted to leave. I thanked Abassi for the tea and told him we'd talk in the morning.

Chiheb left with me. He had a lot of work to do before he went to San Francisco for his conference. We walked up to his apartment together. I knew I had to make up with him now. Once in his apartment, I apologized.

"Tamer, you have to see that he is of this *Dunya*," he said. "I agree with what he is saying, but I believe that he is just buying time to enjoy this world and its possessions."

"Let me ask you something, Chiheb," I said. "If I told you that there was a Jew that could supply us with the bombs we needed for Operation Happy New Year, would you tell me to buy them from him?"

Chiheb considered my question for a minute.

"I would tell you to buy them," he said.

"Then how can you dismiss another Muslim, the one who started you on your path, so quickly?"

"Tamer, you should have seen him after you yelled at him," Chiheb said. "We each went to our own apartments and before I could sit down, he was at my door. He was so upset. He started giving me all of the technical stuff about the projects. That was the proof that he was of this *Dunya* and not the afterlife."

"Sincerity is only in the eyes of Allah," I said. "While you are in San Francisco, I will spend some time with him. I will properly vet him, okay?"

I said it like I was asking his permission. I wanted him to know that he was still in charge.

"I will report back to you and you will ultimately make the final determination," I said.

As I was leaving, I stopped at the door. I wanted to make sure Chiheb knew I was still with him.

"Don't be mad at me, brother," I said. "I lost my cool there a little bit."

Chiheb put his arm on my shoulder.

"I could never be mad at my brother," he said. "The only time I could be mad at you is if I felt that you were losing your sincerity."

"Am I?"

"No," he said. "I'm just saying that that's the only time I will ever be mad at you."

Stay on the path of Allah. That was his shot across the bow.

CHAPTER 26

Stay True to Islam

Chiheb called me the next morning distraught.

He had stayed up the whole night thinking about Abassi and our projects.

"Because we can't see eye to eye, how about I send an e-mail to Abu Hamza to ask his advice?"

Chiheb wanted him to be the judge.

"I would love to hear his thoughts on the matter," I said.

Chiheb didn't say anything for a few moments. I could hear him breathing. Finally, he told me he would call me back. A half hour later, he called and read me a message in Arabic.

As Salamu Alaikum, my Grandfather.

I have a close friend that I like. He has a very big company and a lot of money, and he uses that money to help the Children of the Mother. His opinion is like my opinion and your opinion. I started with him the travel of research of sincere workers. We found a worker that has a difficult material condition and a new marriage. I agree with my friend regarding the two points regarding the state of this worker. One, he has some of this Dunya in his heart and he is not sincere one hundred percent. And two, he has ideas and knowledge that he announced and can benefit the Children of the Mother. And I disagree with my beloved friend about the way to deal with this worker. I say it's necessary to put the worker far from our path because he lacks sincerity and he can cause our destruction if he has serious problems or tests. My friend says it's necessary to use him because the Children of the Mother have an emergent need of workers particularly if this worker has good ideas and is able to help. Please, my grandfather, look carefully on the issue and judge between us what is right. And if the issue is difficult with you, no problem if you take the opinion of someone that you presume is able to give the solution. The disagreement comes between me and this friend. And I am afraid that these issues will go to an ending that we don't want.

"What did you mean by the last sentence?" I asked.

"Many bad things can happen, for example, our relationship could be broken, our work can be disturbed, Ahmed could give us up to authorities or hurt us," Chiheb said, exasperated by the argument. "What if he gets arrested by the police or FBI? What if he gives you to them? I cannot have that."

Then it dawned on me. He was worried about me. Not because

of any loyalty to me personally, but because of what he believed I meant to the mujahideen overseas.

"Don't worry," I said. "Ahmed could tell the FBI anything he wanted. All I did was sponsor a brother to come in to help me with my company. The FBI can never pin anything on me. They could never know my true intentions."

After we hung up, Chiheb sent the e-mail. Later that day, I picked him up outside of his apartment. He was flying to San Francisco for a conference. I grabbed him and gave him a big hug.

"I want you to know that I'm with you, dear brother," I said as I held him. "We're together no matter what."

Chiheb looked at me with a reassured expression on his face. We got in the car and I merged with the traffic heading uptown. I needed him to believe that I was still on Team Chiheb and that he didn't need to go anywhere or do anything without letting me know first.

"You are a trained al Qaeda sleeper and I am just a business-man," I said. "You gave Ahmed all the tests and he is not sincere. He is of this world and not true of heart."

"Yes," Chiheb said, his chest puffing out. "He cares too much for this world."

But Chiheb said I should test him while he was in San Francisco. He wanted me to find his true heart and make sure Abassi understood Chiheb was in charge.

"Even though I am not a trained al Qaeda operative, I promise I will take this week to give Ahmed my businessman test. I will test him. Even though you haven't heard from Grandfather yet."

Chiheb got quiet. I knew he had received an e-mail response

from Abu Hamza. Nelly had offered to let me read it, but I passed. I wanted Chiheb to tell me. I needed my reaction to be natural.

"Tell me something, brother," I said. "Twenty-four hours ago, you were dead set against Ahmed. Now you're giving me specific instructions on how to properly vet him and to make sure he knows who is in charge. What's changed?"

Chiheb smiled and looked away.

"You know me too well, brother," he said. "Grandfather responded to me."

I pretended to be upset with him.

"How could you keep that from me?"

"I had no intention of keeping that from you," he said. "I just didn't feel like the time was right for me to tell you. I don't want to tell you exactly what he said yet, but I will tell you when the time is right."

"Has Abu Hamza ever responded to any of your e-mails this quickly?"

Chiheb shook his head no.

"That's because this is the first time you ever asked him about something of substance," I said. "The first time you weren't whining about talking to El Massoul or the identity of the American sleeper. You weren't needy. You presented him with a well-thought-out argument while pointing out the fact that you now have financial support to fulfill your mission and like-minded brothers around you ready to strike. In his eyes, Chiheb, you are a good worker. Look at all that you have accomplished in one year. That's the image they have of you right now. Don't taint that image with an e-mail littered with counterpoints. Don't come across as combative or insubordinate."

He looked out the window.

"I'm not going to send anything to him until I run it by you," he said.

"Maybe if Abu Hamza knew that you had unfettered access to the West, he would consider hooking you up with the American sleeper," I said. "Right now, he is the one you are in contact with and he is the one that will give you further direction."

Chiheb reminded me Abu Hamza didn't know his location. It was forbidden under El Massoul's rules. But the seed was planted.

He needed a reason to justify breaking operational protocols for the greater good. Chiheb called me from his hotel room in San Francisco later that night. He read me Abu Hamza's e-mail response in Arabic:

My generous brother,

As Salamu Alaikum Wa Rahmat'Allah Wa Barakatu

Thank God for your safety. Thanks to Allah, we are doing well and in good health. I am busy these days in the transportation of the families of the Children of the Mother to some of the liberated countries close to you [meaning Tunisia and not the United States].

Concerning the use of the brother, my generous brother, if we find a person which inside him there is good for Islam and Muslims, we benefit from him according to the need with these difficult conditions and the lack of sincere men who have passed the conditions and who have succeeded the test. And this dear brother, he has the right to use the worker and you should behave with the worker with good behavior to let him ripen and reach a place that he's ready to sacrifice himself for this sake.

We have tested this method many times; replacing men from the beginning is very harmful and brings mistakes. The best thing is to advise them and show them the path and that this is the life. This is the biography of Mohammed, peace be upon him.

More important is to take benefit from this brother just according to the need to allow yourself to bring the good for him. And, insha'Allah in the future, he will be a sincere brother for you.

May Allah give you success. Give Salam to this dear brother, our new friend.

As Salamu Alaikum Wa Rahmat'Allah Wa Barakatu

It was clear that Abu Hamza agreed with me. The only thing that Chiheb was happy about in this e-mail was the fact that Abu Hamza sent me greetings and appreciation for my efforts to the cause. Chiheb still wanted to argue against using Abassi, but I cut him off.

"Don't worry about that right now," I said. "We have his attention. Ask about the American sleeper."

He sent out the following e-mail to Abu Hamza:

As Salamu Alaikum my Grandfather,

The brother who traveled and didn't return back informed me before that one Child of the Mother is staying now in America. Do you know him or know the address of that Child? My beloved friend wants very much to enter the Children of the Mother to America through his big company. If you or anyone else know of Children of the Mother in Jordan, Egypt, or something like that that are trained to produce sweets or are ready to get the training, please send me their names and addresses with the three brothers.

May Allah reward you.

When Chiheb was done reading, I asked what he meant by the "three brothers" comment.

"That is how many brothers I would like," he said, meaning he was looking to recruit three more men to his plots.

"Okay," I said. "Call me when you hear back from him."

I had to focus my attention on Abassi. The next day, I met with the team and the assistant U.S. attorney. Unlike in past meetings, the assistant U.S. attorney was upbeat. Even happy. Abassi had opened the door when we talked at his apartment after visiting the September 11 memorial.

"When Abassi suggested that you help him get a visa to stay in this country under false pretenses, specifically for facilitating acts of international terrorism, that is a serious charge," the assistant U.S. attorney said.

"It's like how they got Al Capone," I said. "Tax evasion instead of murder."

"Exactly," the assistant U.S. attorney said.

It wasn't my first choice. Abassi was a dangerous guy. I wanted him charged with terrorism, but it was better than nothing.

"What's the penalty?" I asked.

"It carries a twenty-five-year sentence."

That sealed it for me. We talked about getting the final pieces of evidence the rest of the meeting. I was scheduled to get together with Abassi the following day. His visa was my first order of business.

"You said a lot to me this past week," I said after we'd met up at his apartment. "Where do we begin?"

"My visa," Abassi said. "I can get the application. Can your company be the sponsor?"

I was hoping he'd say that.

"I spoke with Farris," Abassi said. "He is studying computer science in Las Vegas."

"Should we go see him?" I asked.

"Absolutely," Abassi said.

During the course of the next two weeks, Abassi got the necessary paperwork for his visa application. He lied about his purpose for obtaining it and told me of his plans to recruit like-minded brothers to plan and carry out multiple terrorist attacks across the United States. All of the elements of the crime were met. But I didn't want any confusion as to what was happening. I sat down with him before he signed the documents and did an abridged Christian burial speech.

"Are you sure about this?" I said. "You're lying on federal

documents here. Maybe you should actually get a job and work for my company for real?"

Abassi didn't want to work unless it was on a terrorist attack.

"This is the only way to accomplish our mission," he said.

As he signed the documents, I felt a sense of relief. He mailed the applications out himself, and our charges for visa fraud with a terrorism enhancement were secured.

A few days later, we flew to Las Vegas to meet his "like-minded" brother from the study group. We checked into our suites at the Venetian. Kenny, Johnny, and Joey took a room on the hotel's top floor. We don't like the agents to have rooms in the same hotel as the target, but it was the best we could do on short notice. Nelly stayed behind to finish Abassi's arrest warrant.

Abassi and I met Farris that night in Abassi's suite. He was tall with a thin beard, olive skin, and short-cropped hair. His khakis and shirt were baggy in an attempt to hide his bulging muscles. His English was very good. *Shit,* I thought. This guy was smooth and blended in perfectly.

After we prayed, we sat on the floor and talked. Abassi and Farris caught up. Abassi gave him a quick rundown of what happened with his visa. He was spewing venom about the evils of the West, but Farris never echoed his sentiments. I couldn't tell if he was just being careful.

The next morning, I received an e-mail from Chiheb.

"Call me right away, brother," it read.

Chiheb was back from San Francisco. He was staying at a friend's apartment—who was also an RCMP undercover—in Montreal. I called his cell.

"Tamer, Gidou [Grandfather] sent me an e-mail," he said, the excitement forcing his voice to rise to an uncomfortable level. "He has agreed to meet with us and give us everything that we need."

"Calm down, brother," I said. "What do you mean?"

"Abu Hamza wants us to join forces with the American Child of the Mother so that we could accomplish our mission," he said. "I told him we were lacking proper guidance."

I asked Chiheb to read me the e-mail from Abu Hamza.

> My dear brother, we are very proud of the work you have ac-
> complished. We believe it is time for you to be united with the
> Child of the Mother by you. I am inviting you and your beloved
> friend to meet with us in Dubai as soon as you are able to
> travel. Insha'Allah, we will give you all that you need.

"We need to plan a trip to Dubai now," Chiheb said.

"Is the American sleeper there?" I asked.

"They won't give me that information over the phone or through e-mail," he said.

"So who are we meeting?"

"Abu Hamza," he said.

"I'm in Vegas," I said. "But when I get back to New York in a few days we can book a trip."

"Hurry," he said.

I hung up and called Nelly. He had the e-mail and was waiting for the translation. I filled him in on my call with Chiheb.

"Holy fuck," he said.

Nelly went to meet with FBI executive management about the latest development while the Canadians were also digesting the e-mail. This part is pure speculation on my part, but I know the Canadians got this e-mail as well and they weren't going to let Chiheb go to Dubai. They had their own agenda that wouldn't come into focus for a few more days.

The next three nights I spent with Abassi and Farris, but my mind was in Dubai. We had dinner, walked the Strip, and prayed. When we were in private, Abassi preached about the sixth pillar of Islam. He started out relatively vanilla the first night and then progressed rather quickly with each conversation. Farris would argue about the justification of killing innocents. I mainly sat quietly and chimed in only when asked. I wanted Abassi to do his thing, and I needed to gauge Farris's true feelings. On our last night, Abassi told me that he planned on pushing Farris hard.

"What happened to that guy I knew back in Tunisia? Where is that fire?" Abassi asked Farris.

"My dear brother, we were stupid kids angry at the Tunisian government," Farris said.

"Fuck the Tunisian government," he said. "It was never about them. It's about our religion and every Muslim's obligation."

Abassi told Farris he was resurrecting the study group to carry out attacks on the West. But Farris wasn't buying it. He kept shaking his head as Abassi spoke.

"Nowhere in the Quran does it justify taking innocent lives," Farris said. "No matter what."

Abassi just stared at his friend. "You are very, very wrong," he said.

I had seen enough. Farris wasn't a threat.

"I'm hungry," I said. "Who wants to get dinner?"

The buffet was closed, so we headed for the first open restaurant. I held the heavy glass doors of L'Atelier De Joël Robuchon for

Farris and Abassi. As soon as the doors shut behind us, the cacophony of slot machines and gamblers disappeared. There was red velvet everywhere. A hostess greeted me.

"Reservations?"

I looked around the dining room. The place was almost empty.

"Do we need one?"

She smiled politely.

"It will be one minute," she said, ushering us into the lounge. The dining room's red velvet turned into purple suede. The couches looked so nice I couldn't sit on them. Abassi and Farris checked the menu.

"Tamer, I think this place is too expensive," Farris said. "Maybe we should go somewhere else?"

"Don't be ridiculous," I said. "It's tax-deductible."

Kenny, the co–case agent, still laughs about that line, especially after we were warned to keep costs down on the trip. The case had already blown past its budget by tens of thousands of dollars.

Farris looked at Abassi, who just smiled. He liked having a powerful friend. Price didn't matter to Tamer. The hostess brought us to a table near the front of the restaurant. Dinner was surprisingly pleasant. Abassi tried to sprinkle in some jihad, but it was clear that neither I nor Farris was in the mood. The bill was more than a thousand dollars. No alcohol. FBI management was going to lose their shit.

On the way back to the room, Abassi stopped to use the bathroom. Farris grabbed my arm and pulled me away. He wanted to be out of earshot when Abassi emerged.

"Tamer, I want you to know that it was truly a pleasure meeting you and spending time with you, dear brother," he said. "You will always have a brother here in Vegas if you ever need anything. Anything at all."

I told him the same thing, but he cut me off with a squeeze of my arm. He looked me in the eye. This wasn't about pleasantries.

"Ahmed is a very angry and confused brother," Farris said. "Don't let him take your religion. Stay true to Islam."

It took all my training to keep me from hugging him.

That night I debriefed the team at the Venetian, but no one was thinking about Vegas. All our minds were with Attorney General Eric Holder and his meeting with the Canadian prime minister. After learning about the e-mail, the administration had sent him to Ottawa to talk with the RCMP about a Dubai trip.

Joey checked in with Headquarters before we ended the debrief.

"We won't know until tomorrow morning before our flight," Joey said, wrapping up the meeting.

My mind was already planning the overseas operation.

CHAPTER 27

The End

The next morning the whole team met in the suite. We were hanging around bullshitting when Kenny got the call from Headquarters.

We all watched him talk, trying to read his body language. He said little. His body language was neutral. A bad feeling fell over me. Kenny thanked the person on the other side of the call and hung up.

"It's over," he said. "The Canadians are executing their arrest and search warrants. They're going to wait until you and Abassi get to JFK. Nelly is heading the arrest team in New York."

I went numb.

It was April 22, 2013. The week before, two homemade bombs had detonated twelve seconds apart near the finish line of the annual Boston Marathon. Chechen-American brothers Dzhokhar Tsarnaev and Tamerlan Tsarnaev killed three people and injured hundreds of others.

Everyone was on edge. No one wanted to let a terrorist slip out of our grasp.

"They are aware of the latest intel about the American sleeper, right?" I said.

Kenny nodded.

"They know everything," he said. "It's over."

Joey crashed on the couch and made a blanket out of the *USA Today*. He closed his eyes. Kenny and Johnny sat down and stared blankly out the window overlooking the Strip.

"How could we let the fucking Canadians dictate our national security?" I said, taking Joey's place pacing around the room.

Kenny leaned back in his chair.

"Headquarters actually congratulated us just now," he said. "We should be proud of this case. We saved lives, they said."

While management on both sides of the border were high-fiving, everyone in that suite, along with Nelly back home, felt like someone had kicked them in the balls. I collapsed on the bed and tried to make sense of what was happening. A small part of me was relieved. It was over. I could go back to my life and all the other cases the Bureau had on hold. But mostly I was angry.

I felt like the Canadians and the FBI wasted all of our hard work. We had a platform set up to actively vet any and all known threats on both sides of the border. What about the American sleeper?

Looking back, I understand the impossible position our government was in with the Canadians. We never had any concrete proof of the American sleeper. For all they knew, Abu Hamza was a fifteen-year-old kid in Iran stringing Chiheb along. The cop in me knows that. The boss in me knows the decision had to be made.

The case was done. We took three terrorists off the street, and our government could preserve an important relationship with a foreign partner that was already strained because of multiple extensions.

But this wasn't a victory. Best case, we tied. But really you could say we failed. Every time I hear about someone committing a terrorist act on U.S. soil, I wonder if that was the American sleeper. Chiheb was a lot of things, but he was never a liar. Personally, I have no doubt that there was an American sleeper. My biggest regret is that I couldn't find him.

I spent months imagining what the American sleeper looked like. Every time the image was the same. He was the real Tamer Elnoury in my mind. In my daydreams, he was always in a business suit. I could see him watching the press conference announcing Chiheb's arrest on the flat-screen in his office. Rattled, he dumps his cell phone in the trash outside his building and disappears into the crowd walking down the street.

I was in a bad mood when I met Abassi in the lobby a couple of hours later. He couldn't stop fidgeting as we stood in line to get a cab to the airport. He was giddy with purpose. Even though Farris wasn't receptive, Abassi was energized by the trip. I think he liked being on the road trying to recruit like-minded brothers and making plans.

I pretended to care about all his visions and plans, but it was hard because I knew what was waiting for us when we landed. The more he spoke, the happier I became about ending the case. I couldn't get arrested fast enough.

At the airport, I upgraded to first class as one last fuck-you to executive management. I decided to blame them for the case ending. I was acting out instead of taking the blame. It's embarrassing looking back on it now, but it did make the flight back to New York more comfortable. Besides, it was the only way Abassi and I could sit together.

About midway through the flight, it hit me: I was probably never going to see Chiheb again. We weren't friends and it wasn't like I felt sorry for him. It was just strange knowing someone so well. I knew more about him than his family. I had seen his dark side. But I'd also met a brilliant scientist with girl troubles. A goofy guy who liked lobster. I knew the terrorist and the man. While I was happy the terrorist would never be free, I felt sorry for the man. I felt bad that a man with so much to offer to the world got duped by murderers posing as holy men. It made me sad that they'd used my religion to pollute him. I was still frustrated I couldn't save him. What a waste.

When the pilot told the flight attendants to take their seats for landing, I got anxious. I knew what was coming. Getting arrested is an unnatural act. Even though I knew it was fake and I had been arrested many times, it always left me with a peculiar energy. Not anxiety or stress. A mix of both with a side of adrenaline. My skin started to tingle and my legs felt rubbery as I left the plane and walked toward the gate.

We were first off the plane. It was cold as we entered the airport. Abassi was still talking at me while I scanned the airport. I noticed seven or eight agents dressed in plain clothes following us as we walked from the gate toward baggage claim. I recognized a couple of them. Nelly was standing near the baggage carousel. We made eye contact.

I watched the bags on the belt. Abassi got his bag first. I could feel the agents close in a little when Abassi reached down and grabbed it. A few more suitcases passed me. I shot a glance at Nelly.

He looked calm. My big, gaudy Samsonite silver hard case parted the rubber flaps and trundled toward me a minute later. I took one more look around and noticed the surveillance guys getting closer. I grabbed my bag and started walking to the exit with Abassi. The surveillance guys surrounded us as Nelly blocked our path. He slid his suit jacket open to show us his shield.

"FBI," he said. "Would you folks please come with us?"

"What's this about?" I asked.

Normally, I would have put on a song and dance, but I was exhausted.

"Please come with us and we'll explain everything to you," Nelly said.

Nelly and another agent bracketed Abassi. Two agents I didn't know stepped next to me. They took us toward two different SUVs.

"Where am I going?" Abassi asked. "Where are you taking him? Why are we being separated?"

Abassi gave me a confident look, as if to reassure me that he was in control. He knew the drill. We were taken to separate interrogation rooms at JFK. Nelly left Abassi and came to see me. He took my cuffs off and gave me a hug.

"You good, *habibi*?" he asked.

"I will be."

"What do you want to do?"

FBI protocol was to keep me under lock and key until the dust settled. I knew I couldn't go home till at least the next day, but I didn't want to be around anyone. I just wanted to be alone.

"You have someone who can take me to my undercover apartment?" I asked.

Usually, I would get my gun, credentials, and phones back at this point, but I wasn't ready to plug back in just yet. I took the backpack with my true identity in it but didn't turn on my phone.

One of the surveillance agents drove me to my apartment. The poor guy was feeling pretty good about being part of this "huge success," but he wasn't getting that vibe from me. I didn't say a word the whole ride back.

The agent dropped me off and I called over to the operations center and asked them to take the cameras off-line. I didn't want anyone watching me anymore. I turned the TV on just in time for the breaking news alert. The Canadians were holding a press conference. It felt rehearsed, and no one on that screen had a clue about what had actually transpired over the past year. ABC News was the first to connect the Abassi arrest to the VIA Rail plot in Canada a few days later. But I still wasn't sure why the Canadians were in such a rush to end the case.

The very next week the Canadians announced their version of the Patriot Act, which passed swiftly through Parliament. This was the win they needed and just cause for this new legislation.

I found out later Chiheb was arrested in Montreal outside a McDonald's. He was flown to Toronto and informed of his right to counsel, but he declined. Chiheb told the Canadians he refused to be judged by man-made laws and that he only wanted to be judged by Sharia Law.

During the interrogation, Chiheb spoke freely. He even corrected his interrogator about the plot details. He was trying to find a bridge with as little water as possible to maximize casualties. He pointed to the officer's notepad and told him to write that down. When Chiheb was told that I was an undercover FBI agent, he didn't believe it. He protected me through every interrogation, but gave up Jaser and Abassi. He even talked about Abu Hamza and El Massoul. But he wouldn't give me up. The money Tamer was providing to the mujahideen was critical. It was so important Chiheb dedicated his doctoral thesis—his life's work—to me and my company instead of his professors, family, and research partners. It was his way of thanking me and acknowledging that nothing else matters besides helping the brothers overseas. When they played recordings from our conversations, he just assumed that the government wired us up and I had nothing to do with it. Chiheb was given enough discovery documents to finally believe that I was an FBI agent.

A month after his arrest, Chiheb gave an interview to a Toronto newspaper. Nelly forwarded me the link. Chiheb was savvy enough not to discuss the particulars of the case, but I was confused why he would break his silence to the media, until the last paragraph of the article. Chiheb told the reporter that despite being in jail, he was eating, sleeping, and praying. He had all he needed. Translation: *Fuck you, Tamer.*

Jaser was arrested in his home the same day the RCMP got Chiheb. A SWAT team executed the search and arrest warrants. He lawyered up right away and didn't say a word.

I didn't get much sleep the night of our arrests. I started packing up the apartment before dawn. The FBI told me I was clear to leave in the morning. I took one last look at the white Egyptian porcelain teapot on the stove I'd used so many times to make tea and left shortly after the sun came up. On my ride home, I got a phone call from my supervisor at the National Security Covert Operations Unit—the Dirty Arabs Group.

"I know you must be exhausted, but is there any way you could get to Portland tomorrow?"

In all my years in the FBI, I never said no to any other case. But this time, I did. I didn't even ask what the case was about.

After a few weeks, I came out of my funk and dove headfirst into my caseload. About a year later, I received a subpoena from the Crown Counsel, the prosecutors working the case. Chiheb's refusal to even acknowledge the charges forced the Canadians to give him a trial. He and Jaser were being tried together, despite Jaser's lawyers' argument for separate trials.

I called Nelly.

"Is this for real?" I said. "They're really taking this to trial?"

I'd testified many times in drug cases but never in a counterterrorism trial. The defendants always pled guilty. I stared at the subpoena in disbelief, my heart rate rising. I thought about my family. This was the nightmare I worried about before I took the case. Vinnie's words echoed in my head.

This case is going to change your life.

He had no idea.

I called Heidi in our National Security Law Branch. The subpoena was legit. The Canadians' case was based on my investigation. It was impossible to prosecute Chiheb and Jaser without me. But before I could testify, Heidi told me the Canadian courts had to rule on her thirty-three-page affidavit, signed by the assistant director of the FBI, requesting that the Canadians honor the same protections afforded to me in the United States. The RCMP had already agreed to it, but the court had to now. It didn't take much convincing for the Canadians to agree.

The court let me testify as Tamer Elnoury. The prosecutors,

defense team, and court personnel all signed a nondisclosure agreement promising not to reveal anything about my identity. The media wouldn't be able to cover my testimony in the courtroom, but
they could listen to it.

The Crown and FBI were happy, but now I had to be Tamer in
front of Chiheb and Jaser, one last time.

CHAPTER 28

T-Bags

The trial started the Monday after the 2015 Super Bowl.

Nelly and I arrived in Toronto the Thursday before for trial prep. We flew out of a small airport near my house on the RCMP's jet. This way, we didn't have to deal with security or any cameras or biometrics. The flight was short and when we landed in Toronto, there were no other planes in sight. The pilot handed me a ski mask and asked me to put it on before he opened the door to the plane. Nelly got out first, carrying one large duffel bag. I climbed down the retractable stairs next and met several large, burly men dressed in all black carrying assault rifles.

When the pilot opened the back, the RCMP SWAT guys started unloading my bags. The team leader, Hal, pulled Nelly aside.

"How many people are on the plane?"

Nelly laughed as the security team unloaded my bags into the back of an SUV.

"They're all his," he said, pointing at me.

I didn't realize they were flying me home every weekend, so I had two large suitcases, a garment bag, a carry-on, and my backpack. I can't pack light. I like options, especially for court. I found out later I earned my code name that day. The guys called me "T-Bags." I laughed every time I heard it on the police radios.

"T-Bags is on the move."

For the next three weeks, I lived in a bubble. Hal and his men became my family. They protected me at the safe house, which overlooked Lake Ontario. On Super Bowl Sunday, they even rigged an antenna so we could watch the Buffalo, New York, feed instead of the Canadian feed without the commercials. It turned out to be an amazing game—New England beat Seattle. Or more like Seattle beat Seattle. At one point, I made a joke about a guy getting used to having a security detail, but I was sexually frustrated and I needed them to address it. The next day, when I got back from court, they had a blow-up doll in the living room with her ass in the air.

She was pretty hot.

The prosecution—called the Crown in Canada—was led by Croft Michaelson. An experienced prosecutor, his cochair Sarah Shaikh was overseeing my testimony. Sarah was of Pakistani descent and a Muslim. We had met a few months prior in New York to start my trial prep. After I landed, they met me at their office in downtown Toronto for a few days of last-minute prep. I had let my hair and beard grow on Heidi's suggestion. The Crown wouldn't let me wear a disguise—even fake glasses—and I wanted to change my appearance.

"Why the fuck do you look like that?" Sarah asked.

She always cursed.

"You look like a Neanderthal jihadi."

She sent me to a salon to get a haircut before starting trial prep. It lasted twelve to fifteen hours a day leading up to my testimony. Initially, I tried to sound too professional and proper, but the words sounded phony. After a few hours, Nelly spoke up.

"Sarah, I apologize for interrupting," he said. "Ask him whatever you want and let him be himself. It will come across more natural and he will be a much better witness for you."

He then looked at me.

"No one in the world knows this case better than you do," he said. "You lived it. You were there. Just be yourself and everyone will love you."

That was exactly what I needed to hear. Sarah tried it Nelly's way and the trial prep got much smoother. Nelly saved me, again.

I was nervous as Hal and his team drove me to the courthouse the first day. They ushered me into the courtroom from the jury's door so I could avoid the media. When I first entered, my eyes went right to Chiheb. He was sitting on the opposite side of the court-room encased in a glass bowl, a goldfish without water. He was wearing the black and blue ski jacket he was arrested in with a blue button-down shirt on underneath it. His jeans were rolled up into thick cuffs.

Chiheb looked me dead in the eye and didn't blink. It was the blankest stare I've ever seen. For a second, I wanted him to smile or say something. I wanted him to understand. My heart sank. I felt sorry for the human inside him. Not the monster. No, the monster was going to jail. It was the lost puppy that I felt sorry for, but it was Allah's will that I stop him and this was the final step.

To his left, closer to me, in another empty fishbowl, was Jaser. He was wearing a suit with a neatly trimmed beard and glasses. I almost didn't recognize him. He looked like a businessman or a lawyer. Jaser couldn't wait to get my attention. His hands were palms down on the desk in front of him as he leaned forward, begging me to look at him. When he caught my attention, Jaser looked around the courtroom to make sure no one else was looking and then looked me in the eye.

"I will find you," he mouthed.

Nelly saw him do it and looked at me with a smirk. I relaxed immediately. Jaser was desperate. He knew we had him. I couldn't wait to get started.

All the attorneys arrived wearing black robes like American judges. Sarah and Croft sat to my left behind a wooden table. To my right was a lawyer the court appointed to help Chiheb. In front of him was John Norris—Jaser's lawyer. Norris came over to greet me before we started. I had no idea what to make of that. The niceties started early.

I arranged my notes and introduced myself to the court clerk— an older man who made sure I always had a glass of water. Justice Michael Code took the bench soon after and court was called to order. Code reminded me of the judge from *My Cousin Vinny*. He had a reputation for being one of the most brilliant legal minds in Canada. I had also heard that he was one hell of a prosecutor back in his day. The judge greeted the court and looked at the cameras and greeted the media sequestered in another room. They couldn't see me; they could only hear my testimony. Code instructed the clerk to bring in the jury. They filed into the jury box.

I was introduced to the jury as Special Agent Tamer Elnoury of the Federal Bureau of Investigation. Tamer Elnoury was burned. His apartments were gone. His company dissolved. Tamer didn't exist anymore, so the FBI agreed to let me testify in that name. My training and experience were discussed without ever mentioning where I was from or where I was currently assigned and without giving away anything that could disclose my true identity. It was a very well-scripted opening that was agreed to by both sides.

I had great chemistry with Sarah from the start. It began the same way every day.

"Good morning, Agent Elnoury."

"Good morning, Ms. Shaikh."

After lunch was the same thing.

"Good afternoon, Agent Elnoury."

"Good afternoon, Ms. Shaikh."

Croft must have said something to her, because after the first couple of days she started right with her questions without the pleasantries. But I interrupted her.

"Good morning, Ms. Shaikh."

She blushed, smiled, and replied in kind. The entire jury laughed. They were waiting for it too. Croft was pissed. I found out later that he told someone I was an American witness but it was still a Canadian courtroom.

The entire trial was about the conspiracy to attack the train from Toronto. Sarah would ask me questions to set the stage and then play a recording for the court to hear. The courtroom was wired with surround sound and multiple flat-screens that showed videos or transcripts. A translator sitting at the prosecutor's table would scroll down and highlight the transcript.

This was the Crown's way of playing the recordings in court

even if the conversations were in Arabic. Very smart, because there's nothing like hearing the words coming out of the defendants' mouths in surround-sound stereo. A lot of it was in English, which just highlighted the horror even more. During some of the recordings when we were laughing and joking, Chiheb sat back and smiled and laughed. He was reminiscing and enjoying it.

After the first few days of testimony, we wrapped up early enough for me to catch the local evening news at the safe house. I hadn't seen any of the coverage so far and was shocked to see what was happening. The focus was on Islamic extremism. Nothing about true Islam. In the media's defense, all they were hearing were Chiheb's and Jaser's interpretations.

The next morning, when Sarah came into the courthouse break room, I told her about the coverage.

"I know, I've been watching," she said. "What can you do?"

"I could state the obvious," I said.

"What do you mean?" she asked, focused more on the day's testimony than my editorializing. "You can't say anything. What are you going to do? What are you going to say?"

We were getting to the Christian burial speech, where I gave Chiheb a chance to back out of the attack. I told her there was a pause in the middle of the conversation. After the pause, I told her to ask me what was going through my mind.

"What are you going to say?"

"I'm going to say that his thoughts and rationalizations are not indicative of true Islam."

Sarah was good with that explanation and agreed to ask the question. We wrapped up for lunch right before the Christian burial speech. After lunch, I was excited to take the stand. This was a point I wanted to make. I needed to make it. Islam was never the cause, and I wanted the jury to hear it. I wanted the world to hear it. Just as I got comfortable, Croft and Sarah walked over to the witness stand.

"Tamer, Sarah mentioned to me what you wanted to say about Islam," Croft said. "I don't think it's a good idea."

"Have you been watching the media coverage?" I said. "They are making it about Islam. The world needs to hear from me that this is not Islam."

"Yes, but that's not what this trial is about," he said. "We're going to leave your personal comments out of it."

I leaned closer because I didn't want the whole courtroom to hear.

"Croft, I am your witness, not your fucking puppet," I said. "Either ask me the way that Sarah and I discussed, or I will blurt it out at some point while I am on the stand, and that could get awkward. Your choice."

Croft backed away. He looked me in the eye and then put both his hands up.

"Ask him what he wants," he said as he walked away.

Sarah smiled at me as she walked back to the table. When the pause came, she stopped the tape.

"I have one more question for you, Agent Elnoury," she said. "You also said prior to the break that this particular part of your conversation with Mr. Esseghaier stuck out in your mind, and you provided a justification for that. What was really the reason that this bothered you?"

I sat up a little straighter in my chair.

"These religious views that are presented are a complete desecration of my religion," I said. "So it stands out to me when I am having a discussion about rationalizing killing innocent women and children."

Chiheb kept quiet for most of the proceedings. He knew to wait for Justice Code's permission to speak, but my comments set him off. I wasn't talking about the facts of the case anymore. I was talking about Islam. He jumped out of his seat and was waving his hand at the judge to get his attention. Code removed the jury and then let Chiheb speak.

"I want to address what that witness agent just said," Chiheb said. "He is very, very wrong. There is no interpretation of Islam. There is only one Islam. Either you get it or you don't."

I couldn't have said it any better myself. *His* interpretation was wrong. Chiheb went on and on about religion but was eventually cut off by Code so we could all get on with it.

"Your religious explanation is duly noted on the record, Mr. Esseghaier," Code said.

The media coverage shifted that night. TV reporters were interviewing Imams at local mosques who echoed my sentiments. That was one of my proudest moments throughout this entire case. The Muslim community had a platform, and their ally was an American FBI agent. Al Qaeda and ISIS weren't the only ones with a voice anymore.

Two weeks after I took the stand, Sarah was done. We were confident in my testimony. I wasn't allowed any contact with the Crown from this point forward. It was now Jaser and Chiheb's turn to defend themselves.

But so far Chiheb hadn't even tried. During parts of the trial, Chiheb fell asleep in the prisoner's box. He didn't cross-examine witnesses and declined to even present a defense. Before the trial began, he argued the Quran should be used in place of the Canadian criminal code. Code asked if the Quran would lead to a different outcome for murder.

"Just wait and see who is in truth and who is in falsehood," Chiheb said.

When Code asked Chiheb if he had any questions for me, he didn't move or say anything. He sat in silence before turning to face the back of the courtroom.

Justice Code asked Jaser's attorney, John Norris, if he was ready. Norris smiled politely as he stood.

"Yes, Your Honor."

Like Sarah, he said good morning before he started. In Canada, defense counsel was a "friend" to the court and he was always polite. That was so foreign to me. Every defense attorney I had run-ins with in our courts had always tried to trick me, yell at me, discredit me. I never met one I didn't want to fight in the parking lot afterward. I welcomed combative, nasty exchanges. I knew how to navigate that. What if Norris lulled me with his kindness?

Norris started with how I met Chiheb.

"There was an ongoing investigation into Mr. Esseghaier?"

"Yes," I said.

"And as part of that investigation, you were tasked with forming a relationship with him?"

"Correct."

"You engaged with Mr. Esseghaier and the two of you exchanged Islamic greetings?"

"Yes, sir," I said.

"You were portraying yourself as someone who shared views with him?"

"Yes, of course."

Norris talked about my five days with Chiheb in San Jose.

"You shared with Mr. Esseghaier how meeting him had had a real effect on you, how fate had brought the two of you together?"

"Well, fate had nothing to do with it," I said.

"Because of meeting him, your life had a purpose now," Norris said.

"Something like that."

"That's the gist?"

"That's the legend," I said.

Norris had been instructed to stay away from any sensitive techniques, so when he asked me if the FBI orchestrated the whole initial meeting, I balked.

"Mr. Norris, I cannot confirm or deny that," I said. "If you would like to know whether or not I knew if Mr. Esseghaier was going to be on that flight, I can answer that question."

This went back and forth for a while. Heidi and I made eye contact. She was fidgeting and Nelly was almost out of his seat. Norris looked to Code for help. Code took off his reading glasses and looked at me.

"Agent Elnoury, any reasonable person can infer what your answer would be in this situation," he said. "I don't think you would be jeopardizing national security by answering this one simple question. I think you are taking your oath a little too seriously."

I could feel my blood pressure rise. It felt like Code was siding with the defense from the start. They seemed to win every objection. He was kicking out our legs at every turn.

Code called for a twenty-minute recess so that counsel could discuss it. He released the jury and I went back to the break room. I was livid. Heidi reworded the question so it better fit the FBI and Norris's agenda. As we were leaving to go back to court, Heidi grabbed my arm and asked me if I was okay. I nodded and she squeezed my arm.

"Calm down before you go back up there," she said. "He's just trying to get to you."

I was more pissed at the judge than at Norris. I had to say something. I wouldn't be able to go on unless I addressed this with him.

"I trust we reached an agreement with this matter?" Code asked when court resumed.

"Yes, Your Honor," both attorneys said.

"Okay, let's have the jury," Code said as he sat down behind the bench.

I interrupted him.

"Judge, I'd like to address the court before the jury enters, please," I said.

He turned to me, annoyed, and said go ahead.

"Your Honor, I want you to know that I was highly offended by your inference that I take national security and my oath 'too seriously'"—and yes, I used air quotes here. It was the most respectful way I could be disrespectful. "Of all the people in the world that I would think that meant something to, I would think that would be you, sir. I do take national security and my oath very seriously."

He was onstage and the cameras were rolling. Everyone in the media was there and this was his show. So he couldn't just apologize to me.

"I never implied that national security or your oath wasn't a serious matter," he said. "I am very appreciative of how serious you take these matters. I'm sorry you feel that way. It was never my intent to insinuate anything like that."

Sarah had a very proud look on her face and Nelly winked at me. I felt like I could breathe again.

"Thank you, Your Honor."

He called for the jury and we continued. Norris asked the question the right way and we moved on from there. It wasn't clear what Jaser's defense would be until we got to our first meeting at his apartment. Norris's argument was that Jaser was a con man looking to get money from Tamer. If that meant pretending to be a jihadi, so be it. He left the train plot because he wasn't going to be able to get any money from me, not because he was spooked by the police and afraid to get caught.

There were two major holes in that defense.

Jaser was part of the plot from the start. He checked out a possible site with Chiheb before I even entered the picture. I got to hammer that home repeatedly during cross-examination. I kept getting nods from Sarah every time it came up.

The second point was going to be trickier, but I needed Norris to open the door. During my testimony, Sayyid Qutb's name came up a few times. He was the author of *Milestones,* one of the founding jihadi texts. I told Sarah after the second day of testimony to ask me who he was so I could explain it to the jury. She did, but Norris objected. He argued I was an expert in counterterrorism and law enforcement but had no literary expertise. Code agreed and Sarah was forced to move on.

I brought his name up every single chance I got, but we never got to explain how his writings inspired jihadism. After a week of questions, Norris was wrapping up his cross-examination by asking me a bunch of short questions that forced me to answer yes. It's a common ploy used by defense attorneys to get the jury to hear the prosecution's witness repeatedly agree with the defense. It sounds stupid, but it works. Toward the end of this barrage, he circled back to my first meeting with Jaser.

"From the moment he met you, he knew you were a wealthy businessman and—"

I cut him off. That was the crack of the door I'd been waiting for.

"No, actually, that's not true, Mr. Norris," I said. "When your client first met me, he had no idea what my legend was. But he made sure to let me know who he was with his reverence of Sayyid Qutb."

Norris's face was beet red and his carotid artery was coming out of the side of his neck. He opened the door and Sarah went through it during redirect.

"Agent Elnoury, we keep hearing about Sayyid Qutb and Mr. Jaser's reverence of him," she said. "Could you explain why, as an experienced counterterrorism operative, that was a red flag to you?"

Perfect. I couldn't have worded the question any better. Norris jumped out of his seat.

"Your Honor, we covered this already."

But Code just shook his head.

"I believe you opened that door during your cross-examination of the agent."

Code then looked at me.

"Isn't that right, Agent Elnoury?"

"Spot-on, Your Honor," I said, without taking my eyes off Norris.

"Your Honor, with all due respect to Agent Elnoury, I did no such thing. He sort of kicked that door open on purpose."

My second proudest moment of the trial. Code allowed the question, but cautioned me to be brief.

I explained that Qutb was a radical cleric seen in the mujahideen community as a founder of the jihadist ideology against the Western world. He was Osama bin Laden's idol.

It doesn't get much shorter than that. I'd been waiting to say that for two weeks, and I didn't have to cause a mistrial to do it. I got to tell the jury that before Jaser even knew who I was, he was quoting excerpts from *Milestones* and telling me about how he aligned himself with that philosophy. There was no con.

Sarah wrapped up redirect in a couple of days. I was on the stand for more than three weeks. After I was done, Code thanked me for my time and professionalism. After the jury was dismissed for the day, Norris came over to shake my hand.

"You were a formidable opponent, Agent Elnoury," Norris said. "I wish you all the best."

My bags were already packed and in the car. Hal and his men ushered me back to the break room, where I changed out of my suit and into jeans and a sweatshirt. Nelly was late getting back there. He walked in with a grin on his face.

"Code stopped me in the hall and asked if I was going to see you," Nelly said. "He wanted me to relay a message. He said to tell you that you're not only a hero in your country, but in his. Your service and commitment will forever be appreciated. He told me to take care of you."

I finally got it. Code wasn't against us. He was giving the defense every benefit of the doubt because he didn't want them to have any grounds for an appeal. The evidence was insurmountable and he knew it. I felt bad for being so angry with him.

It took us a while to get out of the courthouse. I shook a lot of hands. Some of the courthouse staff and the Crown came down to the break room to thank me and Nelly. Each handshake and kind word was humbling.

Nelly and I got on the plane with bottles of high-end Canadian liquor, patches, coins, pins, hats, stuffed Mounties, and maple syrup from the Crown and the RCMP. As the plane started to taxi, I looked out the window. The entire security detail was lined up and saluted us. That's when I cried like a baby.

Nelly did too.

It was finally over.

We're Everyone

The jury deliberated for ten days.

I started to sweat after the first two days. Everyone was still positive through day four. After that, I didn't get any more updates. When they came back on the tenth day, Chiheb and Jaser were found guilty of conspiring to commit murder for the benefit of, at the direction of, or in association with a terrorist group. They were sentenced to life in prison.

As of this writing, Chiheb remains in solitary confinement. He refuses to get strip-searched. I think it has something to do with the San Jose airport. It's a fuck-you to me, because I'm a munafiq in his eyes. No more living amongst them, as them, to defeat them. He's now going to die alone. In a way, he got his martyrdom. I was told Jaser is doing well in general population. He finally got to be the Imam with a bunch of minions hanging on his every word.

Abassi was charged with two counts of fraud and misuse of visas to facilitate an act of international terrorism. After seventeen months in jail, he pleaded guilty to lesser charges, including making a false statement to officials upon his arrival at Kennedy International Airport. As part of his plea, he was deported to Tunisia. The U.S. attorney backed off the terrorism enhancements, in part because the FBI didn't want to expose me to another trial.

"I hope that you will think very seriously about the events of the last year and will decide to always abide by the laws of the United States," Judge Miriam Cedarbaum said during Abassi's July 2014 sentencing. It may not sound ideal, but it sidelined Abassi because it put him on law enforcement's radar no matter where he goes.

After the trial, I returned to work. So did Nelly and the team. We are all still fighting the fight. Terrorism didn't go away when we locked up Chiheb and Jaser.

There are about sixty designated foreign terrorist groups on the State Department's list. I would say that more than half of them are radical Islamic factions with the same essential goal: bring down the West. So when I hear people debate whether it's politically correct to call it "radical Islam," I laugh. There's nothing wrong with calling it what it is. I am a Muslim. I am American, and I am fucking appalled at what these animals are doing to my religion and my country.

But giving them a label is just words. How do we defeat an enemy who is willing to die for a cause that they believe in? That is the question I ask every one of my students at the FBI undercover school before I start my lesson on radical Islam. Over the years, I have heard many different answers, but never the correct one: education. In order to defeat your enemy, you must first understand them.

The problems start when every Muslim gets painted with the jihadi brush. Jihadis are using a peaceful religion to further their agendas. That's not religion. It's politics. The reality is that radical Islam is a very small minority that twists the Quran to fit its needs. Just look at Chiheb, Jaser, and Abassi. Chiheb thought the Quran justified the murder of innocent men, women, and children because he chose not to honor the Prophet's rules of war. He knew the rules. He just ignored them. Jaser thought Allah wanted him to kill Jews, and Abassi interpreted Allah's call as a war against America. None of them were right. That is why "radical Islam" is a fine blanket term, but the key to defeating it is learning the differences among those who believe radically—as evident in Chiheb, Jaser, and Abassi. They're not all the same, and understanding the fault lines between the different groups will be radical Islam's undoing.

Banning Muslims from the United States throws gas on the myth that the United States is at war with Islam. I believe there should be a strict vetting process, but our world becomes more dangerous when we shut our doors to immigrants.

I was born Sunni Muslim in Egypt and came to the United States when I was just a child. I remember the day that I became a naturalized U.S. citizen. I missed most of field day. My dad dropped me back at school and I ran through the halls so I wouldn't miss the whole day. My fifth-grade teacher stopped me.

"Congratulations, son," he said as he shook my hand. "Today is a big day for you."

I was ten years old and I will never forget the day I became an American. But my parents still sent me to Islamic school every Sunday to maintain my religion. We traveled back to Egypt almost every summer so I'd never forget my culture. My mother only spoke Arabic to me so I'd always know my native language. None of that made me less patriotic. I've served my country for

twenty-two years and counting. Keeping America's doors open en-
sures that when we are threatened by an enemy, we will always have
someone who looks like them to help defeat them. Our best defense
is inclusion.

America is everyone.

ACKNOWLEDGMENTS

To my family, who spent most days and nights throughout my career not knowing where I was or when I'd be home. You'll never know how much your love and support means to me. You carried me through every case.

To my father and my sister, thank you for making sure I always knew the true tenets of Islam. I love you both very much.

To my extended family, thank you for always being there for me.

To my lifelong friends—Mikey, Sugar, KB, Chicken, Bone, and Muscle—thank you for your friendship and loyalty over the years.

To my agent, Frank Weimann, who believed in this story and the message and never rested till the job was done.

To Joe Pistone, for being a mentor and showing me the way.

To Ben Sevier, without you, this story would never have been told.

To Kevin Maurer, a brilliant, gifted author and journalist from whom I learned so much. I love the way you see the world, and I am honored to call you my friend.

To the folks at Dutton—Ivan, Christine, John, and Amanda—you took me in and helped me tell my story in the most incredible way. Thank you for making it so easy.

To Billy, Al, Mike, James, and all my Narco buddies, you taught me how to be a cop and what it means to bring a case home.

To Howard, who taught me how to tap into my emotions.

To my home law enforcement agency, for giving me my start and supporting my move to the FBI.

To the Federal Bureau of Investigation, for giving me the opportunity to serve my country.

To my team, in all the years that I have worked criminal and national security matters, this case will always stand out to me for a variety of reasons. But the main reason is the core of our team: Nelly, Joey, Kenny, and Johnny. I miss working with you on a daily basis. It's rare that a group of all-stars is assembled on one case. You are true professionals and American heroes. Nelly, your gut and instincts are never wrong, and, Joey, you were our director.

To the men and women of CT-1, you lived up to your reputation. Thank you for your tireless efforts and for fighting the good fight.

To the National Security Covert Operations Unit, you are the backbone of the counterterrorism undercover world. Thank you for always looking out for us.

To the men and women of the NYPD, especially the Counterterrorism Division, the greatest police department in the world.

To the men and women of the FBI undercover program, our fraternity within law enforcement is unlike any other. Thank you for keeping America safe. It is an honor to do this job with you.

To FBI Executive Management (New York and Headquarters) and the Southern District of New York, you make tough calls every day while always having our back. And a special thank-you to Big Mark for watching out for us every step of the way.

To the FBI legal attachés in Ottawa, Canada, specifically Sho and LJ. Without you, I never would have gotten in front of the subjects.

To the National Security Law Branch, specifically Heidi, for always protecting my identity and making sure I can do my job over and over again. You were always my last line of defense, Heidi, and you never let me down.

To the FBI unit that backstopped all my legends, specifically Dave, thank you for always going the extra mile for me and making sure I was always "real" no matter where I was in the world.

To our FBI forensic accountant, Lindsay, for taking care of our finances and making sure all our audits went smoothly.

To our FBI analysts, especially Brett, for finding our bad guys and keeping us informed throughout the investigation.

To our FBI linguists, who had to endure hours and hours of listening to me and relaying the information to the agents on the ground.

To our Canadian partners the Royal Canadian Mounted Police—Doug, Johnny A., Christine, Frank, Omar, Benny, Brady, Simone, Marwan, and Rich—and the Royal Crown Prosecutors—Croft, Marcy, and Sarah—whose dedication and professionalism was inspiring. Two countries working together for a common goal.

To the Canadian warriors, my security detail—Hal, Souki, Kenny (JJ), Geoff, and the rest of the team—thank you all for watching my back. There's no one I would have wanted doing the job other than you.

ABOUT THE AUTHORS

TAMER ELNOURY was born in Egypt and immigrated to the United States before his fifth birthday. Elnoury began his career in law enforcement in 1995. After a brief stint with a fugitive task force, he began working undercover narcotics. Elnoury worked in more than 2,500 narcotics investigations as well as political corruption, gun trafficking, and child abuse cases. In 2008, Elnoury began working with the Federal Bureau of Investigation. He joined an elite, covert counterterrorism unit. Elnoury has worked cases all over the world for multiple government agencies.

KEVIN MAURER is an award-winning journalist and the best-selling coauthor, with Mark Owen, of *No Easy Day: The Firsthand Account of the Mission That Killed Osama bin Laden*. He has covered war and terrorism for more than a decade.